Music & Literature
an arts magazine

Gerald Murnane

Vladimír Godár

Iva Bittová

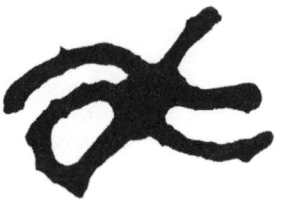

Number Three

Music & Literature

Number Three

ISSN: 2165-4026
ISBN: 978-09888799-2-8

Editor-in-Chief: Taylor Davis-Van Atta
European Editor: Daniel Medin
Social Media Manager: Madeleine LaRue
Online Reviews Editor: Jeffrey Zuckerman
Proofreaders: Julie Hersh
Cover Design & Visual Identity: EA Projects, Brooklyn, NY

A version of Will Heyward's interview with Gerald Murnane previously appeared in *Higher Arc Magazine* Issue 2.

"Far Enough: The Peculiar World of *The Plains*" © Wayne Macauley, 2012. First published by the Text Publishing Company Australia.

"The Interior of Gaaldine" first appeared in *Emerald Blue* and is reproduced here with permission of its author, as does the excerpt from *A Thousand Windows*.

"On the Work of Giya Kancheli" is taken from lectures given at a compositional seminar in June 1988 in Dolná Krupá. It first appeared in Slovak in *Hudobný život*, vol. XXII, 1990/3.

"Encountering the Poet" was originally published in Slovak in *Slovenské pohľady*, 1993/2.

The photographs on pages 181-188 appear courtesy of Vladimír Godár, with the exception of the photograph on page 187, which appears courtesy of Peter Breiner.

Vladimír Godár's original manuscript scores appear courtesy of the composer.

Music & Literature, Inc. is a 501(c)(3) charitable organization.

Individual U.S. subscriptions: US$15 (one issue); US$25 (one-year, two issues); US$45 (two-year, four issues)

Individual international subscriptions: US$25 (one issue); US$45 (one-year, two issues); US$75 (two-year, four issues)

Issue Four: Mary Ruefle / Clarice Lispector / Maya Homburger & Barry Guy
Issue Five: Can Xue / Kaija Saariaho / Stig Sæterbakken

For more information visit www.musicandliterature.org

Acknowledgments

The editor wishes to recognize each of the writers and translators whose work appears in these pages as well as Iva Bittová, Pavel Fajt, Katarina Godár, Michael Heyward, Maria Im, Ivor Indyk, Leah Kaminsky, Nathaniel LaNasa, Mark Molnar, Colin Stokes, Vladimír Václavek, Emil Viklický, and Evan Ziporyn for their special contributions to the project.

A hearty thanks to Gerald Murnane for the time and energy he devoted to responding to letters from a host of people involved in bringing this volume together.

Finally, a note of deepest gratitude to Vladimír Godár, whose close collaboration is as much an inspiration as his compositions.

Contents

II. Vladimír Godár

III. Iva Bittová

The Complete Published Works of Gerald Murnane

Tamarisk Row (1974)

A Lifetime on Clouds (1976)

The Plains (1982)

Landscape with Landscape (1985)

Inland (1988)

Velvet Waters (1990)

Emerald Blue (1995)

Invisible Yet Enduring Lilacs (2005)

Barley Patch (2009)

A History of Books (2012)

Border Districts (forthcoming)

A Thousand Windows (forthcoming)

April 6 2013

Dear Mr Murnane,

I am finally writing the letter which I have for so long
intended to write. I write to you in the first case as
an admirer of your writing. But I also write — as does
anyone who writes a letter — in the hope of a response.
For this latter, I feel a little guilty, because I know
it is a demand on your time; and yet both guiltily
and guiltlessly I crave your indulgence and live in

hope.

This matter of being a fan, of being an admirer: each
admirer of an author feels, in stony disregard of the facts,
that the author writes for him or her alone. The work
feels personal, feels, in fact, like a letter, written by
one person, singular, intended for another, singular.
In the case of your work the effect — perhaps not an
effect at all but rather a reflection of the reader's solipsism
——— is even more pronounced, for at least two reasons.
The first is that the one who reads you in the United
States, where I live, must seek your work out. Other

Dear Mr Murnane,

I am finally writing the letter which I have for so long intended to write. I write to you in the first case as an admirer of your writing. But I also write—as does anyone who writes a letter—in the hope of a response. For this latter, I feel a little guilty, because I know it is a demand on your time; and yet both guiltily and guiltlessly I crave your indulgence and live in hope.

This matter of being a fan, of being an admirer: each admirer of an author feels, in stony disregard of the facts, that the author writes for him or her alone. The work feels personal, feels, in fact, like a letter, written by one person, singular, intended for another, singular. In the case of your work the effect—perhaps not an effect at all but rather a reflection of the reader's solipsism—is even more pronounced, for at least two reasons. The first is that the one who reads you in the United States, where I live, must seek your work out. Other writers of your caliber are promoted by large publishing houses, promoted by bookshops, and make themselves available for book tours, magazine profiles, and political commentary. The fan of Gerald Murnane must search in a large library, or visit the shelves of a well-curated bookshop, or order from a book-delivery service. So, already, this sense of having a minority taste, indeed of having a minority taste within the minority taste we call "literary fiction." Now the admirer has the book in his hands ("his" because the admirer in question is me). He begins to read, and notices, as he has with all other Murnane books and stories he has read that, regardless of the subject at hand, the narrator is always concerned with the process of narrative, specifically the aspect of narrative that concerns the transfer of sensations from the mind of the narrator into the mind of the reader. In fact—if this isn't too broad a claim to make, but that's admirers for you, always making broad claims—the central literary project of a Murnane narrative is to place into a mind (into my mind) the mental events in the mind of the author and his amanuensis, the narrator, at the moment of writing. In this specific sense, you have for many years now been writing directly to me—this is not the first letter that has passed between us but, rather, a belated response to the many I received from you in the form of your published writing and failed to answer since the day some ten years ago when I read "When the Mice

Failed to Arrive" on the sixth floor of Columbia University's Butler Library.

One quality I have treasured in all your writing is its sense of distance. The pages seem to be crossing the space between here (Australia) and there (where the reader happens to be; say, New York) by presenting thinkers, persons, narrators, personages, who are themselves crossing imaginative, imagined or imaginary space such as the plains (the Plains, I mean), the Alföld, or Nebraska.

It is Sunday afternoon here in Brooklyn, New York. The winter officially ended more than two weeks ago but, emotionally, only yesterday, which was, like today, a warm and clear day with a gentle breeze. I am sitting in the kitchen of the small apartment I share with my wife. I have no children. In a little over two years, I will turn forty. I am a novelist and a photographer, with two books so far, and a portfolio of color photographs. I have decided, just now, not to attend tonight a party to which I was invited and to which I have been looking forward since mid-March. I worry that my handwriting might cause your eyes fatigue. I need to think about lunch. My wife's telephone is ringing. I am thinking of the man who will hold in his hands this very page on which I am writing and who will read these words. My wife is in the shower; she spent the morning gardening. I never answer her phone and, on mine, the ringer is always switched off. From the room in which I write, I can see my neighbors' houses, the blue sky above them and, beyond, in the farther distance, but only if I get up and go to the windows, the Upper Bay of New York City.

When I give a reading to an audience, as I am sometimes asked to do these days, the moderator of the event asks the audience if there are any questions, and often clarifies that audience members ought to ask a question rather than make a comment, for a comment can be irrelevant, longwinded, and even incoherent, creating a productive discomfort in which we, author and audience, all marinate together until the moderator rescues us by calling on another audience member. Nevertheless, this letter has mostly been in the form of a digressive comment, and I'd like to close it with an actual question.

In books like *The Plains*, *Inland*, and *Barley Patch*, and indeed in all those works of yours with which I am familiar, there is a particular style of sentence-making that is, as far as I can decipher, unique to you. This style is as follows: without fear of repetition, you attempt to give in each sentence an account of the circumstances that led to that sentence. You try to say no more than can be justified in each sentence. You prefer nouns to pronouns, and in many cases where the vast majority of writers of English prose would choose to use a pronoun, you opt to repeat the noun from the previous sentence. This gives your writing a meticulous and testimonial quality that seems to me—your only reader—to mimic the process of thought. After all, whenever I walk into this room, I register not an "it" but "the long wood table that we clear of papers and use when guests come to dine with us" or, at least, "the table." Objects repeat themselves each time they are encountered. Like your prose, they do not avail themselves of shortcuts. So it is that your prose echoes the operations of a mind going about the process of describing, the mind of the author, the mind of the narrator, the mind of the reader, all of which, in the quiet moment in which the written paragraph is being read, becomes an apprehension of a single vivid image—described by one, understood by another <u>as an action of description</u>, a moment of magical idealism. What this scrupulous prose style conveys is an allergy to carelessness and a loyalty to the transfer of mental events, through the medium of prose, from one mind to another. Here then is the question: how did this habit of meticulous written description first arise in you?

Yours truly,

Teju

16 April 13

Hello, Teju

I collected your letter from my post-office box an hour ago. I expected to have
about two hours free today for going on with my latest piece of fiction, but I'll
cheerfully allot that time to answering your letter. Two hours is about what I
get for writing on an average day. I reckon I can give your letter the answer it
deserves if I give up my writing-time for the next few days.

Yours is an admirable letter. I found the handwriting mostly clear and remarkably
even. If I were to reply to you in handwriting, the neat strokes of my first
few paragraphs would have soon turned into scrawl as I felt the pressure of all
my unwritten thoughts. Your script remains even throughout and you hardly crossed
out a letter or a word. The shapely, measured sentences set me thinking of their
writer as someone likely to share many of my beliefs about prose fiction. (I was
thinking thus long before I reached the later pages of the letter and your detailed
question about my own prose, which question, of course, confirmed my suspicions.)

So, Teju, I feel rather at ease with you already. You would understand, for example,
my bafflement while reading, every Saturday morning, the book reviews in the
AUSTRALIAN. I make no pretence nowadays of keeping up with new titles, but I still
look through the reviews in my favourite newspaper and wonder how seemingly
intelligent reviewers can discuss books as though they consist of subject-matter
or ideas or scenes or whatever when the obvious fact is that a book consists only
of words arranged in sentences. But I must not get started on that, or this
letter will never be written.

People have sometimes commented that I can never report an anecdote or tell a funny story
without much explanation as to the background of the chief characters: how they
came to be where they were at the beginning of the story and that sort of thing.
I got a hint from your letter that you might do somewhat as I do when I tell a
story or write a letter to a stranger. You explained to me in your letter what
you could see around you while you wrote and what was happening on the day when you
wrote. I feel driven to do likewise.

I lived contentedly as a husband and father in a quiet suburb of Melbourne from
1969 until about 1999. During those thirty years, I expected to die as a man of
the suburbs. This in itself did not trouble me, but I thought often about the
question of where my ashes could be strewn or buried after my death. This might
have seemed an odd obsession for a healthy young man, but I believed, as the poet
Robert Bly, once asserted, that one should trust one's obsessions, and so I went
on adding different messages to my Last Will, naming one place after another as
the resting place of my ashes. Even then, the places were all far from Melbourne.
In the late 1990s, when I first visited Goroke, my designated strewing-place
was the racecourse at Bendigo, in north-central Victora, Bendigo being the actual
counterpart of the fictional Bassett in my first published book of fiction, TAMARISK
ROW.

In 1996, my eldest son bought a stone cottage in Goroke, which is about 230 miles
north-west of Melbourne and near the South Australian border. I had travelled
through the surrounding districts but had never seen Goroke itself. On a cold,
cloudy day in October 1997, I drove there alone to visit my son.

Much of the countryside around Goroke is level, but the township itself is
surrounded by low hills. As I approached Goroke for the first time from the
direction of Melbourne, I saw that the hill beside the township was the site
of the cemetery. The sun was setting behind clouds far ahead of me, and the
shapes of headstones stood out against the pale sky. Calmly and wordlessly I
understood, as ome understands things in dreams, that my ashes would one day
be buried in Goroke Cemetery.

Hello, Teju

I collected your letter from my post-office box an hour ago. I expected to have about two hours free today for going on with my latest piece of fiction, but I'll cheerfully allot that time to answering your letter. Two hours is about what I get for writing on an average day. I reckon I can give your letter the answer it deserves if I give up my writing-time for the next few days.

Yours is an admirable letter. I found the handwriting mostly clear and remarkably even. If I were to reply to you in handwriting, the neat strokes of my first few paragraphs would have soon turned into scrawl as I felt the pressure of all my unwritten thoughts. Your script remains even throughout and you hardly crossed out a letter or a word. The shapely, measured sentences set me thinking of their writer as someone likely to share many of my beliefs about prose fiction. (I was thinking thus long before I reach the later pages of the letter and your detailed question about my prose, which question, of course, confirmed my suspicions.)

So, Teju, I feel rather at ease with you already. You would understand, for example, my bafflement while reading, every Saturday morning, the book reviews in the AUSTRALIAN. I make no pretence nowadays of keeping up with new titles, but I still look through the reviews in my favourite newspaper and wonder how seemingly intelligent reviewers can discuss books as though they consist of subject-matter or ideas or scenes or whatever when the obvious fact is that a book consists only of words arranged in sentences. But I must not get started on that, or this letter will never be written.

People have sometimes commented that I can never report an anecdote or tell a funny story without much explanation as to the background of the chief characters: how they came to be where they were at the beginning of the story and that sort of thing. I got a hint from your letter that you might do somewhat as I do when I tell a story or write a letter to a stranger. You explained to me in your letter what you could see around you while you wrote and what was happening on the day when you wrote. I feel driven to do likewise.

I lived contentedly as a husband and father in a quiet suburb of Melbourne from 1969 until about 1999. During those thirty years, I expected to die as a man of the suburbs. This in itself did not trouble me, but I thought often about the question of where my ashes could be strewn or buried after my death. This might have seemed an odd obsession for a healthy young man, but I believed, as the poet Robert Bly, once asserted, that one should trust one's obsessions, and so I went on adding different messages to my Last Will, naming one place after another as the resting place of my ashes. Even then, the places were all far from Melbourne. In the late 1990s, when I first visited Goroke, my designated strewing-place was the racecourse at Bendigo, in north-central Victora, Bendigo being the actual counterpart of the fiction Bassett in my first published book of fiction, TAMARISK ROW.

In 1996, my eldest son bought a stone cottage in Goroke, which is about 230 miles north-west of Melbourne and near the South Australian border. I had travelled through the surrounding districts but had never seen Goroke itself. On a cold, cloudy day in October 1997, I drove there alone to visit my son.

Much of the countryside around Goroke is level, but the township itself is surrounded by low hills. As I approached Goroke for the first time from the direction of Melbourne, I saw that the hill beside the township was the site of the cemetery. The sun was setting behind clouds far ahead of me, and the shapes of headstones stood out against the pale sky. Calmly and wordlessly I understood, as one understands things in dreams, that my ashes would one day be buried in Goroke Cemetery.

I do not have to rely on memory alone as I write this account. Soon after I had returned to Melbourne after my first trip to Goroke, I wrote about my trip in one of the long letters I write often to my handful of regular correspondents. (Most of the letters are of several thousand words. The longest letter in my archive comprises twenty thousand words.) I wrote in October 1997 that I felt while I drove back to Melbourne not that I was returning home but that I was travelling away from my true home and into unfamiliar territory. That was nearly sixteen years ago, when my wife and I were both active and healthy. We visited Goroke for many years, and we bought a plot of land in the cemetery, and I often daydreamed of living in the township but with no thought that this would ever happen. After my wife had been told, in 2008, that she would die of cancer, almost the first thing we agreed was that her ashes would be buried at Goroke and that I should live there for the rest of my life. She died in 2009, and a few months later I moved into the stone cottage where I sit typing this letter.

My son lives in the main rooms of the cottage. I have a large room at the rear, with its own toilet, shower, and sink. The room is half-filled with filing-cabinets: eleven four-drawer cabinets, most of them full of letters, manuscripts, and typescripts meticulously ordered. The most significant of interesting items are marked by coloured signposts, as I call them, protruding up from among the sheaves of papers. I have never learned to use a computer. I even dislike using the telephone in my son's part of the house. (I have a mobile phone that sits in the boot of my car in case of emergency. The phone is switched off for year after year. I don't even know its number.) Almost all my dealings with people are in writing. For more than fifty years, I have kept and filed all in-coming letters. As soon as photocopies became available, I began to copy every item of out-going mail. In recent years, several of my correspondents from the years before photocopying have sent me back collections of letters that I sent them in the 1960s and 1970s. So my chronological archive, as I call it, is a pretty complete record of my copious letter-writing during the past fifty years. But the archive contains much more than letters, which are often less than honest accounts of the writer's thoughts and motives. Although I have never kept a diary, I have filled many thousands of pages with autobiographical fragments, accounts of my views and beliefs on many subjects, reports of my sexual fantasies, and oddities such as a report of forty thousand words listing events in my life that I consider miraculous and a report of seventy thousand words listing all the persons that I have felt attracted to or have fallen in love with, even if I never spoke to the persons or even learned their names. But my chronological archive is only one of three archives, even if it happens to be the bulkiest. My literary archive comprises thirteen filing-cabinet drawers, most of them full and all of them, like the drawers of my chronological archive, meticulously ordered and labelled. I have had ten books published to date. An eleventh is with my publisher. I have begun work on what I hope will be my twelfth. Each of these twelve has a drawer allotted to it in my literary archive. The thirteenth drawer contains the work that I abandoned in the early 1990s, O, DEM GOLDEN SLIPPERS, and the many other fragments that came to nothing.

Also in that drawer are the hundred or so poems that I wrote many years ago before deciding that I could better explain myself in prose than in poetry. Most of my books were hard to write, and most of the drawers in the literary archive contain hundreds of pages of discarded notes, drafts, and even two book-length works that have never been published. The third archive fits into two drawers only, but its few thousand pages contain an immense amount of detail. I call this archive the Antipodean Archive, which takes a bit of explaining. Since early childhood, I have had glimpses of races being contested by horses I do not recognise on racecourses I do not recognise. These glimpses are likely to occur at any time but more likely when I listen to certain passages of music or when I find myself alone in an empty landscape. The far parts of my mind hold for me the same sort of interest that far countries probably hold for travellers. For many years, I longed to know the names of those racehorses that I glimpsed, the colours worn by their jockeys, and the whereabouts of the racecourses where they vied and strove. In the mid-1950s, when I was still a schoolboy, I drew a map of an island not unlike Tasmania, marked half a dozen racecourses on the map, and then drew up a list of a hundred or more horses, together with their trainers and jockeys and their racing colours. For about a year, I devoted much of my free time to compiling records of races run by my imaginary horses in their imagined island-state. Results of races were determined by a simpler version of the method used by the fictional Tasmanian character in 'The Interior of Gaaldine', the last piece in EMERALD BLUE. I still regret my having destroyed all my records of this enterprise after I had brought them forward for more than a year. I have no memory of the actual destruction or of the reasons for it, but I count myself lucky that I can still recall, nearly sixty years later, a few names and colours and race-results. These details, which might be called remembered imaginings, are more precious to me than most of my memories of actual places and events. I began to report the details of the Antipodean Archive in 1985. As I wrote earlier, these details are complicated and far-reaching. Much time is needed to bring the archive forward. Months or years have sometimes passed without my finding time to add to the archive, but during the 1990s, when I wrote no fiction, I enlarged the archive greatly. I have never felt obliged to explain the provenance, so to call it, of all my conjectured racecourses and trainers and horses, but I have sometimes described them as belonging to an alternative universe differing from this universe only in that Australia and New Zealand are missing from it whereas the space now occupied by the Tasman Sea is occupied by two island-dominions of the British Commonwealth of Nations, by name New Eden and New Arcady and known collectively as the Antipodes.

So, Teju, here I sit at my tiny student-desk, crowded into a corner of my room by cabinets stuffed with most of the words I've written during my long life. When I moved here nearly four years ago, I supposed I would spend much time looking into my archives and reflecting on the past. This has not happened. I've been drawn into the community of Goroke. I'm secretary of the Golf Club and an office-bearer in three other organisations. I barely get time to write letters such as this, let alone my latest work of fiction. The reward for my involvement in the community is that I'm a respected member of that community. I was something of a hermit during the forty years when I lived in my suburb of Melbourne. My few friends were scattered around the far-reaching suburbs. The dense motor-traffic kept us mostly apart—I mean, we visited each other only occasionally at weekends. Here in Goroke, I chat every day on the steps of the post office or under the veranda of the store with friends, acquaintances, and with people I hardly know. Perhaps you wonder how I survive as a writer with no other writers near me. Well, I have never had writers as friends and have hardly ever wanted to talk about writing. Yes, there was a hotel in an inner suburb where I drank sometimes in the 1980s and heard gossip from publishers and journalists and even a few writers, but for most of my life, if I've wanted to discuss what might be called writerly matters, I've written to someone. I've sometimes tried to explain to interested non-writers or non-readers that what I write about is what I never want to talk about. I've borrowed most of my theories about literature from Marcel Proust, and I value especially his notion of le moi profond. The author of my books is my deep self. The man who serves as secretary of the Goroke Golf Club is affable, hard-working, whatever, but he is no writer of fiction. Neither is he a hypocrite—I mean, he is not pretending to be who he seems. However, he possesses a deep self: a rather different sort of person who comes to life only when he gets to have a typewriter and a blank page in front of him.

I'll mention two other details about this room. The walls are of unlined stone. My son's house was built in the 1970s from large blocks of Mount Gambier sandstone. Mount Gambier stone is a white stone quarried from the district around Mount Gambier, a large town a hundred miles away in South Australia. Our cottage is, of course, fire-proof and also well insulated—cool in the hot summers of this region and warm in the freezing winters. (They are freezing by Australian standards—the coldest morning in Goroke would be about 25 Fahrenheit, and no snow has ever fallen here.) The other detail concerns the bar-fridge resting beside my sink. The fridge contains two or three bottles of home-brewed beer. Almost every evening, I feel the need to sip glass after glass of my strong home-brew. Its average alcohol content is 7.5%.

Ever since I began this letter, I've assumed that I'm taking part in a sort of interview. I mean, Taylor wrote to me long ago as though you were going to interview me for his magazine. I supposed you would send me a list of questions, but you only asked me the one question in your letter, even though it was a profound question. I'll get to answer your question soon, but I've spent more than four hours already on this letter in the belief that my doing so is providing Taylor with what he needs. Heaven forbid that I'm wrong and that you intend to follow up your letter with more questions. I could never afford the time or the energy to write any more than what I'm writing today. As much as I'm enjoying this engagement with you, I have to make clear to you that this letter is very much a one-off, a once-only.

I made a few notes while I was reading your letter for the first time yesterday. You wrote about your feeling as though my writing—my fiction, I mean—was directed at you alone. This is a strange matter. When I write fiction, I very much feel as though I'm writing for one person alone. I have hardly any notion of the appearance of that person. I think of the person as being at a great distance from me, as being more likely a female than a male, and as being someone I am prevented from ever meeting up with. Although I can hardly visualise my reader—indeed, I feel most reluctant to try to do so—I feel, nevertheless, as though… I don't know whether I can finish this sentence or even whether I should try to finish it. I feel as though I prefer never to try to finish the sentence: as though my leaving the sentence unfinished is a condition of my being the sort of writer that I am.

You wrote about a feeling of distance in my writing. You are a perceptive fellow. Notions of space or distance are nearly always in my thoughts. I tried to explain this in my essay 'The Breathing Author' in INVISIBLE YET ENDURING LILACS. I have to know always where I am in relation to certain other places of importance to me. While I was waiting for the electric jug to boil a few minutes ago, I stared through the small window over the sink. I saw only clouds to the north-west, and I found myself at once trying to visualise the district to the north-west of Goroke as it might look from ten miles up. I have this urge to reduce all sorts of matters to the status of maps or diagrams. I'm uncomfortable with the fact of the universe itself being three-dimensional—I would like to turn it into an endless steppe or grassland. Of all my eccentricities, as they seem to most people, my dislike of travel seems best known. I have never been, nor could ever bring myself to be, inside an aeroplane. I have travelled only about a dozen times out of Victoria, which is roughly the size of Kansas or Nebraska. I travel freely in the western and south-western parts of Victoria, which I think of as my native territory and where I can nearly always learn which direction is north and in which direction lies Melbourne, my birthplace, but I have hardly ever visited the mountainous east and north-east of this state and will never again do so. For a long time now, I've felt no urge to explain or to justify these traits of mine. When some people accuse me of posing or posturing, I recall those days that I have been obliged to spend sometimes in Sydney or Adelaide when attending writers' festivals or the like: days when I was left to myself and when I might have gone sight-seeing or pub-crawling but when I stayed instead in my hotel-room, cowering almost, and trying to learn from maps what was outside my window.

I hardly need to remind you that I think of mind as space. I long ago rejected the popular theories of the mind advanced in the twentieth century. For me, mind is <u>extent</u> and, quite possibly, endless, that is to say, infinite. This would entail, I suppose, the belief that all minds are one or even that everything is mind, but that sort of speculation is not for me. I have enough to do during my lifetime with uncovering the patterns of imagery in my corner of mind without seeking further.

Near the end of your letter, you finally ask me a question. How, you ask, did my habit of meticulous description first arise in me? How, indeed? I mean, what a question to have to answer on this quiet Thursday afternoon of sunshine and intermittent cloud, with my clock ticking near by (that's how quiet Goroke is—you can hear a clock ticking in your room) and the only other sounds the occasional screeches of a corella or a galah strayed from its flock!

My way of writing had to develop, as I hardly need to remind you. Although I was always acutely aware of writing itself—of the shaping of sentences and such matters—my actual writing developed during the first ten years or more of my career, so to call it. While I'm proud of TAMARISK ROW, A LIFETIME ON CLOUDS, and THE PLAINS, I can never look back over those works without wanting to correct some of the writing in them. I think I was still too anxious, while I wrote those works, to find the exact, the appropriate, word or phrase, as though certain words or combinations of words were richer and more potent than others. During the two years and more while I was writing LANDSCAPE WITH LANDSCAPE, I seemed to find at least the confidence to rely mostly on nouns and verbs and, most importantly, on the order of words in each sentence and on the repetition of important nouns.

All this happened thirty and more years ago, and I would be deceiving you if I claimed to recall it happening. All I recall is a vague concern that affected me sometimes while I struggled to write what was a very complicated book. (It still awaits its proper recognition as one of my best books.) But luckily I recall a certain few minutes from the many, many hours while I was writing the last piece in the book, 'Landscape With Artist'. I was about to write that I find it remarkable—my still recalling after all those years a certain few minutes at my desk. But then I reflected that such events have not been uncommon with me. I can still recall from early childhood my first reading certain passages. Anyway, the occasion that I recall was my inserting a new sentence into the final draft of the text. I had shut myself up for a whole weekend in order to get the text ready for sending to the printer. The time must have been late on the Sunday, when I was looking through the last pages of the book. I cannot recall what was the sentence that I replaced or amended, and I'm too tired now to go to my literary archive and to search through the many folders that went into the making of LANDSCAPE WITH LANDSCAPE. I have never forgotten the sentence that I composed and then inserted into the final version of the text. 'I hear from myself a voice I have wanted for a long time to hear.' I had surely composed hundreds of such sentences before, but for some reason I have never forgotten the few moments after I had composed that sentence above. I felt as though I had discovered a precious secret, as indeed I had, although not such a secret as would make writing any easier in the future. I knew I would always have to struggle while I wrote, but having written that sentence, and having read it aloud more than once, I felt as though I would never again struggle without knowing quite what I was struggling towards; as though I knew at last how I ought to write.

I don't offer my quoted sentence as any sort of exemplary sentence, but in its context, it seemed to me one Sunday afternoon in August 1984 and it seems still today a perfect sentence. (Sometimes I wonder whether I should have included the relative pronoun that between voice and I.) All that I want to tell you, Teju, about that sentence is that it gets its power from a noun and from two verbs, one of them repeated. The sentence contains no adjectives or adverbs. I am not averse to using an occasional adjective these days, but I rarely use an adverb. But how did I come to write such a sentence, you still want to know.

When I was looking just now at the last pages of 'Landscape With Artist' for the first time in many years, I saw that the quoted sentence is one of the most important of all the sentences on these pages. (You can read the piece for yourself to learn the truth of this.) The first-person narrator is at last drunk enough and despairing enough to speak the truth to a female person, even though she happens to be merely a painted image. So, what does he say to her? What is this crucial message that he has for womankind? The sentences around supply more than a few hints as to the content of his message, but the essence of his message is never put into words by the author of the fictional text. He writes only that the narrator said at last what he had wanted for a long time to say.

Now, you wrote that my writing is greatly concerned with the transfer of sensations from one mind (my mind, I assume) to another (the reader's mind, surely.) I'm delighted that you find my writing so effective, but I find it paradoxical that I think of my distinctive way of writing as meant more to suggest than to inform or to transfer sensations, as you put it. Can we explain this paradox? Can we explain why I try to avoid description in my writing and why you nevertheless seem to experience what I experience? Is it because I go to much trouble to report the details connected with some or another feeling or sensation or insight but then avoid naming or describing the feeling or sensation or insight, leaving you to supply your own equivalent and to feel as though you share it with me, which is by no means an inaccurate account of events?

I'm very tired. I've spent all my free time for two days at this letter. I'm not complaining. I could not have written less in reply to your own excellent letter, and I'm assuming that Taylor is going to publish some or all of what I've struggled to explain. (If he doesn't, he need not expect any more from me. I'm written out, buggered.) Moreover, I like trying to explain my views, especially since copies of all these pages will go straight into my chronological archive this evening. I may even consider this letter important enough for a coloured label: a strip of silver cardboard with a lime-green sticker atop and on the sticker words such as MY LONG LETTER TO TEJU COLE. Yes, I'm tired, but I want to mention one more feature of my writing in my later books. This is my extreme reluctance to have my narrator seem to accept any sort of shallow generality. I opened the pages of BARLEY PATCH just now and saw the phrase 'the so-called Great Depression'. I wrote thus because I did not want my narrator to be thought of as according any more than a vestige of meaning to the words Great Depression. My narrators study the particular details of their minds; they try to learn the connections between memories from their childhood or daydreams of remote, grassy landscapes. My narrators have no time for the easy-to-use hand-me-downs of popular usage. No narrator of mine would ever accept that the evolution of species is anything more than a theory or that Sigmund Freud was more than a theorist. No narrator of mine would claim to know what adrenalin is, let alone what it feel like. No narrator of mine would claim to know what a feminist is, although he would readily report that some persons called themselves feminists and claimed to understand the word. Am I explaining myself? No narrator of mine would even report that he or any other fictional personage had fallen in love or felt jealous, these being expressions that beg a thousand questions. Robert Musil once wrote that the writer has to break down the accepted concepts of everyday speech and thought and to show what, if anything, lies within them. I don't see this as my duty—I could never have begun to write fiction fifty years ago if I had not seen it as the essential condition of my beginning to write.

I have forty-five minutes still before I'm allowed to open my first bottle of home-brew, but I think I've written enough.

Yours sincerely

Gerald Murnane

The Three Archives of Gerald Murnane[1]

The Literary Archive

This is stored in four steel filing cabinets with a total of twelve drawers, together with a smaller wooden filing cabinet.

Each of the twelve drawers is at least three-quarters filled with hanging files, all clearly labelled. Each of the twelve drawers is given over to one or another of Gerald Murnane's twelve published books. The wooden cabinet is given over to incomplete or unpublished pieces of fiction or poetry.

The Chronological Archive

This archive fills at present twenty-one of the twenty-four drawers in six steel filing cabinets. Each of the twenty-one drawers is closely packed with hanging files. Labels show the year in which each batch of material was filed. In each drawer, at least twenty coloured signposts draw attention to items of more than usual interest. Titles on the signposts are such as

How I wrote TAMARISK ROW
My wife nearly stops me from writing EMERALD BLUE
About nuclear physics and INLAND
(Yet again) why I stopped writing
The origins of my story 'As it were a letter'
A letter explaining my belief in another world
Peter Craven thinks I could win the Nobel Prize
My struggles with BARLEY PATCH
GM is a character in a novel
The truth about me
The girl who became Denise in A LIFETIME ON CLOUDS
I dream the date of my death
My precious glass marbles

Among the items in the Chronological Archive are

* an album containing sixty photographs and more than 3,000 words of text and being an illustrated biography of Gerald Murnane until the age of seventy

* several thousand letters from Gerald Murnane to more than a hundred correspondents, dating from the late 1950s; many of these letters comprise several thousand words; a few letters comprise ten thousand and more words; the longest letter, which is addressed to a young woman and is dated 1987, comprises more than 20,000 words

* a typescript of more than 75,000 words reporting in detail the experiences of Gerald Murnane from 1951 to 1958, when he was aged from twelve to nineteen years

* a journal of more than 1,200 pages and about 350,000 words recording the life and thoughts of Gerald Murnane between 1958 and 1972

* several hundred pages of notes towards the script for the documentary film WORDS AND SILK: THE REAL AND IMAGINARY WORLDS OF GERALD MURNANE, which was awarded first prize in its category at the San Francisco Film Festival in 1991

* voluminous correspondence between Gerald Murnane and several literary scholars in Sweden, where his books were first noticed in the early 1990s before being afterwards published there

* several hundred pages comprising the complete lecture-notes used by Gerald Murnane during his sixteen years as lecturer and senior lecturer at Victoria College (later Deakin University)

* letters and statements explaining why Gerald Murnane began to learn the Hungarian language in 1996; a report of 3,000 words explaining how he learned the language

* a notebook titled MY SHAME LIFE and containing reports totalling more than 20,000 words of matters that Gerald Murnane is ashamed of

* messages written by Gerald Murnane to an imaginary future reader of his archives and labelled Titkos dolgok, which is Hungarian for 'secret matters'

* documentation of Gerald Murnane's lifelong interest in horseracing and

of his continuing efforts to devise a means of earning a regular income from betting

* a detailed account of the mental game devised by Gerald Murnane in the early 1990s in order to indulge his various sexual fantasies; detailed written reports (comprising 170,000 words) of numerous playing of the mental game

* a typescript of 75,000 words titled <u>Azok akik engem szerettek volna</u> (Those who might have loved me) reporting the dealings between Gerald Murnane and each of more than forty persons whom he courted or thought of courting or who, so he came to believe late in life, were courting him or thinking of doing so

* a typescript of more than 40,000 words titled <u>Csodák</u> (Miracles) and reporting more than forty occurrences in the life of Gerald Murnane that seemed to him more likely to have been arranged than merely to have happened

The Antipodean Archive

This is stored in a two-drawer filing cabinet. In the files are about a thousand pages of maps, charts, diagrams, lists, and sketches describing the organisation, administration, and day-to-day running of horse-racing in two imaginary countries by name New Eden and New Arcady and called collectively the Antipodes. Many of the pages report in detail the results of several hundred races decided in each country. One file contains several letters and essays comprising in total more than 10,000 words and explaining Gerald Murnane's reasons for setting up the Antipodean Archive in 1985 and adding to it continually in the years since.

An Interview with Gerald Murnane

Will Heyward

This conversation took place in person on 25 January 2012.

You have a huge archive of written material. For a long time you published nothing, yet you continued adding to your archive during those years. What makes you want to publish your work, and what makes you want to privately store it?

Well, I never gave up writing, but I didn't write any particular work with publication in mind. This was partly because I didn't think that I had another book in me, so to speak. The other answer is hidden in a story called "The Interior of Gaaldine," in *Emerald Blue*. Because nobody seemed to understand that, or see that, in fact, the text contained an answer to this question, I rephrased the matter, so to speak, or retexted the matter, in *Barley Patch*, trying to explain why a person of my standing, or of my published history, would want to stop writing. It has to do with the part of the archive that you saw yesterday called the Antipodean Archive.

I seemed to discover in the 1990s that all fiction was bordered by a landscape where imaginary racecourses were situated and imaginary horses raced. The word *Gaaldine*, as the matter is explained in *Barley Patch*, refers to an imaginary country on the borderlines of a further imaginary country, called Gondal, which was the world where the members of the Brontë family, as youngsters, used to set fictional works, poems, and histories. It was physically located, I think, in West Africa, but was more or less an English sort of colony or land. And, in a famous sentence, Emily Brontë wrote, "Gondal is discovering the interior of Gaaldine." Or, in other words, people in an imaginary setting are discovering a further imaginary setting, suggesting an infinite progression of imaginary places. And this, in some ways, relates to my seeming discovery, in the 1980s and 1990s, that beyond the fictional landscapes that I saw, if you like, or used as the settings for my fiction, there was a further landscape of imaginary horse racing—and that's the first and last time I'll ever say it this simply and directly, and, for lots of reasons, I'm not even comfortable saying that.

There's another thing I have to say in connection—and I think I mentioned this in *Barley Patch*, but perhaps I didn't—and that is that no critic who read "The Interior of Gaaldine" saw any connection between the Brontës and what I was writing about. The story is the last piece in *Emerald Blue*, and it was intended to be the last piece of fiction I ever wrote, or ever had published, and it was, for many years. *Emerald Blue* was published in 1995. So, for ten years, it was the last of my published pieces. Now, the character in "The Interior of Gaaldine" wakes—and it could be a dream or it could be real—in the middle of the night, and there's a young woman beside his bed—he's horribly, almost deliriously drunk—with a manuscript, or a huge collection of pages. He seems to remember that she gave her name as Alice, spelled A-L-I-C-E in the text, but the astute reader, and I doubt if there are very many of them, is meant to understand that her name is E-L-L-I-S, because Ellis Bell was the first pen name used by Emily Brontë. So, if this woman is Emily Brontë, or pretending to be Emily Brontë, she is using Emily Brontë's fictional name, Ellis, to say who she is, and it's all very complicated and twisting and turning, but that is my answer to your question… And therefore, in the years when I was writing fiction as well as adding to my archives—and I must have written hundreds of thousands of words for my archives—I was also adding to my Antipodean Archive, which is a fictional horse-racing archive.

In certain of your writings, you seem to make reference to a distinction between the "visible world" and the "invisible world." What is that distinction? Is it a distinction between written and unwritten, or something else entirely?

That's a very complicated question, and I don't really think of it in that way. To me, when I write, I'm trying to render visible what is invisible. I don't think of there being a written world. Writing is words and sentences on paper that help to bring into being invisible worlds, or invisible landscapes, or invisible characters, or whatever. I began to realize not that many years ago that when I read a book—and this comes through in *Barley Patch* and *A History of Books*—I don't always pay close attention to the text. The act of reading was a liberating act, or it freed me up to start seeing what I wasn't previously able to see.

When I write I've often said that all I do is report the contents of my mind, and that's about it. "The contents of a mind"—it's a nice, neat little phrase, but the meaning of it, or what it denotes, is something immensely complicated and convoluted, just like your question and my answer. To try and restate it, finally: yes, I see us poised, metaphorically speaking, with one foot in the invisible world—and one foot in the visible world. And writing expands my knowledge of the invisible.

There is something almost fractal in your work: one sentence causes another sentence, one thought leads to another, and something gives rise to the impression of infinity. Does that sound right to you?

That's a nice comment, and a few others have said that, and I do feel that way when I'm writing, because of the multiplicity of concerns that affect me when I'm writing. I'm trying to write about a single subject that is present before my mental eye, so to speak. Of course, as we all know, the mind is a rapidly changing thing, or its landscapes and points of view change rapidly.

I once defined *meaning* as the discovery of connections between things that previously seemed unconnected. One of the happiest moments for me when I'm writing is the moment of discovery: when I find that an image that I'd thought was unconnected with anything else in my writing or my memory is, in fact, the center of a spiderweb-shaped network of imagery.

The other thing, which I will throw in because it just came to mind as I described that, is that I quite often can very clearly remember something that I have written, but I'm unable to remember the book in which I wrote it. In fact, if someone sat down and read all my published works after they read the one I have just written, *Border Districts*, they would find quite a bit of repetition—the same scene, or the same incident, or the same image of something, perhaps treated differently. It is almost because sometimes I have forgotten that I have written about something before. Or, more often, I get a new perspective on something, or an image takes on more meaning, or becomes connected with things I did not previously see. I'm not at all ashamed that I have written about the same things in several different books, in several different ways.

I've read your most recent books and then went back to *Tamarisk Row*, and it seems that you have become more and more concerned with your memories of what it felt like to read things at an earlier time. Is there something driving this return to your earliest experiences of reading?

The simple practical discovery that I have forgotten most of what I read and yet I remember the small things, which I wouldn't have thought were important to me. What follows [in my writing] is a sort of investigation into why this should be so. Also, my attitude to reading has changed. I used to read in the hope of discovering things, but—and I think this is a natural result of being older—I read now in the hope of being reassured. I don't mean consoled. I mean to find proof that what I have previously divined or intimated is actually true. I think that it is natural for a young person to read to learn and discover. But I think now that I'm just reading to reassure myself.

And the books that you talk about in *A History of Books*—for example, Proust—are these the books that reassure you?

Well, when I say *reassure*, what I mean is that these books say to me that the patterns I have discovered are actual, that they make sense, and that it was good for me, that I should have discovered these patterns.

What is the meaning of this preoccupation you have with, for example, certain colors or patterns in, say, the freckles on a face, the racing silks of a jockey, a landscape, etc.? What is it about these visual things that makes you fixate on them?

My way of understanding the world is such that I seem to be handicapped. When it comes to thinking in abstract terms, I feel handicapped or restricted. My way of understanding things usually comes from visualizing or from sight. But part of the answer to your question may be that I was born with what's known as anosmia, which means I have no sense of smell. So, to me, when people describe their sense of smell, and the narrator of *Inland* says this, I see colors. So if you were to say to me that the smell of the lilac was very strong this afternoon, I would see little droplets of lilac-colored moisture floating through the air.

Synesthesia. There was the composer...

Scriabin. Maybe he wasn't so affected, although he had a theory of music that it should affect all the senses. But, in my case, the sense of sight is the overwhelming sense. Smell means nothing to me. And although I am musical—I can play music, simple tunes by sight—music doesn't mean as much to me. Even if I hear something that speaks to me, so to speak, I translate it into visual information. For me, the ultimate discovery would be to see everything. Everything that exists is there to be seen. At least, that's my premise.

You mention the way you visualize the conversations you have. Do you think this influences the way you write? I ask because the rhythm of your prose is so controlled.

Well, if I'm writing a compound sentence with three or four clauses, I actually have a rudimentary map of it in my mind as it unfolds. I can hear the sentence as I'm composing it, I can see the map of it, but, of course, I have to be aware of the sense of it—it has to make sense. I once said to somebody, maybe my wife, that of all the things I claim to be good at— and, you know, most of us think we are good at six or seven things—the thing I'm best at is arranging words into sentences. And not just in English, but in Hungarian.

I think this is a good chance to ask you about something very specific that I have noticed about your writing. You often employ adjectives such as *certain* or *so-called*, as in, "A certain color could be seen." So this color is specific, but it is unnamed. And I haven't made up my mind as to the effect you're generating, but there is something happening.

It's a reluctance to declare, or a reluctance to have myself thought as accepting conventional notions of things. So if I said to you, "We visited one of the leading families of Goroke," and if I meant that seriously and conscientiously, you could assume rightly, unless I was deliberately lying to or deceiving you, that I went along with the notion that in the structure of society there are leading families and there are less-than-leading families. Or if I said to you, "One of the great novels of Australia is Henry Handel Richardson's *The Fortunes of Richard Mahony*," you would assume, and rightly so, unless I was deliberately deceiving you, that I believe there is a hierarchy of books, among which there are those entitled to be called great—but I don't believe either of those propositions. I'll say that to you in ordinary conversation because I'm lazy, and because I want to get along with you, and basically I suppose I half believe it, that there are leading families and whatnot, because it makes for better communication if we can agree on language. But if I were writing this in fiction, I would say, "The chief character of a party from Melbourne went to visit one of the so-called leading families of the district," meaning that I don't believe that there are such things as "leading families," although I concede that many people do. And it makes for a convenient way of writing a report of this event. And I might say, "He was reading Henry Handel Richardson's *The Fortunes of Richard Mahony*, a book called by many one of the great books of Australian literature." Have I made my point?

So there is a distance between this sort of "consensus" meaning of a word, and what the narrator actually means.

Yes, but I don't think it is meant to be restricting. I think it is meant to be more liberating. I can more or less imply a question to you: do you believe there are so-called great books? And if you do, would you include *The Fortunes of Richard Mahony*? I'm allowing the reader freedom. Whereas I think that so many writers just assume we are all on the same wavelength, and take on social baggage and commonplace clichés. What goes right against my whole set of beliefs is worn-out expressions and ways of thinking.

Your sentences are very logical and rational. Would you say your books are logical? There's a line in *The Plains* where you say that the plainsmen got tired of logic and began using it for "ingenious parlor games."

I go back to the word connections. As the narrator says in *Inland*, "Everything is more than one thing." If you look at something long enough, it turns into something else. If you write about something for long enough, you'll find that it is connected to something else. The basic sentence is: the sky is blue. That's as basic as you can get. What that's doing—and it's pretty obvious—is making a connection between something you can see and the quality it possesses, and making a simple statement. Probably the longest sentence I have ever written is somewhere in *Tamarisk Row*, which is trying to make a connection between about ten or twenty different things, all of which one person, the boy Clement Killeaton, has experienced. He has a compulsion or feeling that they're not just random things, that there is something that links them all together apart from the fact that they are all related to him.

Just as you mention Proust as an author who has stayed with you, you mention Calvino in some of your essays.

It's a funny thing. This relates to something I said earlier about how when I'm reading, I'm not really paying attention to the text. I've put this into *A History of Books*, or I've certainly put it somewhere in my books: A lot of the pleasure of owning books for me has been the pleasure of first reading a review, which told me the book was of a certain kind and quality, and then buying the book and putting it on my shelves. Then, during the year, or years, that might pass, I speculated about and imagined the contents and thought, "What a pleasure it will be when I read this book, because it's going to be about X, Y, Z, handled in a manner similar to A, B, C," or whatever, and my imagining the contents of the book sustained me and nourished me and inspired me far more, in fact, than the actual contents of the book when I came to read it. Years later, when I had forgotten what I read in the book, I still remembered the imaginary book I had expected to read based on the review and blurb. Calvino is like this for me. I read *Invisible Cities*, but not long ago I tried to read *The Castle of Crossed Destinies*, and I couldn't keep going. I thought, "I could have written this," and if I could have written a book, I don't want to read it. I just assumed that based on the clumsy beginning. I mean, Calvino died in his fifties of a brain hemorrhage, so I'm twenty years older than Calvino was when he died. Presumably, I'm not Calvino's inferior or his apprentice. I just said, "Calvino, you could have done a lot better with that book."

Invisible Cities, however, did influence me. I don't know where you would find the evidence, but a scholar of genius would find traces of it in my writing. For a few years, I know an influence came to me by way of *Invisible Cities*, which I read from cover to cover. Borges is the same sort of writer. Not much of his writing stays in my mind, but the notion of a blind man in a library, in a country of vast plains, Argentina—that does inspire me. I think: "I want to be Borges and write like that." But when I read him, I don't find much in it that is particularly marvelous.

That idea of the real book never living up to the imaginary book that one reads in one's mind before one even opens the real book—is this your relationship to the world outside Victoria?

Oh, yes. I mean, there are other sorts of practical considerations like fear.

I have been to Sydney and whatnot. Also, I'm very concerned by organization, and I hate packing and unpacking. I hate not knowing where certain things are. And when I do go to places, I'm so overwhelmed—and this is literally true, it's not an exaggeration—that, rather than go sightseeing, to use that horrible expression, I just go into my room and read a book at every chance I get. Sightseeing is just so against everything for me. Sights are only surfaces. What I'm interested in are the sights you see in your mind as a result of other sights. The most precious sights of all could arrive to me just by my glancing at a house like any other.

Your writing does seem to favor an indirect treatment of its subjects—a clear treatment, but an indirect one. The idea that it's more interesting to see something partially…

There is a passage in *Border Districts* in which the narrator sits on a veranda at a wedding in house in Camberwell, although it's not called Camberwell, about to go to a big horse race. This narrator is so affected by the sight of the house with vines hanging over it that instead of going to listen to the race, he just sits there and tries to see the race in his mind as it might be run. He concludes at the end of the experience—although he has other experiences of landscapes and mental landscapes—that "renunciation may be preferable to experience, that solitude may be preferable to company," or something like that. But it is a common [experience]. I'm not the first by a million to postulate like this, especially in regard to females and romantic meetings. The same narrator, talking about idealized heroines of fiction, says—and here I'm writing in the first person:

> And did it never occur to me to search in the so-called real world for actual equivalents to these females? Yes, it did so occur at times, but what happened after the meeting that took place between myself and them was more like the end of a novel than anything that could happen in the real world.

That is meant to be paradoxical, almost self-defeating. As I understand the word *autistic*—and I'm cautious here—it may be an appropriate description of myself in regard to the world. I like to hold the world at a certain distance so that I can turn it this way and that.

Speaking of the real world, I like the author's note to *Invisible Yet Enduring Lilacs*, in which you say: "I should never have tried to write fiction or non-fiction or even anything in-between. I should have left it to discerning editors to publish all my pieces of writing as essays." And you say something similar in *Barley Patch* about rejecting the words *novel* and *short story*.

There's a piece in *Invisible Yet Enduring Lilacs* that I first presented and delivered as a speech. I wrote conscientiously for months about the effect Proust has on me. It started out as autobiography, but most of it is just pure fiction. I can't say that I ever experienced half the things I wrote about in that essay, but it made for a good piece of writing. I presented it as an essay, but I would comfortably put it in a book of fiction. That suggests to me, if not tells me, that there is a very fine line between the two.

This way you have come to understand the act of writing...

I'm no closer. It's a mystery. When you start to put down words, your own personality becomes fractured. You're never quite sure what part of you the words are coming from. It's a fairly trite statement, but you begin to question the reliability of memory or even experience itself. What emerges from the writing is something that could never have been predicted. This is the magic: that writing is unpredictable. It leads to discovery, and that is a word that is overused and has a sort of twee sound, and it's not a word I feel comfortable with. But from writing, you learn things you couldn't possibly learn by any other means.

Mere Dreaming: On *Tamarisk Row* and *A Lifetime on Clouds*

Tristan Foster

A child creates an imagined reality not by viewing an object as representative of something else but by reinterpreting it as this new imagined thing. A cardboard box stops being a box and becomes a boat the moment a child climbs into it, the floor suddenly a vast body of water to be sailed. But there is a point en route to adulthood when this sort of faithfully imagined world becomes inaccessible.

Gerald Murnane's first two works of fiction, *Tamarisk Row* and *A Lifetime on Clouds*, both center around a boy and his acts of imagination. For Clement Killeaton, the protagonist of *Tamarisk Row*, the objects of his world are not merely props in his fantasies; they become the things he imagines them to be. An uneven line of marbles in the dirt represents a moment in a horse race; pieces of pine for kindling become suckling baby dingoes; a horse race heard on the radio is a contest of Olympian proportions, taking place in an abstract dimension beyond the known. The horses charge past distant towns and roll like thunder over dusty plains.

Adrian Sherd, the protagonist of *A Lifetime on Clouds*, faces a dilemma. Adrian is old enough to understand the distinction between his imagined world and reality, but that does not mean these worlds can coexist without friction, nor does it mean that when the day comes, he will be prepared to abandon the realms of his imagination.

Tamarisk Row succeeds not only because within its covers the real and the imagined converge and become one, but also because Clement inhabits a space that is central both to his character and the way he views the world, and to the novel's narrative technique. This is even acknowledged by his father, Augustine, who one night as Clement is playing with his marbles in the house "warns him that he does too much dreaming on his own." Augustine fails to realize that the space in which Clement exists is informed by him and his reality—the so-called adult world.

Clement's Maiden Cup is a rerun of a race that Augustine's horse won when Augustine was a young man. The picture of the horse crossing the finish line hangs on the Killeatons' living-room wall as a sort of religious icon, looming above Clement as he plays; it is a victory that has dictated his family's fate. Horse racing is so essential to Clement's understanding of the world that races on the radio do not encompass the wider world, but are the wider world. His are not imaginings of a mythical, faraway land—Clement's daydreams are grounded in the daily reality of his family's beliefs, desires, and social standing. Above all, Clement's reality is made from the quixotic hopes and dreams of his father.

In many ways, *Tamarisk Row* is a record of the sexual discoveries of a boy as he tries to get a glimpse of the secret hidden between schoolgirls' legs. For Clement, the secrets of girls are the secrets of the universe. Sex thrills the boy nearly as much as do the possibilities of a marble-horse race, so he has difficulty extricating the two, believing that a prospective girlfriend "may even agree to be the wife of a racehorse owner on condition that he leads in the winner of the most famous race in a land of mighty plains." While these ideas and mythologies come from and are reinforced by the adults around him, the excitement Clement experiences at the prospect of a race is one that Augustine has forgotten; it has long been replaced by a joyless addiction. Father and son have their obsessions, but while Augustine is defeated, Clement conquers, which suggests that he will soon outgrow his preoccupations.

Clement does not appear in literature without precedent. One of the character's precursors is found in Proust's *Swann's Way*. The narrator informs the reader that as a child he would hurry to read the names of new plays being performed (plays he would never actually see) and indulge in the evocations of their titles and the colors of their bills, even ranking the quality of actors in imaginary lists, based on nothing but real and imagined hearsay.

"I was a lover of theater; a Platonic lover, as my parents hadn't allowed me to enter one," Proust writes. "Nothing could be more disinterested or happier than the daydreams with which these announcements filled my imagination." The same can be said of Clement's Platonic love affair with horse racing: nothing makes Clement happier than painstakingly staging the Gold Cup in the rare hours he is alone, documenting each leg of the race and the associated network of lives and households and sexual acts linked with the fortunes of each marble horse. It is on this notion that Murnane bases his novel's entire aesthetic.

In the opening pages of James Joyce's *A Portrait of the Artist as a Young Man*, Stephen Dedelus, out on the football pitch with his boarding school peers, experiences a momentary gleaning of just how vast the world is. This insight stirs in him a desire to understand his place in the order of the universe. Clement, however, remains in an earlier stage of development. The world beyond the town of Bassett, where the Killeatons live, is not something he has yet been confronted with, and certainly not on his own. He begins to guess at the meaning of his impermanence in a universe beyond his control, but he does not struggle against this idea or attempt to come to terms with it, as Stephen does; the thought that it might be controlled never occurs to Clement. The outcomes of his marble-horse races are always left to chance.

If *Tamarisk Row* leaves Clement on the cusp of realization, *A Lifetime on Clouds* re-creates the dilemmas of faith that trouble the mind of the teenage Stephen Dedelus. Adrian Sherd shares Clement's tendency to trade reality for an imagined world, spending his days in school and his evenings in complex unrealities. However, marble racing games and attempts to see up a playmate's skirt have made way—entirely—for sexual and religious fantasies.

After dinner, Adrian plays on a model railway that runs over a crude drawing of North America; the spot on the map where the train comes to a halt designating the location where his sexual fantasies will take place that night. Unlike Clement's imagined reality, which is positioned as a unique incarnation of the adult world, Adrian's imagined reality is a realm he recognizes as distinct, which prompts him to question whether his increasingly convoluted sexual fantasies are the musings of a lunatic, because he cannot "imagine any men or women in real life doing such things together." But, like Clement, Adrian willfully spends much of his waking life in fantasy landscapes that are grounded in the real yet are ultimately of his own creation.

Landscape—both figurative and imagined—is key to the narrative of *A Lifetime on Clouds*, though not in the same way that it is important to Murnane's debut novel, nor to his later work. Where *Tamarisk Row* explores both the landscape of the mind of a young boy and the physical landscape of the town where he lives, *A Lifetime on Clouds* solely traverses the mental landscape of a pubescent teen. The novel maps out three interior landmarks in particular: Adrian's desire to uphold the teachings of the Catholic Church, the varying degrees of tension created by sexual discovery, and the accumulating guilt from his acts of sin.

"In a monastery a boy had so many beautiful things to inspire him that he soon forgot about women," the narrator tells us. Adrian expects that salvation will come from beauty—and, for a time, it does. While he waits for religious enlightenment to liberate him from his shame, it in fact arrives in the form of a schoolgirl he sees on the train and idealizes. Soon she is a permanent companion, discovering Australia with him, keeping him from "self-sinning." Though she has saved him, he can never admit to her that "his only regret was that Denise herself would never know his story… In her innocence she could never imagine the filth she had rescued him from." Adrian, in fact, never says a word to Denise, who remains purely symbolic. The simple possibility of her is, for Adrian, satisfying enough.

The feeling of guilt is manifested fully in *A Lifetime on Clouds*. It weighs on the adults in *Tamarisk Row*, Augustine in particular, but Clement neither understands nor fears it, so the feeling goes unqualified and lingers like a conversation that is interrupted before the point is made. But if there is a meaningful thematic link between the two novels, it is that *A Lifetime on Clouds* realizes this guilt and places it at the foundation of all of Adrian's thoughts and actions; guilt thus becomes the narrative's focal point.

In *A Portrait of the Artist as a Young Man*, guilt—maybe the weight of the guilt of an entire people—explodes into epiphany, thus enacting the modernist trope of transcendence. Adrian lives in a run-down but young suburb on the outskirts of Melbourne and is a loner at school. Murnane has at his disposal the shame not of a people but of a single imaginative boy. The guilt experienced by Adrian, then, is positioned in such a way that when beauty fails him, the only way out of his guilt is by engaging its source—that is, by joining the Catholic Church, as Stephen considers doing.

If *A Lifetime on Clouds* is a reframing of *A Portrait of the Artist as a Young Man*, it is one that is typical of Australia in the mid-twentieth century. There is no re-creation of the infamous sermon on hell; in its place are awkward sex-education lessons given by red-faced priests and schoolyard banter about wanking. These scenes make *A Lifetime on Clouds* Murnane's funniest book. His humor appears in touches in his debut novel, but, after *A Lifetime on Clouds*, it takes something of a leave of absence from his work—coinciding with the point at which his characters enter adulthood.

To not mention the autobiographical nature of *Tamarisk Row* and *A Lifetime on Clouds* would be a bit conspicuous, yet to mention it could risk lending it more significance than it deserves. In his note to readers at the beginning of *Invisible Yet Enduring Lilacs* Murnane writes: "I should have left it to discerning editors to publish all my pieces of writing as essays." However, *Tamarisk Row* tells the story of a boy named not Gerald Murnane but Clement Killeaton, and the story takes place in a backyard and a school in a town named not Bendigo but Bassett. Neither Clement nor Bassett has ever existed. All of this is a rather long way of saying *Tamarisk Row* is a piece of fiction. Of greater significance, then, is the usefulness of his first two novels not as autobiographical or semiautobiographical texts but as pieces of fiction and their place in relation to Murnane's later writing.

Murnane's catalog is filled with direct and indirect references to his other work, as if each new story has sprouted from one or more of his others. We might suppose that Gerald Murnane is writing about a life that is both his own and not, as if there is a fictional life unfolding in parallel to his real life, one with a childhood that includes a blurring of the real and imagined, real and unreal horseraces, crippling guilt, sexual exploration, and a father accumulating gambling debts. The events in his debut novel, especially, resonate through his later work. The narrator of *Inland* refers to a childhood spent in a Victorian town where the narrator's father befriends men rich from the gold rush and accumulates so much debt that the family is forced to flee their home. In the short story "As It Were A Letter," from *A History of Books*, the narrator recalls a time in his boyhood when his family left their home due to mounting debt and he was left at a relative's house, where he made up games in the dirt. Likewise, in *Barley Patch*, the narrator speaks directly about the elaborate games of his childhood:

> The sort of game that I played in my own backyard needed weeks of preparation: I had to set up a farming property under each shrub and then to mark out the roads that crossed my rural district and finally to choose the names for husbands and wives who lived at each property.

Tamarisk Row not only tells a story that Murnane revisits time and again in his later writing, as if it is part of the childhood of this parallel life that Murnane documents in his writing, but also explores the kernels of all his writing obsessions: his preoccupations with one thing being representative of another thing, landscape, horse racing, and the real alongside the imagined—obsessions that evolve and are altered with time and age but that ultimately endure.

Despite these lifelong obsessions, or maybe because of them, it is clear that Murnane is a deliberate writer. Of course, all acts of writing are deliberate, but his work suggests that he never allows himself to be surprised by where the pieces have fallen; the limits to which he writes are defined in these first novels. Murnane's oeuvre is essentially a chronological telling of the story of the insular world of a parallel life, with *Tamarisk Row* covering childhood and *A Lifetime on Clouds* covering adolescence. From the beginning, his writing has been built using a precise architecture, and it's a rare occasion when he deviates from it. Maybe, for Murnane, the act of the horse race is in opposition to the act of writing. Perhaps it's for this reason that his attraction to racing has remained—it is literally the territory of chance. It is Clement on the living-room floor with his marble racehorses, in near ecstasy at this act of the gods.

Of *Tamarisk Row*, Murnane has written:

> I seemed to have sensed from the first that to read fiction was to create for myself a new kind of space… [I hope] that an appreciative reader of my book would seem to be viewing fictional scenes and personages as though through colored glass.

As well as his obsessions and his creative limits, present in these early works are sentences that are uncomplicated and unaffected, sentences that read as if, after writing them, the author has run the heel of his palm over them to smooth out the creases. But also manifested in *Tamarisk Row* and *A Lifetime on Clouds* is the maturation of Murnane's writing style and the way he goes about creating this "new kind of space."

It is within *Tamarisk Row*—that is to say, within the character of Clement—that this "new kind of space," a compromise between reality and full-blown fantasy, most successfully comes into being. It succeeds precisely because of the naïveté of the child—it exists for Clement, and thus for the reader, because Clement, in his innocence, knows no better. But Clement, if removed from the page, will grow up, will learn, will begin to see the world as baroque or overwrought or simply as something other than what he'd thought it to be. The moment he becomes aware that his world is informed by something larger, the architecture supporting this space, as it appears in *Tamarisk Row*, collapses. Murnane acknowledges and goes through some pains to deal with the impending problems of this in *A Lifetime on Clouds*. In a moment of lucidity between daydreams, Adrian understands the problem that is at the heart of willfully turning away from reality: "He had spent too much time in unreal conjectures, in devising whole years of a future that would never eventuate." Herein lies the problem with this space as it appears in Murnane's early work. Throwing a sheet over reality, using secret rules to construct the labyrinthine, the modest creation of the new—these acts may have parallels with the writing of fiction, but it is not the typical domain of the adult. As the subject of Murnane's writing ages, acquiring knowledge and new desires, the space in which this parallel life takes place must also change.

Both novels conclude in fantasy. Clement runs the Gold Cup one more time in the hope of bringing Tamarisk Row—the marble, the horse, the embodiment of the hopes and dreams of the imaginary husband and wife who live under the tamarisks in the Killeatons' backyard—home, and Adrian, in his imagined role as priest, is asked for advice by a senior clergyman and hears the confessions of a couple of teenagers with predicaments not unlike his own. But these fantasies are entered into with the knowledge that these imagined spaces will never be quite the same again. And nor will Murnane's writing ever be the same; only in short fiction does he again revisit a fictional world of this sort, with this perfect "new kind of space" that he creates in *Tamarisk Row* and which persists, but is inevitably altered, in *A Lifetime on Clouds*. Closest, maybe, comes *The Plains*, but that is another new space altogether.

Far Enough: The Peculiar World of *The Plains*

Wayne Macauley

The dust jacket of the first edition of *The Plains* describes it as "a lament for an Australian literature that has never been written." Thirty years later, this strange, disquieting, curious little book continues to stand almost alone in the library of alternative Australian fiction. But make no mistake: this is no archaeological artifact. *The Plains* is a masterpiece, and, word for word, sentence for sentence, one of the best novels ever written in this country.

Like all great allegories, its premise is simple. A filmmaker, researching a script to be called *The Interior*, journeys to the flat plains of the inland where, in a remote town, he spends his days in the pub trying to learn what he can about the so-called plainsmen and their peculiar way of life. Because it is peculiar. Like the many other petitioners who have made the journey ("I cannot even say that at a certain hour I knew I had left Australia") in the hope of finding a patron among the wealthy landowners there, our narrator must work hard to understand their culture—detailed, arcane, and to the outsider utterly foreign—if he is to find favor with them.

It is right that a peculiar literary work should have a peculiar publishing history. Murnane had originally written a work of about sixty thousand words, *The Only Adam*, with the opening and closing sections set in a place "that might have stood in relation to the setting of the rest of the book as a mirage stands in relationship to the landscape that gives rise to it." Bruce Gillespie, the publisher at Norstrilia, a small press specializing in sci-fi and speculative fiction (Murnane: "I would have thought that all fiction is speculative"), suggested that if *The Only Adam* failed to find a publisher he would like to include "the plains sections" in an anthology he was planning. The longer work never did find a home, and Murnane decided to explore his mirage further. "It seemed to me," he told me recently, "that I could write more than I had already written about my mysterious plains." In 1982, Gillespie published this thirty-thousand-word manuscript as a handsome hardback.

When I first read *The Plains*, in my late twenties, I noted in my diary that it was "miles beyond most other Australian writing I've read." I had already given [Patrick] White a fair go, and [Christina] Stead; I had read most of [Henry] Lawson and stumbled my way through that other great curio, Joseph Furphy's *Such Is Life*. I'd read some early [Peter] Carey and [Murray] Bail, and was keeping up where I could with the little magazines and journals. But *The Plains* was something else. Here was a stepping-off into an alternative world as exhilarating as anything proposed by Swift, Kafka, Borges, or Calvino, written in a prose to rival the European greats I had already fallen in love with. And, more important, in the subtle cultural investigations going on deep within the book, Murnane seemed to be forging his own way not just toward an alternative Australian literature but also an alternative way of imagining the country. With an eye both to the European and South American avant-garde, combined with hefty doses of Proust and Kerouac—most evident in his extraordinary debut novel, *Tamarisk Row*—he was out on his own making something eccentric, free-floating, and completely new.

Because, let's not forget—aside from its startling originality, *The Plains* is also a very funny book. In the early pages especially, Murnane maps our national anxieties—the paranoia about who we are and what we might be, the idea that culture is always somehow elsewhere—with a withering sense of humor. Where explorers like Thomas Livingstone Mitchell (quoted in the epigraph) saw this continent's inland as a blank slate, *The Plains* dares us to see it otherwise. Yes, the interior, that vast, empty space we coast dwellers habitually turn away from, is forbidding, but it is by no means bereft. While we've been gazing across the ocean, something peculiar has been going on behind our backs. The imaginative leap of *The Plains* is to reverse the comfortable order of the idea of culture being "over there" and to see instead Australia's interior as a richly storied other world. The people who dwell out on the plains are not cringing hicks. They're experimentalists. They're cutting edge. They're everything we coast dwellers are not.

In the dialogues of the landowners, in the narrator's musings in the pub and then as he wanders the vast library of his patron, in the way he watches his patron's daughter and wife ("still beautiful according to the conventions of the plains") moving among the estate's gardens and lawns, we see a world shimmering with speculation and wonder. The plains' history is so rich and its arts and sciences so sophisticated that they challenge anything old Europe has to offer, and the plainsmen themselves—deep-thinking, serious, and culturally alert—"confront even the most obdurate or the most ingenuous work utterly receptive and willing." No, this is not the inland of lonely truck stops and whistling wires and fat guys fishing the last potato cake out of the bain-marie. Out on Murnane's plains you get everything: the great perplexity of human existence, the itch of human flesh, the tug on the heart, the dreamy imagining of togetherness, the comedy of trying. Here is the narrator planning his courtship of his patron's wife:

> As soon as I had finished my preliminary notes for *The Interior*, and before I began work on the filmscript itself, I would write a short work—probably a collection of essays—which would settle things between the woman and myself. I would have it published privately under one of the seldom-used imprints that my patron reserves for his clients' work in progress or marginalia. And I would so arrange the ostensible subject-matter of the work that the librarians here would insert a copy among the shelves where she spends her afternoons.
>
> I foresaw this much of my scheme happening as I had planned it. The only uncertain item was the last—I had no way of ensuring that the woman would open my book during her lifetime…

*

Dear Gerald,

This is a letter I have been meaning to write for a very long time. I first read The Plains *in 1985 and it had a profound effect on me. At the time I was a 27-year-old writer wondering if there was any new Australian literature I was ever going to like, let alone get inspiration from. Your book gave me great faith in continuing to pursue the writing I had been doing—writing, it's true, that never looked like getting published but was nonetheless, I think, true to itself and its creator…*

This is the first paragraph of a letter I wrote to Gerald Murnane in 2002. I was at the time a forty-four-year-old writer about to have his first book published. We are, all of us, at some point, I think, looking for some line of steerage, something to set our course by, some little marker buoy out there that tells us we're not completely lost. This is what *The Plains* was for me. This tiny little book, written in my city by a person twenty years my senior, living in a suburb just a stone's throw away, somehow made everything right. By that time I'd read and loved Hamsun, Walser,

Kafka, Gombrowicz, Beckett, and others, but there was no one in Australia who spoke to me in the same way. *The Plains* became for me an iconic book, a black diamond, a Rosetta Stone.

It was about the feat of imagination—how many Australian books dared go where this one went?—but it was also about the marks on the paper. Few living writers anywhere are as ambitious with the prose form as Gerald Murnane is. He fills his works with sentences so boldly constructed and so beautifully finished that any writer serious about their craft would be well advised to spend some time with them: the subtle unreeling of the narrative, the phrases creeping one by one toward a distantly observed idea, the hand-on-mouth humor, the firm and steady gaze. You might not know where Murnane is taking you, but you can't help being taken.

> The countless volumes of this library are close-set with so much speculative prose, so many chapters after chapters appear in parentheses, such glosses and footnotes surround the thin trickles of actual text that I fear to discover in some unexceptional essay by a plainsman of no great reputation a tentative paragraph describing a man not unlike myself speculating endlessly about the plains but never setting foot on them...

Gerald and I have continued to exchange letters over the years. We have still never met. It is, in the old sense, a prosaic relationship. Late last year in place of a letter, he sent me a photo of a straight road cutting a line through the Wimmera plains toward Mount Arapiles in the distance. His note to me was written on the back. He was, he said, "in excellent health and spirits," had a new work on the go, and would soon have his tenth book published. I looked at that photo for a long time—the straight road, the low horizon, the big blue sky—and saw in it a story that had now come full circle. Gerald Murnane, author of *The Plains*, was writing to me from them.

What, then, is this thing we might call an alternative Australian literature, and what would it look like? The last word might come from one of the earliest passages in *The Plains*. Compelled one day in the pub to tell the plainsmen his own story before they will let him listen to theirs, the narrator says: "I told them a story almost devoid of events or achievements. Outsiders would have made little of it, but the plainsmen understood."

I invite all plainsmen and -women to read, laugh at, enjoy, and be inspired by this extraordinary book.

Gerald Murnane's Exquisite Failures

Matthew Jakubowski

> I saw nothing absurd in what I was doing—sitting at the heart of the scene I had dreamed of fifteen years before and yet dreaming further of another scene that would lead me at last into the real world. I had the pleasant suspicion that I was about to complete a neat pattern I had often admired as a subject for fiction. I might have been about to demonstrate that at the heart of every scene assumed to be real was at least one character imagining further scenes that would be closer still to reality.
>
> —Gerald Murnane

Gerald Murnane's *Landscape with Landscape* comprises six interlinked narratives that echo one another, evoking a sort of chorus of possible lives about an anonymous would-be writer.

The collection's title is one we might expect to find on a gallery wall beside a symbolic realist painting. It might spur us to imagine a layered representation of a panoramic scene, complete in one sense yet with any given image partially concealing several others. Murnane's choice to title this book as if it were a landscape painting is no gimmick: its six narrators are writers in the suburbs of Melbourne who are all obsessed with an abstract notion they call "landscape"—a metonym for a certain purpose in their lives, a far-off yet "peculiarly real" place inside each writer—and who have a common desire to hold such a place in their minds. Protecting the meaning of this private landscape and its purity as an idea secretly alive within them, in order to capture some or another part of it in their fiction, is the narrators' shared tragicomic vocation.

With each successive story, the narrators' collective vision of landscape grows more complex, gaining another enigmatic dimension. At the same time, the importance of each man's story is partially negated as the power of the central metaphor overwhelms their individual narratives. Reading the stories tests our negative capability, sending our attention down parallel and crisscrossing avenues, and creates the sensation that throughout the book and beyond it lies at least one other unique layer. Together with the interstitial nature of the landscape metaphor, which obliges us to look beyond hints of autobiographical detail, we are asked to question the nature and value of narrative.

That Murnane can convey remarkable depth using unadorned language and only a few metafictional devices is one of the great joys of his approach to creating fiction. Many authors lend their texts a layered feeling, but none other than Murnane makes ambiguity surge up from the page with such purpose.

Murnane repeatedly provokes our awareness of the evolving layers and depth of the collection by using metafiction to bind the six narrators' lives together: near the end of each story, the writers all mention the title of a story they have written, and that same story appears next in the collection. Yet none of these narrators is the author of the novel. They are, rather, creations of one another, each a sort of dream contrived by the pen of the writer of the preceding story. Murnane closes the loop when his last narrator, of "Landscape with Artist," states that he has written "Landscape with Freckled Woman," the first story in the book.

Threaded between the links of this structure are various theories the narrators offer about memory and their existence, positing "history as a kind of landscape" and "time as a kind of space." The autoreferential effect of these metafictional devices (fiction is their personal history, based on an evolving definition of landscape) brings on vertigo at times, as if Murnane has pointed a video camera at a TV and projected an infinite image of the narrative on the screen. This parallels the concept the South African author Ivan Vladislavić employed in *The Loss Library*, his linked fiction and essay collection. Vladislavić writes, "I see the pieces folding out of one another like a leporello, or leading from one to another like stepping stones, or facing one another like bookends." With Murnane, the figurative power of the metaphor seems to push the collection's meaning out into the third dimension, much as the accordion-like pages expand out from a leporello-bound book.

Murnane achieves this effect through simple language that reflects the narrators' desire for clarity. There is a lure in their tone, a promise in the prose that a single, logical mind guides their rationales as artists and husbands. The men in these stories struggle with a sense that they are meant to author a monumental saga about landscape, or at the very least to maintain belief in an idea greater than themselves. Yet they also offer intimate details about their lives, and in an open, confessional way that makes them strangely affable. They are shy yet proud. They crave sex but fear their appetite for it. Much of their dialogue with others is reported as internal narrative, often as conversations the men only imagine having with women and with artists they wish to impress. Their vulnerability, along with the disciplined language, counterbalances the abstract weight of the landscape rhetoric to reinforce the novel's verisimilitude. The men seem earnestly united in a struggle, the pain of which we enjoy from a distance, while we marvel at the romantic pleasure they gain from their landscape ideal. It is as if their ambition to give true expression to this abstract notion through fiction meets and parallels our desire to experience something real through the book. Ultimately, both are doomed to fail in an exquisite, nearly ecstatic manner.

As the writers describe their growth from adventurous boys into proud, contemplative family men, we see an evolution in their theories about where this hidden landscape might exist. In their youth, the writers had tried to abstain from the real world and remain lost in "pleasant confusion," conceiving of landscape as an ethereal destination ("a place beyond the crudely imagined dreamlands of the average man," "a distant homeland awaiting me," "my sacred country," "the far-reaching vistas and the intricate topography continually before my eyes"). However, when they are older they encounter the conflict between being writers of landscape and convincing other people that their visions are worthwhile. Now landscape represents a space nearer their bodies ("a whole continent was spread out inside me," "a vast and foreign land behind my face," "a huge projection of some intricate pattern behind my eyes, and it would be my life's work to explore those dark spaces"). Although the men know they must reach their readers, their most crucial flaw is their lack of self-confidence, which inhibits their maturity as artists and pushes them inward, toward narcissism bordering on megalomania.

Their singular focus is to write well enough to attract at least one woman who will be impressed by their theories, particularly those of landscape. Yet time and again, even after they pursue a young woman, marry, and have children, the destination of a cherished landscape proves elusive, estranging them from others and drawing them into depression. Says one of the narrators, "I seemed to be writing my way towards a woman I would never see because every page I filled with words only added to the distance between her and myself."

Believing that a true artist must be a tortured loner, they suffer for their vanity. To no avail they pore over the books of Jack Kerouac, Thomas Hardy, A. E. Housman, Thomas Merton, Carl Jung, and others. They leave parties to vomit or masturbate behind bushes. Mildly empowered by their anguish, when they later understand that the limits of their creative talents prevent them from rendering their precious landscape accurately, their desires have changed as well; they have come to enjoy being observed as they fail to achieve their ideal. Their suffering at once pleases them and blinds them to its inherent danger.

In a scene from "A Quieter Place than Clun," the narrator reminisces about a night of youthful artistic suffering. He drinks whisky, listens to a recording of Jean Sibelius, and then pages through the art section of *Time*, where he happens across a caption below a painting: *"Ralph Borge, with meticulous realism, shows human folly, isolation, and decay."* Rather than change his habits to avoid despair, in blissful paranoia he drinks more and shuns his friends, taking pride in the belief that he is a noble exemplar of a transcendent sort of failure.

The narrators' stubbornness is at times endearing, and at other times harrowing; the crazed narrator of "The Battle of Acosta Nu," for instance, continues to deny the dangers of his obsession even after his neglect indirectly causes the death of his young son. The tragedy is a comment on human existence, where artistic suffering has sublimated into mad, nationalistic fervor. The narrator is so enamored of his otherness that he sees the death of his child as a necessary sacrifice to achieve full awareness of who he is and what "landscape" represents. As a type, in this world, the male artist at the head of a household is most dangerous when he pities himself. Having abandoned hope of connecting with his family, he revels in the image of the self grappling with chaos in order to justify intellectual hubris and moral insanity.

Indeed, through these narrators' experiences, Murnane addresses the dangers of suffering needlessly and of not finding one other person who can relate to a dream. We see the narrators grow to be more aware that their humanity both sustains their sense of landscape and places it out of reach. This sense of impossibility frustrates their ability to accept the nature of the landscape ideal; for us, this gives it great power as a metaphor. Beyond its cathartic aspect, yielding pleasure as we sympathize with the men's fates (as an object lesson), the metaphor has quietly become an all-encompassing, self-reflexive comment about the limits of fiction and its devices. The sense that this unsettling motion is occurring wedges directly into the space of our reading experience because the stories focus on the hunger for a literal representation of place that lives in the minds of the narrators, who come to believe that landscape exists most purely and accurately as a concept in the minds of fictional characters. Their failure to discover a satisfying method to capture landscape in their fiction points to the limits of fiction, as well as, perhaps, the boundaries of reading as an imaginative act. These characters' deepening search for steady belief in this otherworldly plane mirrors what we tacitly acknowledge as readers of fiction: finding truth in what we know to be false should be a fantasy beyond our reach.

But it is not. At least, it does not feel that way when we read. The desire for pleasure from fiction makes such vague intimations of truth feel more real than they should. This sensation gains a singular force within the landscape space Murnane creates inside us as we read, through the figurative power of the narrators' collective desire to express the unknowable through fiction. Murnane mentions this space indirectly at the end of the first story:

> At some time in my imagined future I would have wanted to see my landscape as a private place marked off from all others: a place that distinguished me as surely as a pattern of freckles could distinguish a woman.
>
> There was such a place, although I did not recognise it for some years afterwards. By then it seemed less a landscape than the ending of the only fiction I could write. It was the space between myself and the nearest woman or man who seemed real to me.

This final sentence becomes the space between reader and text, which may also be the narrator's sense of emptiness at the limits of himself as both creation and creator. For him, there may be nothing else. However, we feel upon reading these lines that our act of comprehension contradicts his sense of disappointment and failure. Coupled to this, the first-person narration, which leads us to wonder if the narrators' despondency is Murnane's (it is not, of course), heightens the tension of the stories' plot and charges the text with mystery about the kind of person who could devote himself to such maddening, abstract thought. The fuse of this idea, once lit at the end of the first story, winds through the act of reading the rest of the book. As readers, our conception of the space that comprises these layers yields the sense that we, akin to one of the narrators' fictional characters (a person unknown to him, living beyond the realm of his vision), have become a central element in the success and life of the fiction. We may search for the real and expect a degree of verisimilitude when reading novels. Murnane satisfies this innate desire before subverting our expectations with deliberate purpose. The six narrators' failures elicit our sympathy, but the metafictional device linking each story reminds us that the characters are not only fictional, but fictions derived from fiction, copies of a character obsessed with fiction and seeking obsessive readers.

If writers and readers connect through literature, Murnane seems keen to test the limits of this connection and show how vague and imperfect are the creations we admire in fiction. We are, however, permitted the satisfaction that eludes his narrators: we can escape the prison of the abstract anytime we like and return to the real world, where we are left to question why we seek what is not truly alive on any page or canvas.

The Provincial Imagination

Ivor Indyk

This essay is based on a keynote address given at the annual conference of the Association for the Study of Australian Literature, held on 5 July 2013, at the Wagga Wagga campus of Charles Sturt University.

I use the term "the provincial imagination" in an unembarrassed way, in order to draw attention to the particular power the imagination can have when it is exercised in a condition of isolation or separation; and to the fact that, in such circumstances, the provincial imagination can take on contours and find a way of dealing with images that are peculiarly its own. We know well how isolation breeds strange imaginings. The Christmas ritual that Henry Lawson's isolated shepherd puts together in "The Bush Undertaker" with a dog, two corpses, and a goanna is a case in point—Lawson's closing lines are a fitting tribute to its strangeness: "And the sun sank again on the grand Australian bush—the nurse and tutor of eccentric minds, the home of the weird, and of much that is different from things in other lands."

Yet precisely because its products can be weird, we have trouble talking about the provincial in positive terms, or even talking about it at all. When one thinks about the characteristics commonly attributed to the figure of the provincial—shyness, awkwardness, self-consciousness, obsession—it is to recognize that all of these qualities have negative connotations. I can think of only one quality we allow the provincial that could be thought of as positive—this is the capacity for wonder, arising out of the provincial's innocence of the ways of the world—and even this quality of wonder, which is fundamental to the operation of the imagination, we tend to regard as a kind of foolishness, exposing the person who is possessed by it, to the deceit or manipulation of others.

I define "the provincial" in terms of isolation or separation; in the parlance we have been used to for the past two decades, it is the possession of those who live at some distance from the metropolitan centers of political and cultural power, on the margins, at the edge, in the middle of uncharted or distant territories. Of course, this is as much a psychological as a physical state—there are those, like the most dedicated writers and artists, who hold themselves at a distance, even when they may be close, physically, to the center of things. In this respect, one may think of the imagination as inherently provincial, since it has the capacity to populate, and inhabit other worlds that are only remotely tethered to this one; and because it is the faculty of the mind which is the least responsible to authority, the commands of which it feels only weakly, if indeed it recognizes them at all.

To think of the imagination as inherently provincial in its operation is also to recognize recursion as one of its most distinctive forms. To create and populate a world within or beyond this one, in a province of the mind, is to take the first step in a recursive sequence that is capable of generating other worlds within the imagined world, brought into being by the imagined inhabitants themselves. There is, in principle, no limit to these nestings and expansions. Indeed, one might expect the provincial mind to be particularly adroit in managing these embedded and projected perspectives, since it lives close to the edge of the world or in distant territories to begin with. It is often assumed that those who live in border territories, or out at a distance, will turn their gaze to the metropolitan centers and take their lead from there. But wouldn't it be easier, since you're so close to the border, and the pull of the center is weak, to continue looking in the direction of the border, and out across the distance, to the imagined lands beyond?

Australian criticism has been slow to recognize the inventiveness of its own literature, though it is quick to recognize this inventiveness as an influence exerted by authors in provincial cultures similar to our own— Jorge Luis Borges, for example. We praise the Latin American authors for the richness of their imaginative projections while denying the same richness in our own authors, even though our colonial and postcolonial conditions are similar to theirs. Just as it is difficult for us to speak favorably about the qualities of awkwardness, shyness, or embarrassment in our literature, which it owes precisely to the fact of being a provincial literature, so the elaborations of the provincial imagination, particularly those of the recursive kind, seem too weird or wonderful to justify serious attention.

For those who know Gerald Murnane's writing, it will seem natural that I should take it to exemplify the workings of the provincial imagination. He has, of course, fashioned himself as the great provincial, the man who is reluctant to travel, whose mind inhabits the remote western plains of Victoria, or those of Hungary, or of America, who dreams of writing in a monastic cell, who doesn't wear sunglasses, who has never been in an airplane, who is distressed when he finds himself in a place where the streets aren't aligned in a rectangular grid. His exploration of shyness and embarrassment, particularly in matters relating to the opposite sex, is legendary. His self-consciousness is most evident in the writing itself, which habitually features a writer as its chief character, has an exaggerated awareness of the reader, and displays a high degree of repetition and recapitulation, as well as an obsessive return to favored motifs and topics: the two-story house with a young woman at the window, racehorses and racecourses, marbles and colored glass, ground-dwelling birds, streams, and wells.

And there is, of course, his habit of recursion. The book of Murnane's which is most recursive in its structure is *Inland*. If you read the second half of the book back into the first, then you have a narrator not unlike Murnane's typical narrator—that is to say, a narrator both like and unlike Murnane himself—who lives in the district between Moonee Ponds and the Merri in northeast Melbourne and is haunted by plains and who imagines a wealthy landowner in the library of a manor house in Szolnok County on the great Alföld plains of Hungary, who in turn sends his writing to Anne Kristaly Gunnarson, an editor at the Institute of Prairie Studies in Tripp County, South Dakota, who dreams of a prairie in which a man thinks he is talking or writing to a young woman who is engaged in research on all the different grasslands of the world. When you think that Anne Kristaly Gunnarson is already a fourth-order creation, imagined by a character who is the creation of Murnane's narrator, then the figure in the landscape that her created character imagines belongs to a sixth order of reality—and it's no mean feat, either for the writer or the reader, to keep the orders separate in their minds.

For Murnane, the embedding of realities in *Inland* constitutes a kind of credo. "In the summer of 1986-87, while I was writing my fifth book of fiction, *Inland*," he writes in his essay "Birds of the Puszta," "I asked myself what I remembered most clearly from all the books of fiction that I had read. I decided that I remembered most clearly and with most pleasure what I call spaces-within-spaces." Indeed, the book is peppered with the incantation "No thing in the world is one thing" in various iterations—"Each thing is more than one thing," "Some places are many more than one place"—culminating with the familiar quote from Paul Éluard (familiar because Patrick White uses it as the epigraph for *The Solid*

Mandala, which is where Murnane remembers it from), "There is another world, but it is in this one." In a way, as Murnane notes in his discussion of which world might be referred to as "this one" in the Éluard quote, the sentiment does no more than restate the fundamental premise of all fiction, which is, after all, to assert the existence of another world within this one we know and live in. But his way of seeing the quote, as a sentiment uttered by the narrator or a character in a work of fiction, already places that other reality at two removes—"There is another world, says one of those people deep inside the pages of a book, but it is in—and therefore at one remove further from you out there—this world where I am now." Given the author's propensity to multiply worlds, beyond the second and even beyond the sixth degree, there is clearly more going on here than a simple assertion about fiction's power to create another world in this one.

In the case of *Inland*, where there is such a high degree of recursion, one would be right to expect a mystery at the heart of all these displacements. (I think "displacement" is the right term to use here, because of the way Murnane translates a theme or topic from one space to another that has been created within or beyond it.) Murnane is one for secrets, which is why he admires the furtiveness of ground-dwelling birds and the uncertainties of the racetrack, and why he often presents his readers with the possibility of a revelation that can only be fully disclosed through a process of association and digression, or by displacement into the successive realities of a recursion. The secret is usually a highly emotional or traumatic moment, a scene of betrayal or awkwardness—with a girl, with a close family member or friend, as a young writer—the memory of which is so fraught with implication that it requires the embedded realities of the recursion, or the multiple associations of a sequence of images, to absorb its ramifications.

One of the most striking of these is the depiction, in the story "Precious Bane," of the anxiety Murnane's narrator felt as a young writer on Sunday afternoons browsing in an alcoholic haze in a secondhand bookshop wondering who would be reading a book by him in forty years' time, should he ever be able to publish a book, an anxiety that he imagines in a reader vaguely like himself, "who had failed at what he most wanted to do," standing before a wall of bookshelves in the year 2020, wondering where the book by the writer is that he vaguely remembers reading; at which point the perspective goes into his brain, as if in search of the memory of the book, and imagines its cells as a vast district of monastic cells, with more districts of cells beyond them, in which thousands upon thousands of monks sit reading, surrounded by books and manuscripts, one of whom once read or wrote in the pages around him—which have lain undisturbed for many years in his cell—the location of a book the writer may have written, but it is now forgotten, and no one asks him to look for it. The vertiginous replication of perspectives is a good analogue for anxiety, which, as we know, has a habit of repeating and complicating itself.

One may think of each layer of recursions such as these as representing the original scene in a modified and diminished version, thus allowing the emotion to be channeled and ultimately reduced to a manageable intensity, and even to be mocked, as here. In *Inland*, however, the recursion works in exactly the opposite way. The original scene, which is presented toward the end of the book, after its displaced versions have already been developed, is much more muted and delicate in its expression of emotion than the later versions are. It is an intimate scene of perfect understanding between two twelve-year-old sweethearts, which in a little while will be destroyed forever by the boy's departure. In those other displaced versions, magnified by being set in the midst of vast plains, the theme of betrayal escalates in intensity: it includes the suicide of one young woman (in a well on a landowner's estate in Hungary), the rape and murder of another, and the beheading of a third. As recursions, each of these versions is framed and distanced, but nevertheless they add their emotional perspectives to the scene of first love and betrayal when it is presented, giving it an almost unbearable poignancy. The complex of emotions felt by the man who remembers his actions as a boy—guilt, regret, resentment, embarrassment, sadness—is expanded rather than diminished by its Hungarian and American elaborations, and by the fact that the remembered scene itself is complicated by recursion, because the boy, who once lived in Bendigo, communicates with his girlfriend, who is called the girl from Bendigo Street, through a second girl, who is called the girl from Bendigo, because she had once lived there too. Somehow Bendigo has completely infiltrated the scene, which takes place in a northeastern suburb of Melbourne. When you consider how rare it is for a male and a female to come to an intimate understanding in Murnane's writing, and how closely the distance between them is guarded, it is something of a miracle that this description of first love should shine through all the awkwardnesses involved, and the diffractions and refractions of its representations. This is the power that J. M. Coetzee praised in his review of the *Inland* edition recently published by Dalkey Archive Press in the United States:

> The emotional conviction behind the later parts of *Inland* is so intense, the somber lyricism so moving, the intelligence behind the chiseled sentences so undeniable, that we suspend all disbelief, forgive the boy his imagined sins, and allow the peasant girl from Hungary and the girl from Bendigo Street to shine their benign radiance on us from a world beyond that is somehow also this world.

I dwell on the emotional power of Murnane's recursions in order to stress that their significance is not purely a formal one, a matter only of technique, and to show how they perform a larger expressive function. Just how large this might be, and what the risks involved are, becomes clearer if we follow the lead thrown out in Murnane's essay "Birds of the Puszta," where he mentions that throughout the time he was writing *Inland*, he was thinking about the characters in *Wuthering Heights*, the novel that he admires most among all the works of fiction he has read in English, precisely because of its play of spaces-within-spaces. One of the most powerful moments in *Inland* is when the narrator remembers the scene in *Wuthering Heights* when its narrator, Lockwood, dreams that the ghost of Catherine Linton is knocking on his windowpane, crying to be allowed in from the other side of the glass. In his dream, Lockwood thrusts his hand through the pane, and when Catherine clings to it, he drags her wrist backward and forward across the shattered edge of the glass until it bleeds and she lets go. In *Inland*, by way of contrast, Murnane's narrator imagines himself unlocking the windowpanes and opening them fully, taking the "girl-woman's" wrist, and guiding her into the room. Brontë's Catherine reminds him of his own lost girlfriend, the girl from Bendigo Street—the violence done to the ghost of the fictional Catherine by the narrator of *Wuthering Heights* represents yet another iteration of the betrayed girl-woman motif, the fourth; only this time, it is accompanied by a gesture of amends. Additionally—remember that for Murnane no thing is one thing—the scene of the knocking against the windowpane in *Wuthering Heights* has an iconic status for Murnane, because it represents the other world pressing for admission into this one. The willingness to be open to this other world, and to be on familiar terms with its inhabitants, is for Murnane the fundamental qualification of the writer of fiction.

Murnane's close identification with Emily Brontë may at first seem a strange one, but of course they are both provincial writers whose worlds are nestled in broad expanses of landscape, and beyond or within those worlds they are open to other worlds again. When Murnane next invokes Emily Brontë, it is in an entirely different context to the recursive triumphs of *Inland*. In 2009 Murnane published *Barley Patch*, fourteen years after his previous book, the collection of fiction *Emerald Blue*. Even earlier than that, eighteen years earlier, in the early autumn of 1991 to be precise, while he was in the middle of a big work called *O, Dem Golden Slippers*, he had decided to stop writing fiction. *Barley Patch* begins with two questions, *"Must I write?"* and *"Why had I written?"*, but a third question, *Why Did I Stop Writing?*, hangs over the whole book. As you can imagine, Murnane takes his time in coming to address the question. When he does, only fifteen pages from the end of the book, it is to refer the reader to a piece of fiction he wrote four years after he had stopped writing fiction, in order to explain why he had stopped writing fiction. This piece, titled "The Interior of Gaaldine," appeared for the first time in *Emerald Blue*, among other previously published pieces. The problem, according to the narrator of *Barley Patch*, is that nobody seems to have gotten the reference to Gaaldine in its title, nor the references to the Brontës elsewhere in the story, so he is now in the awkward position of having to explain his explanation. In truth, it would have been a miracle if anyone had understood "The Interior of Gaaldine" the way Murnane does, so carefully coded is it. But, as I mentioned earlier, a writer for whom every place is more than one place, and every thing more than one thing, will also be likely to have an appreciation of secrecy. The secret, the coded, the guarded—these are all attributes we associate with the provincial. I think a lot more is made of these occult practices in our literature than we recognize.

So Murnane explains it all again: in their youth the Brontë sisters created imaginary countries, one of which was called Gondal. In an entry in her diary written when she was seventeen, Emily reported that the inhabitants of Gondal had set about exploring the interior of Gaaldine. You can see the attraction to Murnane of the inhabitants of an imaginary world imagining a world beyond their own, and exploring it. In a tribute to *Wuthering Heights* earlier in *Barley Patch*, he notes how he had paused often during his first reading of that novel "to savour my astonishment at the unexpected appearance of certain perspectives in far parts of the place that I call my mind." In the story called "The Interior of Gaaldine," a narrator very much like Murnane travels across the sea for the first and only time, to join a writers' tour of Tasmania. He has the provincial's terror of travel, which he assuages at length with measured amounts of alcohol over a long sleepless night and much of the following day. Finally he reaches his hotel room and falls into a deep slumber, to be awoken by what seems to him to be the sound of a branch knocking against the window of his room (an allusion to *Wuthering Heights*), but is in fact someone knocking on the door, a young woman, who tells him her name, which he takes to be Alice. In fact, as the narrator of *Barley Patch* kindly explains, it was really Ellis—Ellis Bell being Emily Brontë's pen name, the name under which she published *Wuthering Heights*. The young woman carries a briefcase, and in it is a two-thousand-page manuscript of a work of fiction—actually it is only the introduction to the work of fiction—written by an author who has some of the characteristics of Murnane's narrators, and indeed Murnane himself, and which imagines a world called New Arcadia, primarily in terms of its horse racing from the late 1950s until almost the present moment, which it portrays in the finest detail. Some of the trainers and owners are inhabitants of Gondal, which country seems to be embedded in New Arcadia. The author described by the narrator of "The Interior of Gaaldine" has created this world by what he calls *decoding* and *gutting*—that is to say by mashing up preexisting texts—in order to create the horse races which make up much of the activity in New Arcadia. Lest you are in any doubt about the reality of this, Murnane himself has stored in one of his many filing cabinets folders containing details about the horse-racing history of a country called New Arcadia, obtained by just such methods of cutting up texts as described in "The Interior of Gaaldine." He even has a second cabinet full of files relating to a second country, the name of which I don't remember, except that it is similar to New Arcadia in having a strong association with the heavenly.

What are we to make of this strangely embedded parable as an explanation of why the author of *Barley Patch* stopped writing fiction some eighteen years before? At its most basic, "The Interior of Gaaldine" simply restates Murnane's commitment, for which he claims Emily Brontë's support, to the idea of spaces-within-spaces. As its narrator notes:

I have always been interested in what is usually called the world but only insofar as it provides me with evidence for the existence of another world... I have always written fiction in order to suggest to myself that another world exists... I have always read with the purpose of suggesting to myself that a world might exist beyond the world suggested by the fiction.

But just as the belief in the existence of another world beyond this one has religious connotations—specifically Catholic connotations in Murnane's case, though of a lapsed and secular kind, which has perhaps only served to intensify them—so the recursive power of fiction to create worlds beyond even the world beyond this one suggests an encyclopedic ambition that knows no bounds, and wouldn't particularly welcome them.

In discussing this prospect in *Barley Patch*, Murnane's narrator mentions two anecdotes, the first from Turgenev, the second an account of an experience with the psychedelic psilocybin, the active ingredient in magic mushrooms, which was championed by Timothy Leary in the 1960s. Turgenev recounts how many of his characters came to him in dreams and appeared to be pleading with him to be allowed into his works of fiction. Murnane's narrator, however, sees it otherwise—that the characters were standing on the outermost border of their native territory and pleading with the author to put away his writing and join them, in their far-reaching countries or continents. Under the influence of psilocybin (in a hospital bed under medical supervision, it should be noted), the narrator of *Barley Patch* recounts how the narrator of the aborted *O, Dem Golden Slippers* saw "a series of richly coloured images," one of which, a soldier beetle with orange-yellow markings on a dark brown wing case, seemed to be sending signals to him in a series of tiny flashes; he soon came to understand that the author of these signals was God. The flashes stopped and the narrator understood that he had been dismissed, though without any hard feelings between him and God. In any case, the soldier beetle carries a whole range of associations for Murnane, of which God is just one; the beetle rises from its origins under a bush in the garden of his ancestral family home near Warrnambool, the place where he took his summer holidays as a child. In his wonderful tribute to Marcel Proust in the essay "Invisible Yet Enduring Lilacs," the same garden is evoked by a large fly buzzing near his ear (described in Proust-like fashion as "a parcel of a few moments of lost time"), together with the memory of his first race meeting; the tiger lilies in the garden, which bear the same colors as the soldier beetle; his father's inscriptions on the cliff face near the house (the only evidence of his father's writing, and therefore freighted with emotion); the wall in the garden; the relation between the name *Murnane*, the cliff above Murnane's Bay near the house, and the word for "wall" in Latin, which is also the language of his father's religion; and so on, until it comes back to the image of lilacs, and to Proust.

In other words, there is no end to the array of prospects, or to the extension of their dimensions, that an imagined detail might open up. I've got no doubt that it was this prospect of endlessness, for all its religious and psychological consolations, that helped put an end to the writing of *O, Dem Golden Slippers* and created a substantial hiatus in Murnane's writing career, and presumably could have ended it forever. Whether the prospect of countries beyond the countries of fiction caused a crisis of confidence in the author, especially since all that seemed necessary to reach those countries was the cutting up and reconstituting of existing texts, or whether it was the sense that the author had done his job and gotten as far as he could in writing fiction, and so needed to write no more, we will have to wait to find out.

What is interesting is the sense of vertigo Murnane's writer feels in contemplating the perspectives that open before him suddenly in the writing of *O, Dem Golden Slippers*:

> I felt the sort of giddiness that I might have felt as a child if I had crept towards the brink of a tall cliff overhanging an ocean or if I had climbed to the topmost vantage-point in a building of several storeys and had seen still no end to the level grassy countryside all around.

I don't think we give enough importance to giddiness in Australian literature, and not just because I suffer from it, especially when preparing a paper on recursion in Gerald Murnane. Giddiness is often experienced when you stand at the edge of things and look at the possibilities that may be active beyond, but it is a very different experience from the romantic sublime, which is often invoked at this point. Instead of elevation and expansion, there is awkwardness and self-consciousness. In Murnane's case the perspective is as likely to open up behind him as in front—and even more likely to appear in a sideways glance—and since in most cases it has a complex emotional charge to it, in turning and turning about to take it all in, there is always the possibility of disturbance and giddiness. That is the reason Murnane gives for preferring the solidity of the plains underfoot when he is exploring the landscapes of his mind, and for his hatred of the sea.

I would like to return finally to considering recursion as a mode of expression, partly to insist that what we are dealing with here is an aspect of a larger aesthetic and not simply a novelistic technique, and partly also to correct the impression that Murnane is a purely cerebral writer. It's important to know that he moved house twelve times between the ages of six and twenty as his father fled from his creditors on account of his gambling debts, because it gives the fact of his insistence that each place is more than one place a really poignant quality. Recursion in this respect is a way of reassembling or reintegrating the different places that hold the elements of his identity. There is a moving instance of this in *Inland*, when the narrator comments on looking at a photograph of himself as a three-week-old baby lying in his father's arms:

> The place where I stand to look at the photograph is many more than one place. I am standing in one place after another where those men stand who see themselves as a child in the same photograph that I hold in my hand but who were never taken away as small children from their native district. I am standing on one patch of lawn after another under one fruit tree after another and remembering one after another all the patches of lawn and all the fruit trees I have stood under as a child and as a boy-man and as a man in the district where I have lived all my life between the Moonee Ponds and the Merri.

But there is more to Murnane's use of recursion than the reconstitution of identity. In his essay "The Breathing Author," first published in 2002, Murnane give another reason for deciding to stop writing fiction while engaged with *O, Dem Golden Slippers*, a reason other than the prospect opened up by the countries lying beyond the countries of fiction that I have been discussing.

> My drawing back from *O, Dem Golden Slippers* had something to do with my being a husband and a father of adult children. If I had been, as Marcel Proust was, neither a husband nor a father, or

if I had been, as D. H. Lawrence was, a husband but not a father, I might not have drawn back…but in 1991, in the fifty-third year of my life, I drew back. I drew back partly because what I was about to write might have seemed to certain readers to have revealed more than was seemly for a man of my years, a husband and a father, to have revealed.

As I've mentioned, in instance after instance in Murnane's writing recursion marks the revelation, and the absorption, of scenes of emotional turmoil. The father necessarily looms large as the cause of much of this turmoil. There is a very moving scene in the story called "Stream System," after place has been piled on place, when the perspective suddenly opens on what you feel must have been the moment toward which the whole stream of association was leading, with Murnane's narrator sitting for most of the day before his brother died, with his arm around his brother, who was mentally "backward" and friendless, in the hospital where he resided. There is another set of scenes in the story "Acosta Nu," about a descendant of William Lane's Paraguayan settlers who dreams of a place called Australia, and all the recursive opportunities that offers, while his son's sore knee turns slowly into the fatal condition of septicemia—only a parent who has nursed a sick child, and considered the possibilities, could tell it the way Murnane does here. There are many other examples, particularly to do with the fictional representations of Murnane's youngest uncle and his youngest aunt, both of whom remained unmarried; his mother in *Tamarisk Row*; his wife, in fleeting but extremely intense glimpses, in *A History of Books*; the close friend called Kelvin Durkin in *Landscape with Landscape*; and in many places his torturous and embarrassing maneuvers in relation to the opposite sex, as a young man. There is joy and expectancy in Murnane's work, contentment, anxiety, shame, anger, fear, regret. I think the problem with emotion in Australian literature is that we often don't recognize it for what it is, because its expression, in the manner of provincials, is often guarded and coded, and only reveals itself fully to close acquaintances.

Undiscoverable Countries

Emmett Stinson

> Not only is there no such thing as the past; there is almost
> certainly no such thing as a foreign country.

> —Gerald Murnane, *Velvet Waters*

1

In the fourteenth paragraph of the first story of the book that he published in 1995, Gerald Murnane explains an essential principle of his writing to a university student who has come to visit him in his office: "I would point out to my student that the subject of nearly every sentence I had written was a noun or a pronoun or a noun phrase denoting a person." While I was writing the previous sentence, I realized I had made two errors that would need to be corrected. I was wrong to say that Gerald Murnane explains this essential principle, since, as the narrator of the story notes, although he may resemble the real, flesh-and-blood man who is also a well-known author of books named Gerald Murnane, and may even share many of his memories and experiences, he is not Gerald Murnane, but rather the "implied author of this piece of fiction," a term that he borrows from the writing of the literary scholar Wayne C. Booth. But I would still have been wrong if I had said that *the implied author* of Gerald Murnane's story was explaining an essential principle of his writing to a university student who had come to visit him in his office, because the implied author does not explain anything to anyone, but only *imagines* what this conversation would have been like if it had happened, so that what he says is not a record of a real conversation that has occurred, either in a story written by Gerald Murnane or in any other reality.

But whether the implied author and Gerald Murnane are the same person, and whether the conversation he records is imaginary or has occurred in either the reality of the story written by Gerald Murnane or another reality, the flesh-and-blood Gerald Murnane, who is a well-known author of books and taught creative writing for many years at Victoria College, which would later become part of Deakin University, does write almost every one of his sentences according to this formula in which the grammatical subject of the sentence is either a noun or a pronoun or a noun phrase denoting a person. The real Murnane, as many former students have attested, would tell those in his writing classes that they should never be afraid to repeat an important noun. While recently reading the book that Murnane published in 1995 and another book that he had published five years earlier, I tried to keep track of all of the sentences he wrote that varied from this pattern, and, although I could not be certain of the exact number because often my mind became too occupied by the images unfolding within the books to note the precise grammatical subject of every sentence, I found that only one out of every ten or so sentences contained a subject that was not a noun or a pronoun or a noun phrase denoting a person.

Many readers—whether they are readers implied by the text or actual readers of Murnane's fiction—may find this surprising, because even though not very much seems to happen in Murnane's stories, almost every one of his sentences describes a person who is doing things or thinking things or saying things or imagining things, so his stories in which nothing much seems to happen are actually full of people and their actions.

2

In the second paragraph of the second story in the book by Gerald Murnane that was published in 1990, the implied author of the story—who resembles Gerald Murnane but is not him—describes "two bodies of yellow-brown water, each of which seemed roughly oval," which are meant to resemble—although they do not—a figure on a map that is composed of "two bodies of pale blue, each with a distinctive outline." The implied author notes that these bodies of water, both the yellow-brown ones that the author sees and the blue ones on the map, are called "STREAM SYSTEM," a name that is also the name of the second story in this book.

I know these bodies of water that the implied author of Murnane's story calls "STREAM SYSTEM" very well, because on many occasions I have taken my daughter to them with a loaf of stale bread to feed the ducks and the various other birds, whose names I do not know because I do not know the names of birds and which I have not tried to find out because I am not particularly interested in birds except inasmuch as they are objects of delight for my daughter. I had fed the ducks and the other birds at these unassuming pools of yellow-brown water with my daughter many times before I realized that they were part of the grounds where the boy who would become the well-known author of books named Gerald Murnane spent many years of his young life. I know that the boy Murnane lived there because the implied author of the story called "Stream System" tells me that his father tended to the grounds of Mont Park Asylum, a facility for people that the implied author's mother sometimes called—when anyone who might be offended by such talk was out of the range of hearing—"loonies."

But when I say that I know that the boy Murnane lived at the grounds of Mont Park Asylum because of what is said by the implied author who resembles the well-known author of books called Gerald Murnane, I also know that I may not be quite right in saying this. I know that the implied author's testimony might resemble and yet be different from the reality of the life of the actual boy Murnane, in the way that the two bodies of blue called "STREAM SYSTEM" on a map both resemble and do not resemble the two bodies of yellow-brown water that are "STREAM SYSTEM" in that other reality where I take my daughter to feed ducks and various other birds.

3

Gerald Murnane has published nine books whose contents might be described as fiction, and another book whose contents might be described as either essays or creative nonfiction. Of the nine books of fiction that Murnane has written, five are works whose contents might be described as novels, while four are works whose contents might be described as short stories. I am not certain that any of these descriptions is useful for understanding the content of these books, which resemble one another more than they resemble such abstract categories. Of the ten books that Murnane has published, seven are currently in print and readily available from publishers in either the United States or Australia. Of the three books written by Gerald Murnane that are not currently in print, one—the second book he published whose contents might be described as a novel— is due to be republished by Text Publishing later this year. The other two, whose contents might be described as short stories, comprise the only books that Murnane published during the decade that directly proceeded the first decade of the new millennium, and have the titles *Velvet Waters* and *Emerald Blue*. Although these books were published in the final decade of the twentieth century, some of the stories were published as many as eleven years before the start of that decade. After the second of these books was published, Gerald Murnane—who had published seven books of fiction over the previous twenty-one years—would not publish another book of fiction for fourteen years.

4

I know that the fourth story in the book that Gerald Murnane published in 1990 takes its name from a quotation out of Thomas Livingstone Mitchell's *Three Expeditions into the Interior of Eastern Australia*: "We had at length discovered a country for the immediate reception of civilized man, and fit to become the abode of one of the great nations of the earth… Of this Eden it seemed that I was the only Adam…" I know this because the passage is reproduced in full within the story, which takes as its name the last three words in the above quotation. Because the book that contains this story is also the first book by Gerald Murnane that I read, it was only later that I would discover that the first fourteen words of the above quotation also comprise the epigraph of Gerald Murnane's third book of fiction, entitled *The Plains*. But because I had read Gerald Murnane's books out of order, I already knew an important fact about *The Plains* before I had ever read it— or rather I could suspect such a fact based on the testimony of the implied author of the fourth story in the book that Gerald Murnane published in 1990, who states that "much of the text of *The Plains* was formerly part of the text of a much larger book. The larger book was the story of a man who had lived as a child in a place named Sedgwick North." Before I ever read *The Plains*—the novel that most readers of Murnane consider to be his best and most important—I knew that I could read *The Plains* and yet would never be able to read *The Plains*, or, more accurately, that the *The Plains* that I was reading was only one version of *The Plains*, derived from a larger book that may or may not have had the same title and that, as a book that would forever remain to me only a possible book, could contain any of an infinite number of variations on the book that I know as *The Plains*. I have often longed simultaneously both to read the version of *The Plains* from which the novel I know is only an extract and to never read such a book, so that the actual longer novel, from which *The Plains* was excerpted, will never intrude on the possible book that I have imagined *The Plains* being excerpted from.

5

Critics have not spoken kindly of the two books that Gerald Murnane published in the final decade of the twentieth century, which were also the last two he published before a fourteen-year hiatus from publishing books of fiction. In what I have often heard referred to as the most important survey of Australian fiction from the last decade of the twentieth century and the first decade of the twenty-first century, Ken Gelder and Paul Salzman, the authors of this work of scholarship called *After the Celebration*, said:

> In his more recent work, however, a certain narrowness of vision overwhelms the stylistic brilliance, and perhaps also offers a retrospective unravelling of some of the more disturbing aspects of his earlier work: for example, his depiction of women as rather old-fashioned Muses, empty vessels waiting to be filled by male desire; or his sense of landscape as somehow virginal and fulfilled only through pastoral settlement.
>
> In *Velvet Waters* (1990) and *Emerald Blue* (1995), Murnane concentrates on epiphanic personal experiences, rather than the meditations on landscape and history that characterised [his] earlier novels… Circling and re-circling a series of solipsistic reflections, his fiction can be seen either as hypnotic and evocative, or as monotonous and claustrophobic.

I can only say that Murnane's two books from the final decade of the twentieth century seem to me to resemble both the books that preceded them as well as those that would follow after a fourteen-year gap, while being different from them as well. Moreover, I do not recall any discussion in them of women being "muses," or being "filled by male desire" (although I accept that there is something that could certainly be described as "male desire" in these two books), or the notion that "virginal" land is "fulfilled only through pastoral settlement." While I do not recognize these statements from the two books I have read, I can, however, see their resemblance to aspects of the books I have read, in the way that the perspective of a landscape is flattened out when it is turned into the image of a map that both corresponds to but is different from the reality of the land to which it refers. I will have nothing further to do with any objections. I accept the reality that Gelder and Salzman describe, even if it is not one that I have seen, but I can only conclude that we have read two entirely different sets of books that happen to be named *Velvet Waters* and *Emerald Blue*, which happened to be published in the years 1990 and 1995, respectively, by two different well-known authors of fiction who happen to share the name Gerald Murnane.

6

I do not know of any of Gerald Murnane's writing that has been more frequently anthologized than the third story from the book that he published in 1990, which is called "Land Deal." Those who live in Australia or know about its history will immediately grasp that aspects of the story were not at all divorced from a set of debates in the 1980s and 1990s—often called the "history wars"—about the need for contemporary Australians to acknowledge the atrocities that Western colonization inflicted on Australia's indigenous peoples. I know that the epigraph to this story by Gerald Murnane refers to what is known as Batman's Treaty—a deal made in 1835 between John Batman and several elders of the Wurundjeri people to purchase a six-hundred-thousand-acre tract of land that comprises much of what is now Melbourne. The implied authors of this story (for the story is told not by a single implied author but a collective of implied authors, referred to variously as "we" and "us") describe an outlandish proposition put forward by some foreigners, whose mad desire was "to possess the land." For us, there could be nothing more ridiculous, since it is clear that these foreigners know nothing of the land at all: "When they moved even a short distance across it, stepping aside from places that invited passage and treading on places that were plainly not to be intruded on, we knew that they would lose themselves before they found the real land." Having witnessed such events, we come to the only conclusion we can: that we are dreaming, and that we have dreamed a people who believe they are able to possess the land, and that these people remain unaware that the entirety of their history is little more than our dream, from which one day we will inevitably awaken.

I had, many years before reading this story, read a short story by Jorge Luis Borges called "Tlön, Uqbar, Orbus Tertius," in which a scholar—happening on a stray encyclopedia entry for a city named Uqbar—uncovers what he believes is a massive conspiracy by a group of scholars to write the history of an imaginary country called Tlön, before he realizes that he can no longer distinguish between his own reality and that of Tlön, that the two have interpenetrated such that, "the world will be Tlön." I recall finding this story funny and clever, but it was not until I read "Land Deal" that I understood that Tlön, the real Tlön that is separate from an imaginary place called Tlön in a story by Jorge Luis Borges, actually exists, that it is, in fact, where we live, and that it is as incomprehensible to those who live in other realities as the Tlön in Borges's story is to us.

7

I have been many times to the grounds of Mont Park Asylum, where the boy who would grow up to become the well-known author of books named Gerald Murnane lived for several years, though I have not been there either as a patient or to visit someone who is a patient, nor has anyone visited the grounds of Mont Park Asylum for either of those purposes in many years, because the grounds of what was once Mont Park Asylum have now been converted into apartments, which I have seen because they are located very close to a shopping center where I occasionally shop for my groceries. Although the landscape has inevitably been altered by these new developments, all of the façades and brickwork from the old hospital have been maintained, so that—even though the purpose and contents of the buildings differ from their former use—the outside of the apartments that have been created out of the buildings of Mont Park Asylum still resemble the Mont Park Asylum as it existed when a young boy who would grow up to be the well-known author of books called Gerald Murnane lived near there.

8

I have often heard words associated with Murnane's writing that, although they appear to be neutral and analytical, contain the implication of something pejorative, a suggestion that his work belongs, in some simple or uncomplicated way, to a tradition called aestheticism that is self-indulgent, apolitical, elitist—an entire litany of sins that are meant to be characteristic of art that has been inspired in some way by the spirit of what has often been called modernism. I will not claim that such arguments are wrong, or without merit, or that they have no basis in some reality, but it is hard for me to find a resemblance between this portrait of Murnane's work that I have occasionally encountered and the work itself.

For those who have never been to Australia, the places Gerald Murnane writes about may seem or sound very exotic. But such a person would be quickly disabused of such notions by spending even a small amount of time in any of the areas that Murnane writes about, such as Kinglake, Macleod, or Preston, the suburb in which I live. For those who know Australia, the places Murnane writes about may seem banal. But such a person would be disabused of such notions if he or she had spent time in these areas and had seen them as one might surmise that Murnane has seen them. Many of the places Murnane writes about, including the suburb in which I live, are what might be termed working-class suburbs, and many of the people in his fiction are what might be termed working-class people. I find myself frequently thinking about, more than any other character in his book published in 1995, a man known only as "the man with his chin in his hands," who is employed in an engineering works, where he taunts the apprentice workers. Already in his forties, the man with his chin in his hands still lives at home with his mother. As we learn, he will never marry and will die of cancer while he is living with his mother. In the well-known country in the northern hemisphere where I was born and raised, such characters are rarely associated with works grouped under the classification of "aestheticism" but rather with genres like the "southern gothic" or the "blue-collar fiction" of minimalist realist authors such as Raymond Carver. But in Murnane's fiction, "the man with his chin in his hands" exists in the same reality that is occupied by teachers of creative writing, and there is no distinction between these worlds, which Murnane writes about in the true lie that is known as fiction.

9

L. P. Hartley published a book in 1953 that would go on to become a classic of Australian literature. It opens with the sentence: "The past is a foreign country; they do things differently here." I have chosen as the epigraph of what you are currently reading a sentence uttered by the implied author of the second-to-last story in the book that Gerald Murnane published in 1990, who responds to the first sentence of Hartley's novel. While this implied author is not the same person as the well-known author of books named Gerald Murnane, I have heard from people who know the real Murnane that he does not like to be called an "Australian writer," and that, if he had his preference, he would be called instead a "Victorian writer"— since Victoria is the state in which he has spent almost the entirety of his life—or, better still, a "Melbourne writer," since it is on the patch of land that constitutes Melbourne and its suburbs that he has spent most of his life. Regardless, or so I have been told, Murnane does not know what it would mean to be an "Australian writer" beyond a tie to the various localities and landscapes—in both Melbourne and Victoria more broadly— where he has spent his life.

As I was writing the preceding paragraph, I began thinking about what I would write in the next paragraph, and I was tempted to argue that the landscape in Murnane's stories is itself a character. But I cannot argue that landscape is a character in Murnane's stories for the reason that I am not sure that even his characters are characters, since instead they are minds filled with images of landscapes—but these minds that are filled with images of landscapes are themselves constructed like landscapes, or, more precisely, like those images of landscapes that we know as maps. As Murnane, or rather an implied author who resembles Murnane, argues, "A diagram of my mind would resemble a vast and intricate map with images for its small towns and with feelings for the roads through the grassy countryside between the towns." Landscape cannot be a character in Murnane's fiction for the reason that his characters are actually composed of minds that resemble landscapes, or rather those images of landscapes that we call maps, which are themselves composed of other images. Landscapes cannot be characters, and characters cannot be landscapes, and neither can be images, although it appears that all three— landscapes, characters, and images—cannot be so easily disentangled from one another.

10

I first began reading fiction written by the well-known author of books called Gerald Murnane during the fourteen year period when he was not writing books of fiction. At the time, I spoke on several occasions to people in the publishing industry who had known him, to his former students, and to people who had worked with him in various capacities, and everyone I spoke to seemed to think that he would never again write a book that might be classified as a work of fiction. I did not ask, and did not wish to ask or to know, why he had stopped writing, but even though I never asked this question of myself or anyone else, many years later I was surprised to find that Murnane had answered it, or at least answered it in a way that answers it without giving any specific information of precisely the sort that I did not wish to know. Murnane said, just before he published the book of fiction that would be the first book of fiction he had published in fourteen years, that

> I have given up writing a few times, not telling very many people…not with any sense of sadness or solemnity, I just stopped for a while because I didn't have anything more to write about, and I'm not a person who… I would never sit down and just write for the sake of writing. I only write when I feel driven to it.

I have had several opportunities to see Gerald Murnane speak in public, occasions that might also have provided me the chance to speak with him, however briefly. Once he gave a talk at the university where I work, but I was teaching at the same time and could not attend. On another occasion, he spoke at a writers' festival that I was also speaking at, but, due to a prior engagement, I was not able to attend his session. On a third occasion, I was invited along to a lunch that—or so I was told—Murnane would also attend, but I had to turn down the offer because I was traveling interstate on business during the same day that the lunch was meant to occur. At the writers' festival that I know we both attended, I briefly stood next to a man whom I could only make out in the periphery of my vision, but whom I suspect—based on the photos I have seen—may well have been Gerald Murnane, although I decided I did not want to turn my head to look at him in case it was Murnane. I did not turn my head away out of any disrespect for the well-known author of fiction named Gerald Murnane, nor did I turn my head away because I was afraid of discovering that the well-known author of fiction named Gerald Murnane might differ from the various implied authors of his stories who resemble him, but rather because the Gerald Murnane that I was interested in, the Gerald Murnane that I wanted to meet, was the man who did not publish any works of fiction for fourteen years and who had thought, without any sadness or solemnity, that he had given up such writing forever. The Gerald Murnane that I wished to meet was not the man who might or might not have been standing next to me, but rather lived elsewhere, in some undiscoverable country that was neither the past nor the future nor this reality nor another one, where he was imagining, but not writing, books of fiction that would be perfect if only because they would remain possible without ever becoming actual.

Reading Gerald Murnane's Landscapes with Proust

K. Thomas Kahn

> *Quand par les soirs d'été le ciel harmonieux gronde comme une*
> *bête fauve et que chacun boude l'orage, c'est au côté de*
> *Méséglise que je dois de rester seul en extase à respirer, à travers*
> *le bruit de la pluie qui tombe, l'odeur d'invisibles et persistants*
> *lilas.*

—Marcel Proust, *Du côté de chez Swann*

> Like Men and Women Shadows walk
> Upon the Hills Today—
> With here and there a mighty Bow
> Or trailing Courtesy
> To Neighbors doubtless of their own
> Not quickened to perceive
> Minuter landscape as Ourselves
> And Boroughs where we live—

—Emily Dickinson, "1105"

> When you see a rainbow, you're seeing something completely
> subjective. You see it at a certain distance as if stitched on to the
> landscape. It isn't there. It is a subjective phenomenon. But
> nonetheless, thanks to a camera, you record it entirely
> objectively. So, what is it?

—Jacques Lacan, *Seminar I*

I.

In *Invisible Yet Enduring Lilacs*, a collection of essays that were published
between 1984 and 2003 in various venues, Gerald Murnane writes that
"for scholars of the future, if there be any such... I have stored these

reports in what I like to call my archives." When Murnane refers to "these reports" he is being, he admits, "somewhat evasive," despite a physical catalog comprising "about nineteen drawers of steel filing cabinets"; however, since the piece from which this quote comes is entitled "The Breathing Author" (2002), rather that "these reports" are ostensibly reflections on the creative process and how Murnane's writing has been for him a "sort of discovery," offering by way of "a remarkably detailed documentation" an account of "my life and my thinking." To what end is unclear, as no one is privy to the contents of these archives but Murnane himself, yet he is quick to suggest that he has in fact made this discovery, has in fact already arrived at the moment of revelation that his books have been performative attempts to conjure: "My writing was not an attempt to produce something called 'literature' but an attempt to discover meaning," he notes, going on to explain how "I have tried to describe this discovery to several persons" in "hardly less evasive" terms than those he sets forth in "The Breathing Author."

Thus, despite the fact that "these reports" are meant "for scholars of the future" who may be interested in his work, Murnane is clear that—because his writing has been the means by which he has made "this discovery"—those who care to search for them can already find the clues to just such a journey. However, similar to Marcel Proust's, Murnane's discovery is a subjective one, one that uncovers the meanings of images in a way that is only applicable to himself. With that said, though, just as Proust's Narrator in À la recherche du temps perdu is able to retrieve lost time and reconcile the two distinct landscapes that have shaped his life from his formative years onward, a reader can learn to apply the method Proust uses to attempt this on his or her own. This is what makes Proust's novel a memorable (and narcissistic) experience for those who journey with the Narrator to the very end—namely that the experience of involuntary memory that the Narrator's famous tisane and madeleine initiates is one that we all long to reproduce in our own singular way, not just to recover temps perdu but to reflect on our desires, our fantasies, our disappointments, and our successes.

Murnane's Invisible Yet Enduring Lilacs takes its title from the closing pages of the "Combray" section in Proust's Swann's Way, the first volume of À la recherche du temps perdu. Since Murnane's own moment of enlightenment has come through repeated attempts to invoke memory, just as it does for Proust's Narrator, it is no wonder that Murnane calls the French author's masterpiece "the work of fiction that I admire most," and, like the many narrators in his own texts, finds Proust's "Narrator as a man made up mostly of landscapes." In a 2008 interview on Australia's radio program *The Book Show*, Murnane brings Proust's relation to his Narrator to bear on his own quasi-autobiographical narrators, remarking that "the narrator of the fiction that [Proust] wrote is a person that I feel drawn to and I feel most attracted to, so that a version of Proust created the fiction which was a version and not necessarily the whole person." Interestingly enough, although Murnane often refers in *Invisible Yet Enduring Lilacs* to his "books of fiction," the authorial note that prefaces the collection refutes this:

> The author's conjecturing is futile, of course, but it has inspired me to make an even bolder declaration. I should never had tried to write fiction or non-fiction or even anything in-between. I should have left it to discerning editors to publish all my pieces of writing as essays.

Written in 2003, this is indeed a bold statement: it is not only a declaration that aligns Murnane with Proust all the more—insofar as both writers create fictional personae in order to uncover truths about their real and fictional counterparts—but it also intimates that the "discovery" he has finally made through fiction writing has made the division between fiction and nonfiction untenable, has in effect rendered fiction writing a kind of exorcism just as much as it is a revelatory experience, purging the author of the need to continue once the "discovery" has been reached: "Why should I feel surprise or disappointment if the result of my writing seven books of fiction was my discovery of something of much meaning to myself and my deciding that the writing of fiction was no longer of much importance to me?" Murnane asks in *Invisible Yet Enduring Lilacs*. And in *Barley Patch*, Murnane is even more self-condemnatory, as if, although fiction writing paved the way for his "discovery," it somehow postponed the eventual enlightenment: "I can only suppose that I wrote fiction for thirty and more years in order to rid myself of certain obligations that I felt as a result of my having *read* fiction."

Just as the petite madeleine provides the moment of enlightenment for Proust's Narrator, so, too, does fiction writing provide the same for Murnane. Fiction writing is for him a compulsive yet repetitive journey that sees him grappling with landscapes: "landscapes with landscapes" (to bring his essay collection to mind), "spaces-within-spaces," as he phrases it in *Invisible Yet Enduring Lilacs*, the mutable "dream-countries" of *Inland*, and the "image-landscapes" in *A History of Books*. Throughout Murnane's work, there are recurring poetic phrases that are reminiscent of Vinteuil's "little phrase" that recurs throughout Proust's *À la recherche du temps perdu*, which affects M. Swann and the Narrator in myriad ways throughout and is thus symbolic of one's shifting relation to an aesthetic object at the level of cathexis. In the same way, Murnane's recurring landscapes indicate his own shifting relation to these images as he moves closer to the moment of authorial and personal "discovery." As he notes: "I started out wanting to be a poet… I tried to think of myself as a poet of the Australian landscape." Murnane's oeuvre is indeed a highly poetic project, one that takes landscape as its focal point and that is charged with a dauntless obsession with getting at the subjective heart of an image.

II.

For Murnane, it is less about remembering things as they truly were than it is about remembering them as they appear in our often untrustworthy memories. This is especially true with regard to the memory of books and their long-lasting influence on our lives. Of Proust's *À la recherche du temps perdu*, Murnane writes: "I am not writing today about a book or even about my reading of a book. I am writing about images that appear in my mind whenever I try to remember my having read that book." Murnane insists on writing as a means of exploring the significance of a particular image, a method that causes the act of writing to be a performative attempt to unearth the underlying "truth" about that image. In "Why I Write What I Write" (1986), he remarks: "My sentences arise out of images and feelings that haunt me… These images and feelings haunt me until I find the sentences to bring them into this world." And in "The Breathing Author" he elaborates:

> I often tell my students that a writer of my sort of fiction is a technical writer. The task of this sort of writer is to report in the plainest language the images that most claim his attention from among the images in his mind and then to arrange his sentences

and paragraphs (and, if applicable, his chapters) so as to suggest the connections between those images.

Although images remain invariable despite the passing of time, their subjective relation to our sense of individuality morphs continually; thus, Murnane's preoccupation with landscapes can be read as an exercise in exploring the shifting meaning of an image as it relates to his conscious and unconscious lives. His endeavor to explore such meanings both problematizes the image itself and overvalues the image with metonymic weight, insofar as it serves as a touchstone more for the author than for the reader. A close chronological reader of Murnane's work can see how the notion of landscape affords new insights to the writer as he matures. Murnane's continuous foray into the realm of sense memory—wherein he invites the image to yield truths—becomes a focal point much in the same way that Proust's petite madeleine is for his Narrator. These two authors share not so much an ability to impress experience upon their reader as an ability to map out the source of creativity, repetitively focusing on sensory stimulants in the hopes that, as is the case with Proust's Narrator, a flood of involuntary memories will be unleashed "from my cup of tea."

Because what one takes away from a book is subjective in terms of how it relates to one's own personal and artistic journeys, it is telling that Murnane's recollection of *À la recherche du temps perdu*—which he read in its entirety only twice, once in 1973 and again in 1982, after which he "has not read any volume by Marcel Proust"—overvalues the lilacs which he places in the title of his own essay collection. The translation that Murnane read on both occasions was C. K. Scott Moncrieff's, published under the title *Remembrance of Things Past*; there, Moncrieff translates the lilac quotation (which also serves as one of the epigraphs to this piece) as follows:

> When, on a summer evening, the resounding sky growls like a tawny lion, and everyone is complaining of the storm, it is along the "Méséglise way" that my fancy strays alone in ecstasy, inhaling, through the noise of falling rain, the odour of invisible and persistent lilac-trees.

More faithful to the original French, in my view, is Lydia Davis's recent translation:

When on summer evenings the melodious sky growls like a wild animal and everyone grumbles at the storm, it is because of the Méséglise way that I am the only one in ecstasy inhaling, through the noise of the falling rain, the smell of invisible, enduring lilacs.

In his recollection, Murnane has read the phrase as "invisible yet enduring lilacs," which he includes intertextually in *Inland* and which he admits in *Invisible Yet Enduring Lilacs*'s titular essay "ought to be the title of this piece of writing." Because, as Murnane remarks, "I am writing about images that appear in my mind whenever I try to remember my having read that book," he recalls first reading the lilac passage in a dreamscape that combines "the white and lilac flowers of the lilac bushes" with a fantasized country estate owned by a sympathetic "drawler" much like Swann, the visual centerpiece of which are the "enduring lilacs that had previously been invisible." In Moncrieff's translation, "persistent" is less resonant than "enduring"; and in Davis's more accurate translation, the *et* in the original French is not included (i.e. "invisible *and* enduring lilacs") but is rather elided by a comma. That Murnane includes a *yet* in hindsight implies not only a latent urgency implicit in the image of the lilacs, but also that there is something hidden in the image that is meant to be uncovered: in spite of their invisibility, the lilacs endure; they endure even if they are not visible.

That the image has some insight to offer, if one is able to render these enduring lilacs visible by gazing intently at them over time, is stressed in Murnane's iterative use of landscapes in his own work. *Inland*'s narrator also shares a fascination with getting to the heart of images, as seen in his preoccupation with a quote attributed to Paul Éluard: "There is another world, but it is in this one." For Murnane, there is something hidden beneath landscapes that bears repeated exposure and confrontation, and while "maps...confine [his] thinking," as he writes in "Birds of the Puszta" (1988), it is only through incessant subjective glances and obsessive textualizations of these landscapes that the truth can be unearthed: "I seemed to have learned something from a layer beneath the surface of the knowable." It appears that even the young Murnane knew that this was his lot in life: "I was a boy who delighted in finding what was meant to remain hidden." However, the further inland one goes, the more dangerous this task becomes: while "mountains [are] too obvious a place," "plains looked simple but were not so," since in "concealing much of [their] meaning" they beg "to be inspected closely." This may well be why the filmmaker-narrator of *The Plains* refers to himself as "the explorer of a distinctive landscape."

This explains Murnane's textual obsession with landscapes and also his infatuation with Proust, whose Narrator is able to prompt a sense memory from the now famous petite madeleine and tisane. Reading *Swann's Way* for the first time in January 1961, Murnane, writing in 1990, recalls having "just opened the first tin of sardines that I had bought—a product of Portugal" and eating so as "not to waste anything that had cost me money" "while I read from the book propped open in front of me." His experience with Proust, especially as it hinges on the most important scene in *À la recherche du temps perdu* that deals with involuntary memory evoked by the senses, is worth quoting in full:

> For an hour after I had eaten my meal, I felt a growing but still bearable discomfort. But as I read on, my stomach became more and more offended by what I had forced into it. At about the time when I was reading of how the narrator had tasted a mouthful of cake mixed with tea and had been overcome by an exquisite sensation, the taste of the dry bread mixed with the sardine oil was so strong in my mouth that I was overcome by nausea.

Here, Proust's Narrator's experience of "an exquisite sensation" is recalled by Murnane as one encountered while he himself "was overcome by nausea." However, despite this initial noxious correlation and "in my mind at least a mild flatulence whenever I handled the book," after completing *À la recherche du temps perdu* Murnane finds himself going against the Narrator's mandate to, as Murnane puts it, "never deliberately...go in search of" "those parcels of a few moments of seemingly lost time." In not so doing, he finds that he is now able to take from these memories and images "feelings of expectancy and joy."

So while Proust's project is rooted in involuntary sense memory, how—in Davis's translation—"from my cup of tea" "emerged" "all of Combray and its surroundings," Murnane makes an interesting distinction between involuntary and voluntary memory, which is also found in *À la recherche du temps perdu*. It is useful to remember that Proust's Narrator does not have his moment of enlightenment and poetic vision without successive prompting; indeed, the Narrator is compelled to taste the petite madeleine several times, encountering first "resistance" and "the murmurs of distances traversed" and realizing that "all the exertions of our intelligence are useless" when it comes to remembering our pasts before finally "the memory appear[s]," and the Narrator's past along with it. In much the same way, Murnane's performative and iterative preoccupation with landscapes serves to conjure a similar petite madeleine moment, a moment of "discovery" that Murnane suggests he has finally reached after thirty years of writing fiction, embedded less in the taste memory immortalized in *À la recherche du temps perdu* (as taste is so bound up with the sense of smell, and "[Murnane] happened to have been born without a sense of smell") than in "the visual memory," as Proust terms it, of Murnane's beloved landscapes.

III.

It is worth noting here another novel to which Murnane is indebted, "the book that I admire most among books of fiction in the English language, *Wuthering Heights*." Indeed, Emily Brontë's 1847 novel makes its appearance in several of Murnane's books, notably in *Invisible Yet Enduring Lilacs*, *Inland*, and *Barley Patch*, where special attention is devoted both to the novel's structure ("I am fascinated by the *shape* of what takes place," he writes of *Wuthering Heights* in "Birds of the Puszta") and to its evocation of the treacherously sublime landscape of the Yorkshire moors. Juxtaposing the structure with the thematic treatment of landscape in Brontë's novel, Murnane summarizes:

> A man visits a remote district. In that district the man sees a sign of a further district that seems as remote and harsh to the people around him as their district seems to him. Then the man remembers that the further district is linked with his own past.

Remarkably, this reads like a synopsis of his own novel *The Plains*, which focuses on a filmmaker who narrates a journey to "inner Australia" in order to make a film about the plains and the people who inhabit these more interior regions. Although Brontë's Lockwood is linked to the district he visits by way of "his own past," the filmmaker-narrator of *The Plains* is linked to the location he visits solely by a shared (if misunderstood) cultural identity with the inhabitants of "inner Australia," believing somewhat perversely that as a filmmaker he is "admirably equipped to explore this landscape and reveal it to others." His proximity to and obsessive interest in the plains allows him to come to at least some understanding of the complex meanings they can afford, both at objective and, more important, at subjective registers. *The Plains* often plays with this idea of two landscapes, "one continually visible but never accessible and the other always invisible even though one crossed and recrossed it daily." Given Murnane's interest in landscapes—particularly landscapes alongside other landscapes and "spaces-within-spaces"—it is no surprise that *Wuthering Heights* appeals to him as much as it does: the novel's structure makes use of a unique amalgamation of nested, embedded, and frame narratives, wherein one narrator's subjective account of another narrator's account of "the truth" causes the reader to be at least thrice removed from the primary narrative. Thus, *Wuthering Heights* is very much about the individual's subjective relation to knowledge as well as to his or her surroundings—themes that, as I have suggested, are central to Murnane's own work.

Proust is also painstakingly concerned with landscapes, and it is intriguing that the quote from *Swann's Way* that Murnane chooses as the title of his essay collection—the quote he misremembers as "invisible yet enduring lilacs"—is one that serves as both metaphor and metonym: not only do the lilacs symbolize the budding love the young Narrator begins to feel for Swann's daughter, Gilberte, but they also act as a metonym for the Méséglise way, or the way by Swann's, one of the two recurring landscapes throughout *À la recherche du temps perdu*. Quoted above, but worth recalling again here, is Murnane's description of Proust's Narrator "as a man made up mostly of landscapes." In spite of the petite madeleine moment's gustatory centrality to *À la recherche du temps perdu* and the Narrator's flood of memories, Murnane, lacking the sense of smell ("my nose has no power of smelling," he writes in *Inland*), is quicker to focus on the visual components of the Narrator's journey, set up as two oppositional "ways" in the first volume of *À la recherche du temps perdu*. Indeed, much of Proust's novel sees the Narrator experimenting with each of these ways—the Méséglise and the Guermantes ways—and what each way entails before he is finally able to reconcile them internally as he journeys through life "discover[ing]," as Murnane comments, "part of the truth underlying the surface of his life." This is only made possible, however, by an aesthetic approach to life, as Proust's Narrator comments in *Time Regained*, the last volume of *À la recherche du temps perdu*, here translated by Andreas Mayor (who took over after Moncrieff died before he had completed the translation), Terence Kilmartin, and D. J. Enright:

> Through art alone are we able to emerge from ourselves, to know what another person sees of a universe which is not the same as our own and of which, without art, the landscapes would remain as unknown to us as those that may exist on the moon. Thanks to art, instead of seeing one world only, our own, we see that world multiply itself and we have at our disposal as many worlds as there are original artists.

It is through art that Murnane is able to iteratively analyze his landscapes and explore how their visual impressions throughout time relate to his subjective understanding of their relation to his own "few moments of seemingly lost time," as he phrases it *Invisible Yet Enduring Lilacs*'s titular piece. Here, in a phantasmic conversation with his deceased father, to whom he would like to explain why Proust has so affected him, Murnane remarks: "In order to answer this…truthfully, I would have to speak to my father about the thing that has always mattered most to me." This thing, he goes on, "is a place":

> Occasionally during my life I may have seemed to believe that I might arrive at this place by travelling to one or another district of the country in which I was born or even to some other country, but for most of my life I have supposed that the place that matters most to me is a place in my mind and that I ought to think not of myself arriving in the future at the place but of myself in the future seeing the place more clearly than I can see any other image in my mind.

Elsewhere, in "Landscape with Freckled Women," collected in *Landscape with Landscape*, he elaborates on this idea of writing, landscapes, and the subjective meaning of them for each individual: "A writer needs no more than a landscape of his own… He began to form a new notion of his landscape. He thought of it as lying within himself—within some broad but invisible zone composed of his memories (which were mostly memories of dreams)." And the opening sentences of *The Plains* reveal how the parallel between landscape and knowledge is the central theme of the novel: "Twenty years ago, when I first arrived on the plains, I kept my eyes open. I looked for anything in the landscape that seemed to hint at some elaborate meaning behind appearances." The meaning of these landscapes can only be fully signified by the author himself: the reader is allowed to witness the attempts to arrive at truth and meaning, but the ultimate act of signification is too subjective to be granted even textual access. Because of this, Murnane's documented journey as he explores the various meanings of landscape and the "place" that matters most to him sketches the artistic process, privileging it over the act of final discovery and enlightenment.

As Jacques Lacan has observed in the quote I have placed as one of the epigraphs to this piece:

> When you see a rainbow, you're seeing something completely subjective. You see it at a certain distance as if stitched on to the landscape. It isn't there. It is a subjective phenomenon. But nonetheless, thanks to a camera, you record it entirely objectively. So, what is it?

What is a rainbow, and what is a landscape? Despite an objective means of capturing an image—in Lacan's example, a camera—the rainbow remains "a subjective phenomenon." Similarly, despite Murnane the writer's compulsive excavations of landscapes in his work, the meaning they afford him is such a wholly subjective one rooted in phenomenology and individuality that "capturing" them textually hardly subjects them to an objective signified. It is the meaning that Murnane can take away from them that is of importance, even if he is unable to share this with his readers: he can share the *journey* (because it is one that we all undertake at various points in our lives), but not the *truth*, which he discovers along the way, a truth that is his and his alone. Murnane has been able, as Emily Dickinson writes, "to perceive / Minuter landscape[s]," and his books are subjective roadmaps to an interior landscape from which we, as readers, are barred. As with Proust's Narrator, Murnane calls upon us as witnesses. He hopes that his own experiences and his obsessive grappling with the matryoshkan image of the landscape (one that is both external and internal) will benefit us on our individual paths toward knowledge and self-discovery.

Murnane's landscapes are connected to Proust's discussion in *Swann's Way* of "the Celtic belief...that the souls of those we have lost are held captive in some inferior creature, in an animal, in a plant...effectively lost to us until the day, which for many never comes, when we happen to pass close to the tree, come into possession of the object." This eventual "discovery," as Murnane writes in *Invisible Yet Enduring Lilacs* and that I also quoted at the start of this piece, "of something of much meaning to myself" is causally related to "my deciding that the writing of fiction was no longer of much importance to me." Murnane has, in effect, completed the poetic, Proustian project of self-discovery. As the narrator of *The Plains* remarks: "I was trying to discover my own kind of landscape. (And what mattered more than the search for landscapes? What distinguished a man after all but the landscape where he finally found himself?)" Murnane is one of the lucky ones, for whom the day of possession and enlightenment comes: he has found his own landscape.

Some Persistence of Memory

Scott Esposito

My failing was that I could never arrange my subject matter—the arguments and narratives and expositions that kept me talking for never less than half a day—so that it culminated in a revelation that somehow emphasised or contrasted with or prefigured or even seemed to deny all likelihood of the lesser revelation of the land outside appearing suddenly in an unexpected light.

—Gerald Murnane, *The Plains*

There is a very simple question about literary maps: what exactly do they *do*? What do they do that cannot be done with words, that is; because, if it can be done with words, then maps are superfluous. Take Bakhtin's essay on the chronotope: it is the greatest study ever written on space and narrative, and it doesn't have a single map... Do maps *add* anything, to our knowledge of literature?

—Franco Moretti, *Graphs, Maps, Trees*

"Bells rang punctually," said Susan, "maids scuffled and giggled. There was a drawing in of chairs and a drawing out of chairs on the linoleum. But from one attic there was a blue view, a distant view of a field unstained by the corruption of this regimented, unreal existence."

—Virginia Woolf, *The Waves*

The extremes that bloom in the desert depths of winter were what drew me to Death Valley. To travel up thousands of feet from the bottom of the western hemisphere and see snow falling in a place hotter and drier than almost any other on Earth. To walk out miles into the white salt earth where no life could survive. To hear the echoes of a bird's wings scatter the chill air between the crevice stone. Solitude is felt insofar as we are displaced from what we have grown accustomed to, and here was a place of such solitude that I might speak to myself with a rare freedom.

By around 4:30 pm, night had fallen. I drove on for another half hour, climbing out of a deeper valley than I had ever been in, and when I emerged it was once again daytime. Behind me I could see an immense shadow seeping across the lowland, pouring down over the ends of the horizon. I continued driving, and by the time it was once again dusk I'd risen more than four thousand feet and was still climbing up out of the Valley toward the day. Steep rock walls streamed up around me, my little road but a string upon the vast shadow again overtaking the land.

That night, in a small motel, I imagined that I'd stopped my car and looked back into the Valley as it was engulfed by shadow, and there I saw a monstrous film projected onto the towering sheets of desert stone, a theater so gigantic as to be measured by the square mile, where the players might be seen for miles and stand thousands of feet tall. What sort of stories might be told upon this megamedium? How would it hinge against the desert's megaliths to create a fabled space, just as the movie theater had become a place attached to its own mythology? For the arts are rarely made at such a scale. They are products not of nature but of civilization, and thus they are built to its scale: a painting but twenty feet high is a grotesque distortion of an art gallery's space; our plays are performed on stages that can comfortably accommodate perhaps a dozen people; our books fit neatly in the hand, as do our musical instruments. Confronted with so large a landscape as Death Valley, they are asked to withstand a nature much more enormous than anything one would ever encounter in a city. I understood this intuitively when in the Valley I began to listen to Morton Feldman's composition "For Stefan Wolpe," a piece of music I had listened to often, though, I realized, never understood, until I let its towering choirs of vibration and feedback fuse with the desert's eerie cathedrals. I played other music in the desert, but nothing else had the capacity to match the forms I was seeing, to push myself to see within the landscape. The rest just made the desert feel more human, anthropomorphizing it into categories of the bizarre and the beautiful. Only the Feldman made me feel that I was not a presence in the desert but the desert itself.

What might literature look like if played upon the near infinities of a vast geography?

When I had reached Death Valley several days earlier, slowly enveloped by fear before the desert's unrelenting scope, I understood that this was a place in which I could experience geography as it exists in Gerald

Murnane's literature. In many works, Murnane presents a nomad forever voyaging through a landscape built from a lifetime of reading, forever staring out upon Australia's vast interior, finding in the two of them some equivalence: "But I preferred to work by daylight when the tall windows on one side, and the ranks of variegated volumes on the other, allowed me to think of myself as still poised between two enormities." All is mind, gazing into itself as it peers through the books and across the plains.

His novel *The Plains* is about a journey into an Australia made mythical, where a man becomes wrapped up within extremes: the extremes of a land beyond all scope, the extremes to which a mind must be pushed in order to see certain things about itself. The plains are experienced throughout the book as a space against whose scale humanity struggles to make itself felt:

> Unchecked by hills or mountains, the sunlight in summer occupied the whole extent of the land from dawn till sunset. And in winter the winds and showers sweeping across the great open spaces barely faltered at the few stands of timber meant as shelter for men or animals.

The book centers around a filmmaker who has journeyed to the plains to impress one of its aristocratic lords into becoming his patron. From the outset we are in the quasi-mythical, the landowners an obscure group of men of strange habits and age-old animosities, their would-be artist pursuing the kind of conjecture that can rarely bear the weight of becoming material.

These plains are more than just a physical place. They correspond to the human mind, which, with equal ease, refuses our efforts to make its measure. Murnane is nothing if not a cartographer determined to find the tools he must use to map this gray terrain. In *Barley Patch*, he elegantly strikes a balance between the mix of knowledge, mystery, irony, and conjecture that must be used when attempting to chart the geography of thoughts:

> I can only suppose that I wrote fiction for thirty and more years in order to rid myself of certain obligations that I felt as a result of my having *read* fiction. Something else I can hardly believe nowadays: during those thirty and more years, I sometimes recalled my childhood ploy of seeing, or seeming to see, places further

off than certain painted places, and yet what I recalled seemed quite unconnected with what I was doing as a writer of fiction. Not until the afternoon mentioned in the fourth paragraph of this piece of fiction did I understand how many were the blank pages; how ample was the space on the far side of every piece of fiction that I had written or had read.

This quotation typifies Murnane's writing for so many reasons: with that opening ("can only suppose"), we are already within his perpetually cautious, estranged relationship with the contents of his own head. The use of "obligations" implies, as he does frequently, that there is always an element of duress to writing, making it less a desire than a duty. These rhetorical asides set the place for the meal: those closing sentences that recall a childhood memory, the relevance of which was not grasped for some thirty years, while also suggesting that the explanation he has now, after so much time, finally reached is in truth only provisional and should be revised at a later date, amid even clearer vision. Thus we see here how Murnane courts the certainty of truth with a constant suspicion, as though it is a dangerous woman who must be seduced with every last trick available, as though, even if he may have it for an evening of careful orchestration and hard-won, ecstatic release, it will again manage to slip away in the morning and effortlessly draw him forth for another try at possessing it.

The writer is always, in a sense, at work on his compositions. His job is to see not only what is before him but to notice the traces of everything that is evoked or suggested by those things. In so doing, he takes the first tentative steps toward grasping the metaphorical possibilities of his world, possibilities that form the basis for the pages and pages of white space that are then filled in with an ever-emerging realization of the substrate on which these metaphors rest. The narrator of *The Plains* is a filmmaker, but as he becomes more entangled by his work he begins ceaselessly reworking his notes for his would-be film until he secretly believes himself to be a writer. This neatly summarizes what so often happens in Murnane's work, when the metaphors discovered with the eyes inevitably give form to the mental landscape that conjured them. It is in the interplay between what the eyes see and what the mind makes of these images that the gaze is perpetually refreshed.

The writer is the person who gazes out in order to gaze within. The iconic portrait of one shows an individual staring out of the frame, eyes dreamy, head cocked at an angle to indicate that sight which sees at once what is in the field of view and what sits within the skull. Murnane's protagonists indeed gaze dreamily, following the serpentine path of their thoughts that begins with what the eyes see and then moves along a chain of association toward some unforeseen yet strangely inevitable conclusion.

The thing that most often occupies their gaze is Australia's plains. They are vast. They might be explored for a lifetime and still yield up new, untrodden acres. In the play of the golden evening light against their shapes there is always the chance of finding that connection between two mutually intelligible thoughts. The Plains's filmmaker eventually comes to recognize that his camera is only a prosthesis that enables a deeper process he feels drawn toward; he muses that perhaps his patrons, seeing him heft his camera, "felt obliged to make some comment on the irrelevance of such things as lenses and light waves to the creation of those images of mine that no one had yet laid eyes on." It is not the images he makes that enrapture him but the act of looking: "I was far more concerned with those who might one day examine the faulty prints in my patron's jumbled collection and see me as a man with my eyes fixed on something that mattered."

The plains await the mind's expanses, always ready to present us with some new thought that we could previously only suspect was there. Murnane's books are maps of this terrain, maps made out of language, akin to the person who instructs you, in a city free of street names and address numbers, to walk down so many feet, turn left at the grand magnolia, head that way until you reach the dry well, and then turn right and walk for another hundred feet... In this sense, The Plains is a map of a grand, labyrinthine desert; as I read it, I built up my own understanding of the multitudinous connections and associations that Murnane had painstakingly arranged before me, and I realized that once I put this book down it would begin to again be foreign to me, just as have so many labyrinthine mountain towns whose roads I knew so well when years ago I walked them daily, but now would be at a loss to navigate. The Plains also maps a physical territory, although it comes to represent a convoluted, unstable cartography, as though instead of attempting to project a globe onto flat space it wants to represent a sort of Möbius strip in language's narrative.

As recondite as The Plains becomes, however, it seeks poles and direction. Early on, the text makes known its obsession with unifying itself: the colors "blue-green" and "old-gold" represent two sides in a mysterious quarrel among landowners, as if the War of the Roses had been pursued by secret societies ventriloquizing the highest echelons of royal power. Soon the book is locating those colors everywhere, trying to build some sort of binary to order its diverse phenomena, just as the many landforms on the Earth can be reconciled by north and south. Yet against this search for order, *The Plains* remains determined to push "beyond the illusions that could be signified by simple shapes and motifs." Its gaze remains firmly anchored to the fata morgana, forever marking the horizon of a vast land spilling surplus light; I find within it my own fata morgana that draws me toward the next illusion, though I have not yet situated myself within the book's prior pages.

Herein can be found the paradox of *The Plains*: it has no certainties until we read it and discover them within, yet those certainties were always present in the text. This situation reflects that of the plains' inhabitants, who obsess over understanding themselves and their territory yet, despite their endless revelations, never do. Its publishing houses thrive on books dedicated to explaining prior books written by plainsmen. Its rulers spend hours in their enormous personal libraries searching for phrases to capture the plains' shifting metaphors. And still they abhor a full explanation: of one of the lords, the narrator speculates that, "He wants of all that is irretrievable only that it should seem to be bounded on all sides by familiar terrain." I picture the familiar as existing in a constant state of necessity and tension with the irretrievable.

I first set foot in the desert with a fear of committing my body's weight to something I could not trust. I tried to say a few words into the stillness, but each time I spoke, my words were swallowed up. I was abashed by this imposing space, as though I had stepped onstage in front of an audience of thousands and under their hard eyes had forgotten everything I had to tell them. From the eight-lane interstate to the four-lane highway, then the county road and finally the strip of concrete though the dead sands, with each link the land took possession of me more fully. Even in the winter the desert was hot and dry, free from all but the most pitiable signs of life. The thought came to me, first as an inkling and then with greater and greater persistence, that if my car gave out I would be at the mercy of whoever happened to pass by—and no one had in almost a hundred miles. The faint, recursive stirrings of panic and paranoia emerged, arranging the trajectory of each thought. I could only continue by shutting my mind to these sensations, which in practice meant a kind of deadening aphasia. Slowly it turned over into elation.

This frame of mind is not easily reached, and it is fragile. It is the threshold one longs to cross when staring out at a stupefying vista, that instant when the matter of return is brought into doubt. Connections multiply with dizzying energy, ideas otherwise impossible become inevitable; it is a state of suggestibility that opens the mind to the influence of music. Here we reach down past those everyday thoughts to the interred and packed germs. "And I knew," writes Murnane, "that plainsmen commonly consider all art to be the scant visible evidence of immense processes in a landscape that even the artist scarcely perceives."

Maps were once drawn to make fanciful creatures the lords of the white spaces, but those monsters have long since moved from our maps to our books. The indefinite expanses of the mind now harbor the mystery that maps once represented; we can only encounter those irretrievable parts with some risk, and what is found there is only described by symbols. This is what makes Murnane's writing vital: the way he shows us his path by which he reaches the irretrievable; the beautiful, elaborate symbols from which he builds it. It is said that the human mind is the most complex structure in the known universe: in these books we feel the thrill of that intricacy attempting to comprehend itself.

The truth of the valley was beyond the tools I had for perceiving it; the best I could do was to reach it through the language of confusion, fear, elation, and wonder. Though I only ever got a tiny bit of what was there to be had, I did get something of it. The proof are my many sobs and tears, the words I did finally succeed in speaking to myself. I have frequently wondered at their meaning, and at their source. Their overwhelming arrival will never be repeated, though they are an emblem of all that exists within even the driest mind, and they guarantee that the future will yield up other irresolvable moments. One day they too will form a part of what is down there. In some new moment I will see what they become.

"This writer had argued that each man in his heart is a traveller in a boundless landscape," writes Murnane in *The Plains*, though he himself is scarcely a traveler in the conventional sense. With possibly one exception, he has never left his native Australia; nor has he traveled much within his home country. This has not stopped him from writing about South Dakota, Paraguay, Romania, and other foreign lands, even though he places no importance on researching them so as to "get the details right." It seems important to his literary project that his descriptions of these places bear, at most, only accidental resemblance to the actual geographical locations.

Where does literature stand when its mimetic impulse—for I feel certain there is one with Murnane—is aimed squarely at neither the earthly world of phenomena nor the intuited mind of its creator? The degree to which his writing is fictional, autobiographical, novel, short story, essay, or some hybrid thereof is unclear, and Murnane himself has done much to add to the confusion. In his essay collection *Invisible Yet Enduring Lilacs*, he claims: "I should never have tried to write fiction or non-fiction or even anything in-between. I should have left it to discerning editors to publish all my pieces of writing as essays." Yet in *Barley Patch* he states, "My pieces of published writing were called by publishers and by almost all readers either *novels* or *short stories*, but to have them thus called began in time to make me feel uncomfortable, and I took to using only the word *fiction* as the name for what I wrote." He goes to quite clearly, and one would say purposefully, absurd lengths to claim that his work is not autobiographical, as when he writes in *Barley Patch*, "While I was writing the previous paragraph, which is, of course, part of a work of fiction, I remembered for perhaps the first time in sixty years an event in the seventh or eighth year of the life of a person who can never be any more than a personage in the mind of any reader of this writing."

Perhaps this is the secret of Murnane's maps: they prove all the more valuable to us for our inability to say just what he is mapping, though it is quite clear that his accumulated memory and knowledge does play a large role in shaping whatever is this space. We see a clue toward this in his disavowal of the role creativity plays in his work; he instead favors an idea of the writer as a sifter of the mind's contents. He writes in *Barley Patch* that he has for decades avoided the words "*create, creative, imagine, imaginary*, and, above all, *imagination*." He goes on to claim, "I had come to understand that I had never created any character or imagined any plot. My preferred way of summing up my deficiencies was to say simply that I had no imagination." At length, he disavows imagination entirely, saying that "the word *imagination* seemed to me connected with antiquated systems of psychology." Finally, he concludes, "What I called the contents of my mind seemed to me more than enough for a lifetime of writing."

Beginning in 1991, Murnane did not publish any literature for nearly two decades; he has had several such periods of nonpublication throughout his career. He describes the reasons that an author might stop writing at the beginning of *Barley Patch*, the only novel-length work he has published thus far after his fallow period, by introducing the question Rilke famously posed to Franz Kappus in their correspondence: "This above all—ask yourself in the stillest hour of your night: must I write?" Murnane responds: "In the early autumn of 1991, however, four years before I ceased to be a teacher of fiction-writing, and on a bustling afternoon rather than during a still night, and without even putting to myself Rilke's recommended question, I myself gave up writing fiction."

The fact is stated thus, as are so many in his writing, with scarcely any sort of preamble to prepare us for such an immense declaration, and then it is left there, a valise full of questions, never to be directly readdressed—although it is quite clear that Murnane is taking up the matter of the two decades without publication, albeit in perhaps the most tangential ways possible, in *Barley Patch* as well as *A History of Books*. In the five pieces that compose this latest work Murnane frequently remarks about how he, a lifelong voracious reader, has stopped reading new books, instead choosing to focus on a few canonical opuses that he would like to spend as much time with as possible before he dies. This involution mirrors how Murnane's writing has become preoccupied with dredging through his life's memories. It is as though at some moment a tipping point was reached, whereupon he decided that the borders of his map were now fixed.

Though the plains must remain immeasurable, one might attain such a familiarity with them that they would form the basis for a comprehension of one's existence. At that point, no matter where we might look, it would be impossible not to see them. I believe this explains *A History of Books*, an inquiry into what remains after a lifetime of reading. The book's epigraph, from Proust, makes evident just how much Murnane believes does remain, yet it also hints at what has been lost along the way: "After a certain age our memories are so intertwined with one another that what we are thinking of, the book we are reading, scarcely matters anymore. We have put something of ourselves everywhere, everything is fertile, everything is dangerous, and we can make discoveries no less precious than in Pascal's *Pensées* in an advertisement for soap."

If everything is indeed fertile, then nothing will have an individual character. Though a reflection born of *À la recherche du temps perdu* may come to light while we gaze at the toothpaste in the morning, we will fail to remember the first time we encountered it, years ago. We may know that our epiphany came from somewhere, but where?

Murnane has referred to "A History of Books," the longest of the five texts in his latest collection of the same name, as a novella, but it may as easily be an essay, or a memoir, or perhaps it is meant to smash boundaries in favor of a more idealized form that can be all three at once. As he writes within it, "Above all, so the young man said to the young woman, he admired the author mentioned for having written the neglected masterpiece in such a way that no reader or commentator had been able to decide whether the work was fiction or autobiography or a blend of the two." It is more than one hundred pages in length but uses almost no proper names or place names, instead referring to all but a few of the many fictional characters, former acquaintances, authors, and locations that it discusses by way of recurrent tags, as in the following sentence: "The man could recall nothing of what he had learned about the man with the black hair and the black beard from the book where the four illustrations had been printed." Though this language is circuitous, it is truer to how memory works, where we more frequently arrive at our destinations through details and associations. The point this language underscores is that any one place on a map is meaningless on its own: it is only in relation to something else that a place derives significance. This is how *experiences*— like reading the volumes of Proust—that are common to thousands if not millions take on the individual characters that mark them as our own. The lack of proper names in "A History of Books" also has the effect of radically flattening everything, turning living, breathing people into the same image-memories as fictional characters, images found in magazines, myths, and stories. Although this strange hybrid ranges from Murnane's adolescence to his young adulthood to his old age, everything in it seems to exist in the same realm. It is Murnane's brain, or the plains.

As with *Barley Patch*, the logic of the language in *A History of Books* accommodates itself to those memories it is mapping. Interior monologue is not present; instead, interior states are evoked by pointing to aspects of stories and authors' lives: "The man who sometimes recited the poem had first learned it after he had felt sympathy for the poet and after he, the man, had been annoyed that some of the poet's readers had begrudged him his weakness [alcoholism]." Conclusions are arrived at through implication, a series of calibrated words and phrases that nudge a reader toward what is never quite said. At times even the most basic things are obscured to the point of absurdity: I believe that the man in the opening anecdote to the book's second piece, "As It Were a Letter," is Murnane's brother, but he is only ever referred to as "a man," and Murnane gives no direct indication of any meaningful relationship.

This is a kind of language comfortable with the knowledge that we must deconstruct what we know before we can begin to see what else we possess, trustful that forgotten things will persist in radiating their presence within the depths of mind. I once saw a play about a detective who told such a good story that he convinced his two suspects to commit the murder to which he was trying to get them to confess. This roughly approximates our relationship with books. "Everything in my memory," writes Blanchot, "strives to be the recollection of a language that has not yet been invented." Or as Murnane says, "The work finds us, not we the work, and the most we can do is not to turn and flee from it."

Let's say that I was in search of the language to describe what the landscape of Death Valley did to my mind for the few days that I inhabited it. I could write down some particularly meaningful vignettes from those days, as I've already begun to do here. I could then dig into my memories for those things whose traces I have used to construct those scenes. How did I know to start playing the Feldman, out of the hundreds of musicians I might have chosen at that moment? What events first led me, years ago, to try listening to Feldman? How did I create the aesthetic environment in which such an experiment would be possible? Eventually I would perhaps accumulate the necessary reference points to map out a space in which I might essay my understanding of the landscape.

Every writer is after an inexhaustible terrain, the act of writing a perpetual rediscovery of fragments within that terrain. This inexhaustibility is the plains Murnane gazes at with his imperturbable constancy, the place that provides endless inspiration and that forever pushes back at the threat of writer's block. I picture it as two squares, one inside the other. The bordering square is the familiar, that place where writer's block is inevitable, the place where we spend most of our time; and the inside square is that inexhaustible, irretrievable vein. The writer gazes from the familiar into the irretrievable, and the words he uses are snatched from that inner space, though in truth nothing that he utters ever truly describes the inside square.

And then perhaps one more tiny square within the second square, an aperture, an absence, a negation. Murnane has speculated that each of his books is "a postponement," "a sort of faithlessness" by which he has avoided the true work at hand. "Truly, I'll write this first, and afterwards that, and afterwards, yes afterwards, I'll devote myself to my true task." "The writer," he concludes, "knows that he can never declare 'everything,'" instead looking for "one line or paragraph in which I would say in my own style what no one but me could say." One imagines this thing standing outside of the economy of memories whose endless circulation forms the basis of Murnane's work. I do not think he would know this thing when he had managed to say it.

Every journey moves toward the ideal. When reading books like *Barley Patch* or *The Plains*, one butts up again and again against the question of abstract concepts and their physical representation, the conflicting realms of the divine and the earthly, language and that which resists being named. In the middle of "A History of Books," we suddenly find a strange story about the gods and goddesses. Their world is one without any art, because they do not live in a realm of language but rather one where everything is what it is. "No one painted or sculpted or composed music or wrote literature because no one was urged to find so-called meaning behind so-called appearances. Where the everyday was the ultimate, there was nothing to do but play." That play is both the absence toward which Murnane moves and the negation of any movement. In a world in which appearances correspond to reality, there is no possibility of change. It is as static as a chessboard filled with sixty-four tiny pawns. There is no travel in this realm; there, nothing can be foreign.

While I was writing the preceding section, I stood up to have a look at my copy of Murnane's novel *Inland*, assuming by dint of instinct that there would be something in there for me. It is a habit I have developed as a writer, knowing when to trust in the accidental thought that is really more than an accident. (Blanchot: "True automatic writing is the habitual form of writing, writing that has used the mind's deliberate efforts and its erasures to create automatisms.")

It turned out that there was something in there, though it was nothing Murnane had written. I found in there something I had lost. It was a small object, though it meant a very lot to me, and for a long time I had thought I knew where it was, pressed between the pages of a different book. About six months previously I had gone looking for it in that place and hadn't found it. Owing to some persistence of memory, or maybe that is another way of saying *hope*, I went looking for it in that same place several more times, always with the sense that I'd somehow missed it there the last time and would find it now. I never did, of course, because it was in my copy of *Inland* all the time.

When I found it I laughed a little bit, because a few nights before I'd gone looking for it in that other book, and, upon not finding it there yet again, I'd reasoned that I could only have placed it into a different book. You see, I had taken the book it was not in on a trip with me and had thought I had placed the object in that book somewhat poetically, feeling that there was a certain purpose to its being there. I wanted to create the memory by which that thing was in that book, so that one day it would be more of a fiction than a truth—the image of that thing in that book would be a perfect symbol that I could draw on to write something.

I had taken other books on this trip with me, so when I didn't find it in the wrong book those few nights ago, I reasoned that I must have stuffed it between the pages of a different book I had brought on that trip. I tried to conjure the books I'd brought with me, and I looked in between the pages of a few of them, but I didn't find it.

Then tonight I was sitting here working on this essay, and there it was, right in my copy of *Inland*, and I suddenly remembered that, yes, I had brought *Inland* on that trip with me. I had started reading Murnane with *Barley Patch* three months prior. That was roughly a month before a great calamity in my life, and my memory of reading *Barley Patch* was forever changed by that calamity, as though its shockwaves had penetrated back to the events preceding it and had warped the text of the book. (Here we see how strongly time orients our understanding of the world, for in truth the shockwaves might have hit any memories, but in reality they only ended up hitting those near in time.) I can now only read *Barley Patch* with the faint stirrings of the disaster yet to come. I brought *Inland* and the thing I later lost with me on the trip, intending to read both, but in actuality I only read the latter and not the former, and then I stuffed the latter into the former and forgot that it was there until today. I am so glad to have it back now, even though it brings me great pain to read it.

Part of this once-lost item is a postcard reproduction of a Rothko painting showing three rectangles, the ones on the top and the bottom slightly squatter than the one in the middle. The outlying ones are a burnt orange and a dirty white; the one in the middle is a smudged rust color.

I was given this postcard because a few months prior to receiving it I had seen a play about Rothko titled *Red*. The play makes much about the duality of the red and the black in Rothko's work, how the red in the center of Rothko's canvas symbolizes passion and life and the black surrounding it the depression and death that is always trying to dig its way inside. The words written on the back of this postcard made some rather piercing points about this theme as it pertained to my life then, and will always.

Having thought of all this, I now recall that I began listening to Morton Feldman's music because I chanced to discover a composition of his titled "Rothko Chapel," which Feldman made as a musical response to the place of the same name. Loving Rothko's paintings, I immediately purchased the album. On that same disc was "For Stefan Wolpe," which I tried listening to a number of times but could never comprehend as I did "Rothko Chapel," which was perhaps made accessible to me by my having spent hours staring into Rothko's canvases. And now it occurs to me that I put the Feldman on in Death Valley because, gazing into the desert stone, I was reminded of that same mesmerizing absorption that I feel when enraptured by one of Rothko's paintings. I thought to play "Rothko Chapel" in Death Valley, but when I listened to it, the music didn't do what I thought it would. And then the disc continued on to "For Stefan Wolpe," which for the first time ever made perfect sense. I looked up and felt the towering desert stone rush into me.

An Encounter with Gerald Murnane

Hari Kunzru

I hesitate to record my one meeting with the writer Gerald Murnane, since to do so might imply a degree of acquaintance or intimacy that does not exist. However, the editors of this journal insist on the importance of the smallest details of Murnane's life, and since their judgment is beyond question I will describe it as best I can.

It took place on the balcony of a large two-story house, in the western half of the Australian state of Victoria, that looked over paddocks and many acres of flat grassland, all of which belonged to the owner, a breeder and trainer of racehorses. Through a confusing series of circumstances that are unnecessary to relate here, I had been invited to attend a cocktail party. I believe I had been mistaken for another sort of writer, perhaps another writer in particular, someone with a similar face or name, whose opinions on horse racing carried some weight in that part of the world. To my dismay, all the other guests were connected with racing, and all conversation at the party revolved around its technicalities, personalities, and politics. Since horse racing is a subject about which I have no knowledge or opinions whatsoever, I experienced the sort of dismal social failure I last remembered from a literary party in New York at which I had been introduced to two of my heroes, older men with large, universally admired bodies of work behind them. I had, I flattered myself, something in common with these men in terms of my interests, literary style, and general view of life. However, at the moment of our introduction, they were conducting a conversation about baseball, specifically about forgotten baseball players of the 1950s. Baseball is also a subject about which I have no knowledge or opinions whatsoever—not even contemporary baseball, let alone the baseball of a time before my birth. Unlike at the horse-racing party, though, here I could imagine the conversation turning to other matters—many other matters, from art to politics to the nature of reality— about which I might say something of interest to these two eminent men, something that perhaps would cause them to nod in agreement, to let me know that they considered me worthy of their attention, a fellow writer whose future work they might read and respond to, even if it contained no thoughts or information about baseball. However, no such conversational turn came. They continued to name forgotten baseball players, to share details of their careers, their playing styles, their personal lives, even their various manners of dress (it was a world in which sock color appeared to have particular significance), while I stared dumbly from one to the other until my embarrassment became almost physical, and I withdrew.

After a few initial exchanges it became clear to the other guests at the horse breeder's party in Australia that I had nothing to contribute, and they drew away from me, leaving me alone by the bar. On the pretext of looking for the bathroom, I slipped off and began to explore the house. This was how I found my way to the upstairs balcony, with its view of paddocks and grassland. As I stepped out onto it, I discovered that there was already someone leaning on the railing, looking at the view. This man did not introduce himself, but from certain signs I knew at once that it was the writer Gerald Murnane. He did not seem annoyed that I had interrupted his solitary contemplation of this almost-empty landscape, and indeed motioned for me to come and stand beside him. Together we looked silently at the view. After a while I felt I ought to make some kind of conversation, and since I didn't want to startle or annoy him by revealing that I knew who he was, that I was in fact one of his readers, someone who had spent a great deal of time thinking and talking about his books, I thought it best to offer something general, so I asked him what had brought him to that area. He replied that he was there pursuing one of his hobbies, which was the connoisseurship and appreciation of yabbies. The word *yabby* or perhaps *yabbie* was unfamiliar to me. I assumed, given our location, that it was a kind of horse, but Murnane was kind enough to define it for me, explaining that it was an Australian dialect word for several species of crayfish.

Since crustaceans are a subject about which I have no knowledge or opinions whatsoever, I experienced a moment of panic, fearing that I was about to undergo a repeat of my humiliation in New York. However, Murnane began to explain his hobby, and I was content (indeed somewhat relieved) to listen to him as he spoke of his love of yabbies. I assumed that since dealings between humans and yabbies were almost entirely to do with one eating the other, yabby- or yabbie-judging would largely be a matter of weight and flavor. Instead, it turned out that among the fraternity of yabby fanciers to which Murnane evidently belonged, a complex set of aesthetic criteria had been developed. An extensive color vocabulary (slate, chocolate, emerald, greenstone, pearl, and so forth) was accompanied by fierce and occasionally violent debates about claw shape, tail flare, and the length and droop of feelers. Certain esoteric qualities such as "temperament" and "effulgence" were also in play, though it was far from clear to me what they signified. Murnane spoke with such passion that I quite forgot about the dreadful party going on downstairs. I asked him various yabby-related questions, which he answered with erudition and humor. My initial plan, which had been to turn the conversation as soon as possible away from crayfish and toward questions of literary value, completely slipped my mind. After some time Murnane excused himself, making a wordless gesture that I interpreted as meaning that he had to use the bathroom. I waited for some time on the balcony, but he did not return. Eventually I went downstairs, where the party had become quite raucous and drunken. Murnane was nowhere to be found. I assumed he had already left. After a while, I said a perfunctory thanks to the host and followed suit.

—June 2013

The Interior of Gaaldine

Gerald Murnane

A true account of certain events recalled on the evening when I decided to write no more fiction.

For a long time, I used to dream at night that I had gone to live in Tasmania. After the first few dreams, I would spend my last waking hour each evening at my desk, looking at a map of Tasmania or at one or another leaflet for tourists who might be persuaded to visit Tasmania. (I had no books about Tasmania.) I was hoping either to lengthen the sequences or images in my dreams or to introduce into my dreams details that I would afterwards mistake for memories of an actual place I had left many years before but would return to in the future, but I only succeeded in dreaming of myself at my desk in Tasmania.

I was nearly fifty years of age before I visited Tasmania, although I almost went to live in Tasmania at the age of ten. Before I had reached that age, I had lived in six different houses in Victoria. Like many families at that time, we lived in rented houses, but unlike many fathers of families, my father did not intend to live in his own home in the future. One of his many unusual beliefs was that a working man was entitled to a house at the expense of his employer. My father, who was skilled as a farmer and a gardener, read continually the columns headed SITUATIONS VACANT in several daily and weekly newspapers. He looked forward to becoming one day a head gardener or farm manager at some prison or mental hospital in a provincial city with a rent-free house provided on the premises. At one time, he even applied for several positions as a lighthouse keeper on capes of southern Victoria or islands in Bass Strait. He often spoke of the many hours each week that a man would have for his private pursuits if he could live at the place where he worked and if he was free from the burden of paying for his own house, although he seemed to do no more in his spare time than to read books from the Crime Fiction and General Fiction shelves of the nearest circulating library.

One day when I was ten years of age, my father announced that he had applied for the position of assistant gardener at the mental hospital at New Norfolk in Tasmania and that he was confident of being awarded the position. After he had obtained the position at New Norfolk, so my father told my mother and my brother and me, we would all live together in a six-roomed stone house that was more than a hundred years old and had been built by convicts. While he was waiting for a reply to his application, my father called at the office of the Tasmanian Tourist Bureau in Melbourne and brought home and showed us a publication whose pages contained coloured photographs of Tasmania together with short paragraphs of text. I studied the illustrations and prepared to think of myself as a Tasmanian.

My father was seriously considered for the position at New Norfolk. In the jargon of these days, he was short-listed. The persons making the appointment arranged for my father to travel at their expense by aeroplane from Essendon Airport to Hobart and then to New Norfolk and, of course, back to Essendon. These events took place nearly forty years ago. Few people travelled by aeroplane in those times, and my father was so afraid of taking his first air journey that he made his will beforehand. He travelled safely to Tasmania and back in a Douglas DC-2 but would never speak of his experience in the air and never again stepped into an aeroplane. Soon after he had returned from Tasmania, he learned that he had not been appointed to the position he had applied for. He soon became interested in some other advertised position and never again mentioned the mental hospital and the stone house at New Norfolk. I kept for several years the book with the coloured illustrations of Tasmania but lost it during one of my family's later moves from one rented house to another. During the thirty-five years and more since I last saw the coloured illustrations, I have forgotten all but a few of the many details in the illustrations. Those few are some of the details of an illustration showing a young woman with a basket of apples from the trees of the Huon Valley, of an illustration showing a view from an aeroplane of Elwick Racecourse, which lies beside the estuary of the River Derwent, and of an illustration showing the front of a large house built in a style that I have since learned is called the Georgian style and surrounded by level grassy countryside.

On a certain day in a certain year in the late 1980s, when I had not dreamed for many months about Tasmania, a man who was a stranger to me telephoned me from Hobart and invited me to take part with two other writers in a week-long tour of Tasmania arranged by a writers' organisation of which he was an office-holder. This was the first invitation I had ever received to take part in an event outside the state of Victoria.

The man who telephoned me was the first person who had ever spoken or written to me from Tasmania. I wanted to accept the man's invitation, but I had never stepped into an aeroplane and I intended never to do so, and I explained to the man in Hobart that I could only accept his invitation if he could arrange for me to travel to and from Tasmania by sea. The man told me that he was surprised by my request and that he would have to look at the budgetary ramifications. The following day, the man told me that I was welcome to join the tour and that I could travel to and from Tasmania in the ferry *Abel Tasman* but that I would have to spend a weekend in Tasmania before the tour proper began. The first engagement of the tour was in Devonport on a Monday evening, so the man told me, and the other two writers would, in his words, fly in to Devonport on the Monday afternoon, but the *Abel Tasman* arrived in Devonport only on Tuesday mornings, Thursday mornings, and Saturday mornings, so that I would have to amuse myself, so he said, in Devonport from the Saturday morning until the Monday afternoon when the other writers arrived, although his organisation would book me into a comfortable hotel in Devonport for the Saturday night and the Sunday night.

The tickets for my journey to Tasmania arrived in the post together with a note from the man in Hobart telling me that he had paid in advance for my accommodation for two nights at the Elimatta Hotel and that all other matters would be looked after by a woman from his organisation who would call for me at the hotel on the Monday afternoon and would accompany me and the other two writers on the tour. I calculated that I was one year younger than my father had been when he travelled by air to Hobart nearly forty years before. For all my years, I had hardly ever travelled outside Victoria and had only once stayed in a hotel. The nine days that I was going to spend in Tasmania would be my first absence from my family since I had become a married man twenty years before. I packed at one end of my suitcase a bowl and a spoon and nine small plastic bags each containing the measured amount of wheat germ and raisins and walnut pieces and honey that I intended to eat in my room each morning for breakfast after having added water from the bathroom tap. I packed also a bundle of blank pages and the few finished pages of a piece of short fiction that I had been trying to write for several months. I packed also two books. The first book—*The Seven Mountains of Thomas Merton*, by Michael Mott, published in Boston by the Houghton Mifflin Company in 1984—I had owned for several years but had not yet read. The second book—*A*

Life of Emily Brontë, by Edward Chitham, published at Oxford by Basil Blackwell in 1987—I had owned for only a few days; I had ordered the book from my bookseller as soon as I had read a notice of its publication, and my copy had arrived from England by surface mail only a few days before my departure for Tasmania.

I was due aboard the *Abel Tasman* late on a Friday afternoon. I ate my usual breakfast on the Friday morning, but I could not eat lunch. For most of the afternoon, I paced up and down the lounge-room and the hall of my house while my suitcase stood packed and locked at the front door. I was afraid of missing my train into Melbourne or the train from Melbourne to Station Pier, even though the trains I planned to take would bring me to Port Melbourne more than an hour before the first passengers were permitted aboard. At the same time, I was afraid of travelling so far from home. I had always been afraid that if I were to travel out of what I thought of as my native territory, I would become a different person and would forget the person that I had been. Only a year before I was invited to Tasmania, I had read somewhere of a belief among certain North American Indians that a person who travelled faster than a person could travel on horseback would leave his or her soul behind. I would have had to admit that I had held a driver's licence and had travelled by motor car for nearly thirty years and that I had often travelled in trains, but I could have argued that I had hardly ever travelled out of what I thought of as my native territory. If I had left my soul behind me when I travelled by train to Sydney in 1964 or by car to Murray Bridge in 1962, then I had joined up with my soul soon afterwards when I hurried back to my native districts.

As the time for my leaving my house became closer, I began to sweat, and the muscles in my legs felt weak. I knew that I could have kept myself calm if I had drunk something alcoholic, and I had six stubbies of beer and two flasks of vodka in my suitcase, but I was afraid that if I drank even a glass of water during the afternoon I would vomit as soon as I stepped on board the *Abel Tasman* and felt the movement of the sea. I had never been in any vessel larger than a rowing-boat, but I had seen cut-away illustrations of ocean-liners in books I had read as a child, and I supposed that the gangplank of the *Abel Tasman* would lead on to a vast upper deck and that my vomiting would take place in front of numerous promenading passengers.

I have never since remembered anything that might have happened to me between the time when I left the train at Port Melbourne and the time when I unlocked the door to my cabin deep down among the many corridors inside the *Abel Tasman*.

The first thing I saw when I had locked the door of my cabin behind me was that I was sealed off from the world. This made me afraid again. I had expected my cabin to have a porthole with a view of sea and sky, but all I could see was the interior of my cabin and all I could hear were faint mechanical noises. I spent the first few minutes in my cabin trying to learn whether or not I was above the waterline. I listened through the wall that I believed was nearest the hull, but I heard only voices, and I began to understand that I was deep inside a honeycomb of cabins and that I would not know whether I was above or below the surface of the sea for as long as I could not remember how many sets of stairs I had descended on the way down to my cabin or how far above the sea I had been when I crossed the gangplank.

A life-jacket was fixed to the inside of my cabin door. Behind the jacket was a notice with instructions for putting on the jacket and following a certain route through the corridors and up the stairways if the ship's alarm sounded. I took down the jacket and began to fasten it around me. I got the jacket into what I thought was the correct position, but then I saw from the diagram on the door that I had fastened the jacket wrongly. I tried to get the jacket off me, but I could not get it off. I was sweating and trembling. I sat on the bed with the life-jacket still tied around me. I imagined a steward knocking on the cabin door and then entering by means of his master key to welcome me aboard and finding me already in a life-jacket. I imagined myself trying to sleep with the jacket still fastened around me.

I opened my suitcase and took out one of my stubbies and drank. The beer was still cool, and I drank it all in a few minutes and began to feel less anxious. I opened another stubby and began to work at getting the life-jacket off. I remembered the fruit-knife that I had packed in my bag for quartering the apples and scraping the carrots that I intended to eat whenever I could avoid having to sit down in dining-rooms or motels or wherever the writers were going to be fed on tour. I took out the knife and hacked with it at the fastenings of my life-jacket.

The captain's voice spoke from just behind me, and I dropped the knife. His voice was coming through a sound system into the cabin. He welcomed all the passengers on board and gave us a few items of information and then let us hear the sound of the alarm and reminded us of what to do if we heard the sound during the voyage. While he was talking, I went on fiddling with my life-jacket, and something gave way and enabled me to struggle free. But I was not able to put the jacket back on the door in the way I had found it, and I thought I could see signs of damage where I had hacked at one of the straps with my knife.

While I was drinking my third stubby, the vessel began to move. The noise of the engines was loud in my cabin, but I was surprised at how little movement I noticed. When I had finished the stubby, I left my cabin in search of a bar.

I found a bar and drank beer alone there until nine. For most of the time, I leaned against a window with a hand cupped around my eyes and stared out into the darkness. I was still surprised at how calm the sea was, considering that the season was winter. For most of the time, I could see a few lights in the distance, but I did not know where I was.

When I was back in my cabin, I did not feel sleepy. I had eaten nothing since breakfast, but I did not feel hungry. I opened another stubby and took out the two books I had brought. Since I had become the owner of the book about Thomas Merton, I had looked forward to learning the circumstances of his death. Merton had travelled widely as a young man, but after he had become a Cistercian monk he had observed what was called his vow of stability and had never left his monastery in Kentucky. In his early middle age, when he had for long been a well-known writer and had corresponded with people in many countries, he began to ask his abbot for permission to travel to conferences. The abbot refused his permission for some years, but finally allowed Merton to attend a conference in Thailand of persons from different religions interested in meditation. On the first day of the conference, Merton was found dead in his hotel bathroom, having been electrocuted by faulty wires. This was as much as I had learned from magazine articles, and I wanted to learn more. But I expected to learn more also about Merton's life as a monk and a writer. I had been interested in Merton for more than thirty years, as the following paragraph will explain.

While I sat in my cabin during the first sea journey I had ever undertaken, I was aware that the two books I had brought with me were about the two writers who had most influenced me during the first of many years in my life when I spent much of my time wavering between what I saw as the only two courses that my life could take. During the last year of my secondary education, I had read, among other books, *Elected Silence* and *Wuthering Heights*. Soon after the examinations at the end of that year, I forgot the experience of having read every book except the two mentioned just now. I never afterwards forgot my foreseeing while I read *Elected Silence* that I would become a solitary and a writer as Merton had become. (Sometimes the term *solitary* seemed to mean that I would become a priest in a religious order or a monk in a monastery; at other times the term meant that I would become a bachelor living alone among books.) Nor did I afterwards forget my foreseeing while I read *Wuthering Heights* that I would fall in love with one or another young woman who would seem to me to resemble the image in my mind of Catherine Earnshaw before she had first thought of becoming the wife of Edgar Linton. (In order to meet such a young woman, so I supposed, I would have to live the opposite of a solitary life.)

I did not want to begin reading either book at the beginning. I looked at the pages of illustrations in both books and then at the indexes. I read from each book by turns—a page or two from the one, a chapter or so from the other. I remember myself lying back on my bed at some time towards midnight and drinking the last of my sixth stubby and promising myself that I would never again feel obliged to read the pages or the chapters of any book in the order decided on by the author or the editor and regretting that I had read too many books of fiction during my lifetime and too few biographies of writers of fiction. I remember myself at about the same time taking a pen and paper from my suitcase and making a note to remind myself in the future to consider writing a piece of fiction which would be published as though it was a biography, with an index, illustrations, and whatever else might be needed to complete the illusion.

At about the time mentioned in the previous paragraph, so I remember, I decided that I had been mistaken as a young man to think of Thomas Merton as a solitary. I read in my cabin that Merton as a monk had been continually visited by friends. I read that he had fallen in love, as a man in early middle age, with a young woman he had met when she was a nurse in a hospital where he had been admitted as a patient and that he and the young woman sometimes had picnic lunches together in the woods near the monastery when he had left the hospital and gone back to the monastic life. In my cabin I decided that Thomas Merton had posed as a solitary but that Emily Brontë had been a true solitary.

At about the time mentioned in the previous paragraph, I decided that I had been mistaken as a young man when I thought of finding in the future one or another young woman resembling the young

Catherine Earnshaw. What I read in my copy of the book by Edward Chitham persuaded me that Catherine Earnshaw had seemed to the woman who wrote about her to be an inhabitant of the place called Gondal, which was a place in the mind of Emily Brontë. When I had expected as a young man to fall in love with a young woman resembling Catherine Earnshaw, so I recall having decided in my cabin, I ought to have understood that such a young woman could be met with only in the place called Gondal.

After I had finished the last of my stubbies, I set aside my books and put on my jacket. I put my flasks of vodka in the pockets of the jacket and walked to the highest and foremost part of the upper deck. The time was soon after midnight and the weather was fine but cold. The barman who had served me earlier had told me we would not come into sight of the lights of Tasmania until early daylight, but I sat on a seat on the deck and stared ahead of the ship. I sipped from my flask and began at last to feel what I usually felt after drinking, which was a feeling that I need no longer trouble myself with reading or writing, since I would shortly see as a result of my drinking what I had for so long been trying to see as a result of my reading and writing.

Even at that time, a few people still sat or walked on the upper deck, but an hour or so later I seemed to be the only person there. I went on sipping from my flask. I have been a drinker for most of my adult life but never what is called a seasoned drinker. I have never been able to keep pace with men who drink regularly in hotels, and I have often vomited in the toilet of some hotel while my drinking companions were talking quietly and with no appearance of drunkenness in the bar. I have always preferred to drink alone, sipping from stubbies of beer and trying to maintain in myself the feeling I described in the previous paragraph. I have always disliked wine and spirits, but in situations where I could not have at hand a half-dozen stubbies I have usually had a flask of vodka in a pocket. On the upper deck of the *Abel Tasman*, in the early hours of the morning, I began to sing to myself.

Among the many songs that I must have sung, several stay in my mind. I sang what I knew of 'My Old Kentucky Home', if that is its title, as a result of having read earlier of Thomas Merton in the monastery in Kentucky. I sang what I knew of 'The Camptown Races', if that is its title, as a result of my having remembered that Merton's monastery was in the district of Kentucky celebrated for its racecourses and stud farms. I sang what I thought of as a song about Gondal. The tune and all the words but one were from a song I had heard sung by the American group The Weavers. I sang as I crossed Bass Strait that Gondal was a dreadful place where the whalefish did go and the north wind did blow and the daylight was seldom seen. I sang as though I wanted to warn the curious away from travelling towards Gondal so that I might be one of the few to enjoy its pleasures.

Not long before daylight, as the barman had foretold, a tiny light appeared far ahead in the darkness. I sat watching the light. By now I had almost finished my second flask of vodka. While I watched, a few persons came up on to the deck and watched also, but I felt confident that I was the only person who could see the single sign in the darkness of the land ahead.

When the sky began to lighten, I drank the last of my vodka and then went back to my cabin and packed my books into my suitcases. The books were the only things I had unpacked. I was still wearing the clothes I had put on nearly twenty-four hours earlier in Melbourne. I did not clean my teeth or wash any part of myself. I looked at my face in the mirror and told myself that I was not drunk, but I felt strange. In all my life, I had never gone for so long without food or sleep.

I carried my suitcase up to a coffee shop on an upper level and sipped two cups of black coffee and watched the mountains of Tasmania becoming clearer to view. A few other people sat around me, but I believed they could not see me. When the vessel was entering the Mersey River, I stood in a crowd near the purser's office and was surprised when people did not blunder into me.

I walked down the gangplank. The persons waiting all looked through me. I took a taxi to the Elimatta Hotel. I told the driver I was a bad travel- ler and had not slept all night, and he left me alone. I intended to talk to no one for the whole weekend. I believed I was about to resolve some momentous matter if only I could be left alone. I did not want to sleep or eat. I wondered how soon I might buy a six-pack of stubbies from my hotel.

The young woman who came to the reception desk in the hotel after I had pressed the bell several times told me that my booking was in order but that I could not occupy my room before eleven.

I have always preferred to disguise my feelings in the presence of others. I was dismayed by what the young woman had told me, and having stayed only once in all my life at a hotel, I could not understand the reason for my being shut out, as it seemed to me, from my own room. But I behaved as though I had only called at that hour to confirm my booking and to leave my suitcase in her care. I put my suitcase behind her desk and strolled out of the hotel as though I had friends outside waiting to drive me to their home for a shower and a shave and a substantial breakfast. I turned towards the main streets of Devonport. The time was about eight-thirty.

I walked for fifteen minutes and reached the commercial centre of Devonport. I was not unaware that I would be mostly confined to my hotel room for the next two days, and I bought a bag of apples, a few bananas, and a bunch of carrots, but I went on walking with the fruit and the carrots swinging in a bag from my hand. I did not want to eat. I was almost afraid to eat. I felt as though my body no longer needed food: as though my body could be sustained by the powerful thoughts about to enter my mind. Such a feeling was invigorating, but I thought occasionally that if I ate so much as a mouthful I would fall to my knees in the street and would crawl to the gutter and would begin to vomit. The police would be called. I would be taken back to my hotel. My suitcase would be searched. Something in my baggage would enrage the police. It might be my books or something I had scribbled during the previous night. I would be escorted to the *Abel Tasman* and left in the care of the captain until the vessel sailed for Melbourne on Sunday evening.

I went on walking. I. walked for more than two hours, very slowly and with frequent pauses. I walked through streets of houses at first, and later I walked back to the river and then along a path that took me to the headland where the Mersey enters Bass Strait. I believe I walked for ten minutes or more along the ocean before I turned back. But I remember hardly anything of what I saw while I walked. The one detail I remember is the spur-winged plovers. I noticed the plovers first while I walked along the grassy bank of the river from the Elimatta Hotel towards the main streets. Every twenty or thirty paces, I passed a pair of plovers walking up and down the grass and listening or watching for their prey. I had always been interested in plovers. In the early mornings in the suburb of Melbourne where I lived, I would sometimes hear the cry of a plover and would suppose that I was receiving some kind of message. In the streets of Devonport, I would stand at a few paces from a plover, trying to see the eye of the bird. I remember one bird that turned away and would not meet my eye on a neat lawn that I learned a few moments later was part of the surrounds of the library of Devonport.

I cannot remember having arrived back at my hotel. I assume that I arrived towards midday and was shown to my room. Perhaps I ate soon afterwards in my room one or more of the carrots or apples or bananas that I had been carrying for so long, but I suspect that I lay on the bed in my room and slept for a few hours. My room was part of a block of rooms across a courtyard from the main building of the hotel. The first thing that I can recall from the Saturday afternoon is my walking across the courtyard to the drive-in bottle shop and buying a dozen stubbies of Tasmanian beer and two or three flasks of vodka and then taking them back to my room. I can recall from that same afternoon a few minutes when I was drinking from a stubby of beer and when the sunlight-was bright on the other side of the curtains of my room (I had not opened them since I had first entered the room) and when I noticed a radio near the bed that I was lying on. I turned the radio on. I heard part of the description of a football match between two Tasmanian teams. The broadcast was interrupted by a broadcast of a race from Elwick. I listened to the broadcast, but I had never previously heard the name of any of the horses in the race. (I did not often listen to broadcasts of races in Melbourne, but when I listened I would always recognise the name of one or another horse.) I got up from the bed and walked into the bathroom attached to the bedroom. I looked into the mirror and told myself that I should no longer doubt that I had crossed the sea and had arrived in Tasmania.

I can recall also from the late afternoon or the early evening of the Saturday a period of about fifteen minutes when I awoke on my bed, still fully clothed, and supposed the time to be the morning of one or another day. I took out of my suitcase one of the parcels meant for my breakfast on each day of my tour. I emptied the oats and other things into my bowl and added water and ate. The first mouthful was hard to swallow, and I supposed I was about to vomit it up again. I stood at the door to the bathroom and toilet with my food in my hand. I went on eating but I was ready to vomit if I had to do so. After each mouthful, I felt less uncomfortable. I nudged with my foot the plastic lid of the toilet. The lid fell over the bowl of the toilet. I sat on the plastic lid and ate the remainder of my breakfast food.

I can recall a few minutes from a time that I suppose to have been soon after dark on the Saturday evening. I had woken again on the bed that I considered my bed. I was still wearing the underclothes and shirt and trousers that I had put on in my home in Melbourne at least thirty-six hours before. I walked to the small refrigerator in the corner of my room. I opened the door of the refrigerator and looked at the supply of beer and vodka inside. I seem to recall that I saw an unopened flask of vodka and more than six stubbies, but this must have seemed not enough to keep me contented throughout the Sunday. I seem not to have supposed that a guest of the hotel might order drinks on Sunday, since I remember walking across from my room through darkness and buying another six stubbies and another flask of vodka from the bottle shop.

I must have slept soundly at last during the late evening of the Saturday. What I next remember is my hearing while I slept a sound that seemed to me a sound in a dream. I seemed to be dreaming that a branch of a tree was knocking against the window of my room. As I awoke, I understood that someone was knocking at my door.

I got up from the bed. I had covered myself with the bedspread, but I was still dressed in the shirt and trousers and underclothes that I had worn when I left Melbourne. I supposed the person knocking was one of the staff of the hotel. I opened the door. A youngish woman asked me if she could come in and then stepped forward as though I had already invited her to enter.

I stepped back. The woman walked into the middle of the room and then stood and looked around for the best place to seat herself. She walked to an armchair near the head of my bed, as I thought of it, and sat in the chair. She had been carrying in her right hand a bulky briefcase of the sort that men had carried on suburban trains when I had worked as a public servant in Melbourne twenty-five years before. Having sat, she rested the briefcase across her thighs.

I closed the door to my room. The only places where I could have sat were the bed and the other of the two chairs, which was on the opposite side of the bed from the chair where the woman was sitting. I sat in the chair, and the woman and I looked at one another across the bed.

Even before the woman had spoken at the door, she had seemed to give off a certain warmth and friendliness towards me. As she had walked into my room, I thought she must have mistaken it for some other room. She had arrived at the hotel to visit someone she had never seen but had corresponded with for a long time, but she had knocked at the wrong door—that explanation would have fitted exactly.

We looked at one another by the light of the bedlamp. I cannot report that she smiled at me, but her face was composed and her look was friendly. I was sure by now that she took me for someone else.

Every year, I am less able to estimate the ages of persons much younger than myself. The woman in my room might have been any age from thirty to forty. How did she look to me? My instinctive reaction whenever I meet a female person for the first time is to find her either sexually attractive or sexually unattractive. I did not react instinctively when I first met the woman I am writing about. I seem to have noted few details of her appearance. I remember that her hair was neither dark nor fair, but I do not remember that it was brownish or gingery. Her eyes, her skin, her body—none of these I could describe. What I recall continually is an impression I got from her voice and her posture and her manner towards me. I understood from the first that she thought of me as a friend or an ally of some kind. When she looked at me or spoke to me, it seemed understood between us that we had dealt with one another previously and had long since set aside such petty matters as love and passion. Now, we were together once more in order to deal with things that truly mattered.

When I had sat down, she told me her name. I heard it as Alice. She told me that she knew my name already but not as a result of her having read anything I had written. She was interested in writing, she said, but not in the sort of writing that she understood me to have written. She knew my name, she told me, because a man she knew—the owner of the briefcase in her lap—had pointed out my name to her in a paragraph in a newspaper. My name had been printed in a paragraph reporting that three writers were going to take part in a tour of Tasmania. The man her friend, so she said, seemed to know something about me or to have read some of the articles or poems or novels or plays that I had written. Her friend had asked her to telephone the newspaper and to ask who had supplied the details of the paragraph about the writers' tour. She had telephoned and had been told the name of the organisation that had arranged the tour. She had telephoned the organisation for several days afterwards before she had finally spoken to someone. She had asked for details of the itinerary of the writers, including the names of the hotels and motels where they would be staying. She had had to pretend to be a devoted reader of all my writings before the person from the writers' organisation would give her any details. The person was a man, so she told me, and she believed he would not have given her the details if she had not been a woman and had not spoken pleadingly. When she had reported to her man-friend that

I would be staying for two nights alone in the Elimatta Hotel in Devonport before the tour began, he had been pleased. He had then arranged for the visit that she was making at the time of her telling me this.

I wanted at first to ask her why her man-friend himself had not come to show me whatever was in the briefcase. But then I supposed that the briefcase contained a typescript of the same sort of writing that I had had published during the past fifteen years and that I had come to Tasmania to talk about. If I was right, then the friend of the woman was a writer who had not yet been published and who wanted me to read some of his writing and to help him to get the writing published. For as long as I had been a published writer, I had been approached, after I had talked or read to one or another group of people, by unpublished writers wanting me to read their writing and to help them to get their writing published. And for the first few minutes while the woman was talking to me in my room, I supposed that she had been sent by her friend to persuade me to read his writing. For as long as I supposed this, I tried to think of a polite way of refusing to accept from her the contents of the briefcase in her lap.

I can hardly believe, as I write this account, that I was able while the woman talked to me not only to hear her out calmly but to put one after another interpretations on her words. And yet, I recall that I soon decided while listening to the woman that her story of her man-friend was untrue and that she had brought me some of her own writing to read. After I had begun to believe this, I expected that I would not be able to refuse her when she handed her writing to me and asked me to read it. However, as tired and as dazed as I might have been, I was still determined, so I recall, to carry on the pretence that the writing I had been asked to read was the work of a man who was an admirer of my own writing but was unknown to me. This pretence, so I thought, would save me from having to tell the woman to her face that I had not thought highly of her writing. (I had never thought highly of any writing that had been shown to me by unpublished writers of the kind I have been describing.)

She asked me, as I had expected, to read the contents of the briefcase. In a few graceful movements, she got up from her chair, opened the briefcase, let the bundle of pages fall onto my bed so that the uppermost page was conveniently placed in front of me, and then let herself out of my room. The previous sentence may not be an accurate report of events. I cannot remember her leaving her chair or the room, but certainly a time arrived when she was no longer in the room, and she is not in the room with me now, although she will surely return to this room, or to some other room that had already been reserved for me in some other city in Tasmania, in order to collect the briefcase and its contents and to learn my comments on what I might have read.

More strange than my not remembering the woman's leaving my room is my not remembering her having imparted to me the information I am about to record, which information is a summary of the life of the man said by the woman to have been the author of the pages left in my keeping.

He had lived all his life in Tasmania. He was of about my own age but he had never once travelled the few hundred kilometres by sea that I had finally travelled between Tasmania and the mainland. He had been born in Hobart but had lived as a child for an equal number of years in both Hobart and Launceston and had never afterwards been sure of how to answer persons who asked him where he came from. During his years at secondary school, he had been at least an average student in most subjects but among the best few in English and geography. At the age of fifteen he had had a poem published in his school magazine and had confided to one of his teachers that he wanted to be a poet, but no evidence survives of his having written any other poem or any other piece of literary writing, and in his last year of school his teachers commented in his reports that he seemed to lack ambition. After secondary school, he obtained a place in the training college for primary teachers in schools in the government system. He followed the course for the required two years and earned his trained teacher's certificate. At that time, in the late 1950s, teachers were in short supply. His certificate entitled him to a permanent place in the employment of the state government. At the time when his briefcase was delivered to my room in the Elimatta Hotel in Devonport, he had been a teacher in primary schools in Tasmania for thirty years.

In his early years as a teacher, his junior rank had obliged him to teach in schools unpopular among his colleagues: schools in industrial towns or in government housing estates. As he became more senior, he was more able to teach where he chose, and he chose always to be an assistant teacher in a school in a middle-class suburb of a city. He never sought promotion to any position of responsibility, much less to any head teacher's position. Most of his colleagues were driven at sometime during their careers to study by night for qualifications entitling them to enter the higher-paid grades of the teaching service, but the author of the pages at my elbow, who was close to fifty years of age, had been for fifteen years the most senior teacher in the lowest grade in the system of classification used in Tasmania.

The author of the contents of the briefcase had never married. According to the woman who had brought the briefcase to me, the author, as I intend to call him from now on, had never been seen in the company of any person to whom he might have been linked romantically. Most young teachers in the 1950s lived in boarding houses or as boarders in family homes when they were living away from their own homes. The author as a young man would share a bathroom or a toilet with other persons but would always live in a detached or self-contained room with at least a gas-ring and a sink so that he need not observe the mealtimes of others. As his income increased, he began to live in small rented flats. He saved money each year. Most he put aside for a small house for his retirement; some he used to buy cheap furniture and fittings for the rented flats that he began to occupy after about his thirtieth year; the rest he put towards the cost of buying and maintaining the second-hand cars that he began to buy and to maintain after about his thirtieth year.

He had stayed for no more than five years in any one place during his career. The life he lived was simple and blameless, and yet his colleagues and his neighbours could not leave him alone, and their questions and their scrutiny had always caused him to move on. The population of Tasmania had been never more than a few hundred thousand throughout his career, but he had been able to move seven times during his career to a place where he was scarcely known. At the time when I first heard of him, he was planning to make one further move at about the age of fifty and then to take advantage of a scheme for early retirement and to live for the rest of his life in a village more than thirty kilometres from any place where he had taught. He had lived at two different periods of his life in each of Launceston and Hobart, once at Burnie, once at Devonport, once in Wynyard, and once in New Norfolk. In each place, his routine was as reported in the following paragraph.

He arrived an hour early at school and prepared the lessons for the day. He taught his class conscientiously throughout the day and did whatever other duties his head teacher assigned to him. He ate his cut lunch in the staffroom and took morning and afternoon tea in the same place and exchanged small talk there with his colleagues. After school, he shopped for his supplies and then went to his lodgings. On one afternoon each week, he would call at the local library to borrow and return several books, and on Friday afternoons, if any of his colleagues were in the habit of drinking at a hotel near the school, he would join them for an hour. After he had arrived home each evening, he remained indoors; he was never seen at any meeting or gathering by night. On Saturday, if a race meeting was held in the town or the city where he lived, he would always attend. Sometimes in the winter, he was seen at a football match. On other Saturdays, he would walk for an hour in the late afternoon. He attended no church on Sunday or on any other day. His only outing on Sunday was a short walk late in the day. Each year while one or both of his parents was alive, he spent Christmas day in their house. When his parents had died, he ate Christmas dinner at the home of his married sister, who was his only sibling. On Boxing Day each year, he arrived in one or another unfashionable hotel in one or another seaside town and stayed for a week. He took his short holiday partly so that he would be able to satisfy the questions of his colleagues in the first weeks of the new school year but also as a genuine break in his routine. In the hotel, he went to his room only to sleep. Each morning he walked, always in sports trousers and long-sleeved shirt, along the streets nearest the sea, or he sat on the foreshore and looked at the beach. In the afternoons, he sat in the bar of his hotel, drinking beer slowly and listening to radio broadcasts of cricket or tennis or golf or horse races or watching televised reports of those events or talking with any other drinker who might have begun a conversation with him. In the evenings, he watched television programmes with other guests in the hotel lounge, again drinking slowly and talking with anyone who offered to talk to him. At the end of this week, he returned to his home and stayed indoors all day for most of the days until school resumed.

The author sometimes invited to his home one or another of his colleagues. On perhaps one Friday each year, when the author was drinking with colleagues (always males), he would invite to his home some young man whose wife was staying with a sick parent or was in hospital after having given birth to her first child or (as often happened in later years) had recently separated from her husband. The two men would buy a few bottles of beer and a meal of fish and chips and would sit in the author's lounge-room for three or four hours before the visitor would return to his home.

Whatever odd sights the visitor might have expected to see in the rooms of the bachelor who had invited him home, he saw little worth reporting back to anyone who might have questioned him later. The furnishings would have struck most observers as drab and tasteless. There was a portable television set at least fifteen years old, a cheap mantel radio, and an old record-player with a dozen or so records. A few shelves of books were in a corner—mostly books about horse racing in Europe and the USA. The rooms were bare of pictures. There were no vases or ornaments. The only unexpected item in the lounge-room might have been the filing cabinets. (There would have been only one cabinet during the first seven years of the author's teaching career, but the number increased by one every seven years.) The author was never uncomfortable if his visitor stared at the filing cabinets or asked about them. In fact, these casual-seeming invitations to his home were part of a deliberate policy by the author. He hoped his visitor would tell his colleagues afterwards how little of note he had seen in the bachelor's quarters. This, so the author hoped, would bring an end to any gossip that might have circulated about him. Whenever a visitor seemed curious about the filing cabinets, the author would say offhandedly that he did a bit of writing for a hobby. The author then gave one or another brief account of his hobby depending on how much the visitor seemed to be aware of all that might have been denoted by the word *writing*. To someone who had seemingly never opened a book since his years at the training college, when he had been compelled to read a novel, a play, and an anthology of poetry for his literature course, the author would say that he had been taking correspondence courses in the hope of learning how to write a best-selling crime novel so that he could give up teaching. To someone who might have had on his own shelves some of the Reader's Digest condensed books, the author would say that he had had a poem published when he was at school and a poem or two published in obscure places over the years since then and that he had been trying for years to get together a small collection of poems that might one day be published. To the one man of the twenty and more who had heard that the owner of the filing cabinets was some sort of writer and who had then asked such questions as revealed that he sometimes read a novel or even a book of poetry or even that he may once have tried or thought of trying himself to write a novel or a book of poetry or even a single poem—to that man the author said that each of his poems had been published under a different name and that he preferred not to disclose these names, since he believed that the enterprise known as literature had taken a wrong course from the time when pieces of writing first began to be published with the true name of the author attached. From that time, so the author believed, critics and reviewers and commentators and all other persons who claimed to be able to distinguish good writing from bad writing had never had their skills fairly tested. The author wished that all writers of all texts that might have deserved to be considered as literature had either refused to put a name to any of their texts or had put to every text a different name. If the world had been as he wished, the author said to the one man mentioned earlier in this paragraph, readers would have been able to learn about the author of any text only what the text itself seemed to tell them, and persons claiming to be skilled at commenting on texts would have had to spend much effort in trying to establish which of the many texts published each year came from one or another previously published author. In that world, the author had said to the man mentioned above, no person claiming to be skilled at commenting on texts would be able to praise or to denigrate any piece of writing safe in the knowledge that he or she knew who was the author of that piece and knew that other texts by the same author had been praised or denigrated by other persons claiming to be skilled at commenting.

Thus the author had lived for about thirty years. Now, he was within a few years of retiring under an early retirement scheme that allowed teachers employed by the government to leave work in their fifties. He expected to be left alone by his neighbours after he had retired. Anyone who heard that he was some kind of writer would suppose him to be one more middle-aged man trying to do in his retirement what he had dreamed of doing while he had worked for a living. As a retired man, he would be largely free from having to pretend. And yet he intended, as an extra safeguard of his privacy, to tell none of his former colleagues where he intended to live after his retirement. He had been on good terms with many of his colleagues during his career, but he considered none of them a friend. He had no friend, although the woman who had called at my room was somewhat close to him. He had known for many years where he wanted to spend his retirement, and he had made his last move as a teacher to a place far from the place he was going to retire to. When he left his last school, he would tell his colleagues that he intended to take a long holiday before deciding what next to do. In fact, he would use his savings to buy a cottage in the tiny township of N— on the river of the same name. (I had learned only the first letter of this name.)

The man has given much thought to his choice of the place where he would live for the remainder of his life. He knows that Tasmania is considered a place of mountains and forests, but the township of N— is near the centre of the largest district of mostly level pastureland in the whole island. After his retirement, the author will see mountains and forests in the distance, but he will be surrounded near at hand by mostly level and grassy countryside.

In the briefcase that the woman left with me are nearly two thousand pages. In the upper right-hand corner of each page is a date. The earliest of these dates is from the late 1950s; the most recent date is from this year. (In the text on many pages are other dates, but these are from a different calendar.) If the pages comprised a work of literature, I might report that the first thousand or so comprise an introduction to the work while the other pages are samples chosen at intervals from the narrative proper. If the pages comprised a work of literature, I might describe that work as a novel with many thousands of characters and a plot of infinite complications. The author of the pages in the briefcase has imagined an island-country of approximately the same shape as Tasmania but with about twice its area and twice its population. The name of the country is New Arcadia.

The island-country of New Arcadia is situated with its midpoint at the intersection of the 145th meridian east of Greenwich and the line of latitude forty degrees south of the equator of a planet whose geography and history are similar to those of Earth except that the imagined planet contains no country corresponding to the country Australia. I have not yet learned from the pages I have read whether or not New Arcadia is a member of the British Commonwealth of Nations or the system by which the country is governed. The people of New Arcadia have similar racial origins to the people of Tasmania as it was in the 1950s, except that New Arcadia has considerably fewer people of Irish or Scots or Welsh origin. A less noticeable difference appeared to me as I looked through the pages. The persons in New Arcadia who own racehorses (a slightly larger proportion of the population than in Tasmania) often choose names for their horses such as few Tasmanians would have the knowledge or the wit to devise. A note in one of the early pages explains that the author got many of the names of New Arcadian racehorses from the books that he borrowed continually from libraries. Yet, when I read in the pages such names as Scholar-Gipsy, Laurids Brigge, La Ginistra, Clunbury, Das Glasperlenspiel, and Into The Millenium, I found myself thinking not of a primary teacher sitting alone of an evening in a shabby lounge-room but of men—and a few women—leafing through books in the libraries or on the verandahs of sprawling houses set among clumps of trees and wide lawns in far-reaching expanses of mostly level countryside.

The reader should have guessed from the contents of the previous paragraph that the pages I have been looking at or writing about for most of this evening and of the day that preceded it and of the morning that preceded the day are part of a detailed chronicle of horse racing in New Arcadia from the late 1950s until almost the present day. An introduction to the chronicle contains, among many other matters, maps of the race-courses of New Arcadia, lists of all owners and trainers and jockeys in the country, details of all the principal breeding studs, summaries of the annu-al balance sheets of all the racing clubs... By far the bulk of the pages left with me are filled with details of particular race meetings, but throughout the chronicle I found notes written by the author to explain his methods of devising his imagined world. (He seems to have intended from the first that one or another reader would one day see his text.) In addition to all these contents, the pages also include sample pages from a vast index of all the horses that have raced in New Arcadia during the past thirty years, with each race that each horse contested being listed by serial number beside the name of the horse.

About 1400 races are run in New Arcadia each year. I have learned from a note that the author has always fallen short of his ultimate aim, which is to report for every race every detail that is capable of being decided by the method he has devised for running races. (This is the term he uses. One of his notes begins: *I have run three races every night for the past week...*) Such details include the betting fluctuations for every runner; the amount, if any, invested on the horse by the owner(s), the trainer, and the proxy bettor for the jockey; and—what took the most time by far—the position of each horse after each two or three furlongs of each race.

The author runs a race by consulting a passage of prose chosen at random from one or another of the same library books that he scans for the names of New Arcadian horses. After many months of experiment, he decided as a young man in the 1950s that each letter of the alphabet would have a certain numerical value. Before the running of a race, the names of the starters are listed vertically at the left-hand side of a page. The words of the chosen passage of prose are then written in vertical columns adjoining the list of names in such a way that each name soon has beside it a horizontal array of letters. When this array is of a certain number, the numerical value of the array is calculated and the total is written beside the last of the letters. A comparison of the totals determines the progress of each horse up to a certain point of the race; roughly speaking, the horse with the highest total is the leader at that point.

The description in the previous paragraph grossly simplifies the author's method of running a race. A race run by the method described above would scarcely resemble any race in the world where I sit reporting on the author's pages. In a race run by the method as described above, the lead would change constantly, as would most other positions. In a series of races run thus, rank outsiders and short-priced favourites would win with equal frequency. In the short time remaining to me, I can only report that the author foresaw from the beginning the need for corrective devices that would be combined with the evaluation of scrambled texts. The chief of these is a banking system that allows him to hold in reserve for any horse a sudden addition to its total. Thus, a horse running fifth halfway through a race and suddenly earning a large score from the letters allotted to it—such a horse may hold its position for some distance further until it needs to draw on its bank. The author also provides each starter before the race with a bank in proportion to its odds in the betting ring, with favourites receiving much more than outsiders. This is done, of course, so that favourites and outsiders will win about the same percentage of races that they win in the world where I am writing this sentence.

The author has a name for his method of deciding races by consulting books borrowed from libraries. Whenever he runs a race by the detailed method reported in the previous paragraphs, he thinks of himself as *decoding* a certain text. In the years when he was running the first few thousand races in New Arcadia, he would sometimes become interested in one or another book whose pages he was opening at random and decoding and would sometimes begin to read passages from the book. He found in time that he could get little meaning from reading such a book. Instead of reading in the accepted sense of the word, he was decoding the book in his mind: seeing the letters of word after word listed vertically and imagining the forward rush of a field of horses. I believe that the author has not read any book for nearly thirty years. He still scans certain books or consults the indexes of certain books in search of names for the latest crop of two year olds in New Arcadia, but when he walks out of a library nowadays holding in his hand a book that he intends to decode, the pleasure he feels as he closes his fingers around the bulk of the book comes from his thinking of it as the source of the stringing out of the field on the far side of the course in a steeplechase of two and a half miles at Leamington (population 40,000; chief city of the north-west of New Arcadia) or of the bunching of the field on the turn into the straight in a mile weight-for-age race at Killeaton Park in Bassett (population 300,000; capital city of New Arcadia).

The author has always lived close to a library, but when he has retired and has gone to live in N—, he will no longer be able to stroll home with an armful of books each week. He has already begun to prepare for his retirement by buying books. New books would be too expensive, even if he wanted to buy them, and so he looks through the shelves of second-hand booksellers. The books that I would call novels of the Victorian period are what he most prizes. He loves these books, as I can readily understand, for the sheer mass of their texts. A few chapters from a novel by George Meredith or Anthony Trollope can bring to his mind a whole race meeting somewhere in New Arcadia, together with such consequences as that a certain horse will show signs of injury on the following day or that a certain owner will have been enabled by his success to buy a costly yearling for racing in the future.

But the author loves more than the mere wordiness of these books some quality that he claims to find in the prose itself. In a note that I cannot claim to have understood, he seems to state (I have, as it were, translated his note; he uses no grammatical or literary terms, decodable books being for him mere agglomerations of words) that the profusion of realistic detail in Victorian novels gives to the images of horse racing that they cause to arise in his mind an unsurpassed richness and vividness. If my interpretation of his note is correct, then his method of decoding a text must surely be more complicated than I have so far described it. If he merely converts letters of the alphabet into numbers in accordance with a fixed scale, how could the details of his races be in any way affected by what most readers would call the subject matter of the texts he decodes?

Nor is this the only mystery about the author's methods. In another note, he seems to state something similar to Gustave Flaubert's claim that he could hear the rhythms of his unwritten sentences for pages ahead. The author seems in this note to state that he can hear the multiple thudding of horses' hoofs in any text he looks at, and that of all the various kinds of prose (I translate him again), the Victorian novel is best able to generate the slow rising towards the frantic climax appropriate to a horse race. Again, I suspect that his decoding, as he calls it, is more complex than I have so far understood it to be.

When the author has retired, he will be able to run in detail every race in New Arcadia and to keep the calendar of that place aligned with the calendar of the world that contains the township of N—, but until then, he will have to go on running certain races in detail and merely determining the results of all other races. He determines the result only of a race by a method that he calls *gutting* a text. The method of gutting a text is much more straightforward than decoding. He begins to gut a text by looking only at what most people would call the passages of quoted speech. His term for these passages is *junk-mail*. As with decoding, the words to be gutted are written vertically beside the names of the horses in the race. The scale of numerical equivalents consulted when gutting is different from the scale consulted when decoding. I have not yet understood the difference between the two scales, but I suspect that the scale for the method of gutting might be called crude and unsubtle. Its only purpose is to determine the finishing order at the end of a race. It is not required to suggest any of the gradual unfoldings or the multiple possibilities suggested by the method of decoding. In this matter, as in many others, I suspect the author of hiding behind a show of bluff simple-mindedness. His using quoted speech in this way seems to mock the purpose of the authors who use it in their fiction. Such writers, he seems to be saying, suppose that the best fiction is the most lifelike; that the best prose is speech. (The Victorians used quoted speech as much as any later writers, but he seems more tolerant of them for some reason—perhaps because the speech in Victorian novels seems to readers nowadays too formal or too elaborate to be lifelike.)

A different sort of writer from myself might have wondered why the author of the pages in the briefcase had gone to such trouble to invent a duplication of what was already available to him: why he should have invented the racecourses of New Arcadia when he could have bought a racehorse for himself and watched it of a Saturday at Mowbray or Elwick. I have always been interested in what is usually called the world but only insofar as it provides me with evidence for the existence of another world. I have never written any piece of fiction with the simple purpose of understanding what I might call the real world. I have always written fiction in order to suggest to myself that another world exists. And whenever I have read a piece of fiction that seemed to me worthy to be read, whether the author of that fiction was myself or another person, I have always read with the purpose of suggesting to myself that a world might exist beyond the world suggested by the fiction, even if that further world was suggested only by such passages in the fiction as a report of the narrator's reading a text that he could not understand or of a character's dreaming a dream that was not reported in the text.

The author of the pages in the briefcase might have been making a declaration similar to my declaration in the previous paragraph when he made such notes in the margins of his pages as he made after his detailed report of the running, in a certain year, of the Rosalind Park Stakes (1 mile, 7 furlongs; weight for age; run in the autumn at Killeaton Park). In that race, Psalmus Hungaricus (owner/trainer S. T. Juhasz; rider M. L. Quayle) beat Lavengro after having been beaten by that horse by a margin of three lengths at their previous meeting under somewhat similar conditions. The author in his note asked, and was, of course, unable to answer, the question whether the trainer and the rider of Psalmus Hungaricus had agreed not to let the horse run on its merits in the race in which it was beaten.

While I was writing certain passages in the earlier pages of this piece of writing, I fell into one of my ways of writing fiction, which is to write as though I am looking at one or another detail in my mind and reflecting on that detail at my leisure. Certain passages in the earlier parts of this narrative may have suggested that I have been and will continue to be at leisure to imagine what ought next to be reported of the imagined narrator. I beg the reader to be under no misapprehension. While I have been writing this and the previous paragraph, I have felt less and less able to pretend that I am writing one more piece of fiction of the kinds that I have written in the past. My time is short. In a few hours, the woman representing the writers' organisation will call at the reception desk of this hotel, and my tour of Tasmania will begin. (If any reader of these words should wonder about my health, let that person be assured that I have largely recovered. In order to have finished this narrative before I leave the hotel, I have omitted many a paragraph that I might have written to report my having slept for a few hours or eaten a bowl of oatmeal and other things or drunk a few stubbies of beer.) What I intend to do in the time remaining is to pack my suitcase and to be ready for the writers' tour and then to write a last few paragraphs in an effort to answer certain questions in my mind. (The briefcase is already packed, with its contents in the same order that they occupied when I first looked at them. If the woman who left the briefcase has not returned before I leave this room, I intend to put the briefcase inside my suitcase and to lug it around Tasmania until I am confronted by either the Woman or the author, as will surely happen if no one calls on me during the next few hours.)

Why did the woman bring me the briefcase? Who is the woman and what is her connection with the author of the contents of the briefcase?

I list my answers to these questions in the order in which they occur to me and not in the order of their likely accuracy.

The author of the pages sent them to me out of gratitude. One or another of my books of fiction, when decoded, had caused the three-year-old colt World Light to come from last on the turn and to win the renowned Stanley Plate, run over nine furlongs at set weights on the Merlynston racecourse at Inverbervie (second city of New Arcadia; population 200,000).

The author of the pages sent them to me because he wanted to meet me. He had come to believe that I was ready to be converted to his own way of life. Something that I had written or something that I had said in one or another interview had persuaded him that I would be happier decoding and gutting texts than writing them.

The author of the pages wanted to meet me in order to persuade me to write a different sort of fiction in the future. He would never dare to think of interfering in the multitude of possibilities that might affect the running of any race in New Arcadia in the future, but he had observed certain things in all the years while he had been decoding and gutting texts. He would like to suggest to me that a few changes to my way of writing the texts that would later be published as books might one day result in a few more races in New Arcadia ending with what are called by race commentators blanket finishes.

The author of the pages in the briefcase is not a man of my own age, a bachelor who had worked all his life as a teacher in primary schools. The author of the pages is the woman who brought the briefcase to my room for some purpose that I cannot as yet divine.

I have read many texts during my lifetime: many more texts than I have written. Whenever I have read any text, I have had in my mind an image of the personage who caused the text to come into existence: the implied author, as I call him or her. The ghostly outline of this personage has arisen in my mind as a result of my having read certain details in the text. While reading many a text, I have begun to mistrust and to dislike the implied author. As soon as I have begun to do this, I have stopped reading the text. While reading other texts, I have begun to like and to trust the implied author. When I have begun to do this, I have gone on reading and have sometimes felt so close to the implied author that I seem to have understood why he or she wrote the text that I was reading. While I was reading the pages in the briefcase, I seemed to understand that the implied author of the pages—the person in my mind who had written the pages—had written the pages in order to cause to arise in the mind of one or another reader of the pages one or another image of a personage who would seem to the reader more likeable and more trustworthy than any person in the place where the reader was reading.

I have trusted for many years that I will remember from every text that I read the few words or phrases that I need to remember. I remember now the names of the owners and the trainer of the winner of a maiden race in a certain year at Cleveland (population 60,000; chief city of the midlands district of New Arcadia). The colours carried by the horse were an unusual combination: grey and white. The owners were J. Brenzaida and F. de Samara. The trainer was Ms A. G. Almeida.

The text ends at this point.

From *A Thousand Windows*

Gerald Murnane

> The house of fiction has a thousand windows.
>
> —Henry James

The single Holland blind in his room was still drawn down in late afternoon, although he would have gotten out of his bed and would have washed and dressed at first light. At the moment when he became a personage in this work of fiction, I supposed him to be seated at his small desk with his back to the glowing blind and to be reading, by the light of a desk lamp, a sentence that he had written, perhaps only a few minutes earlier, at the head of a blank page. The sentence was his remembered version of a quotation, so to call it, that he had read long before. He recalls, or so I suppose, that the author of the sentence was a male person from an earlier century, but he cannot recall the name of the author. The sentence is as follows: *All our troubles arise from our being unable to keep to our room.*

One of the commonest devices used by writers of fiction is the withholding of essential information. Much faulty fiction seems to derive from its author's having been overly influenced by films, and yet I have to admit that authors were withholding information from readers long before the first filmscripts were written. Long before cameras could record such scenes, solitary characters were reported as sitting in quiet rooms or trudging across lonely landscapes at the beginnings of works of fiction while the readers of those works looked forward to learning, all in good time, the names of those characters, their histories, and even their motives and deepest feelings. The narrator of this work of fiction wants no reader of the previous paragraph to look forward to learning any such details in connection with the personage mentioned there.

How many years have passed since I last watched a film—since I last walked out of some or another cinema ashamed at having wasted an afternoon or an evening and bothered already by the first of the clusters of false images that would occur to me again and again in coming weeks—false because their source was not my own mind but sequences of shapes and colours displayed in the visible world as though shapes and surfaces were all? And yet when young, I had hoped for much from films. I had hoped to see, in black-and-white scenery arranged by persons with mostly European names, visible, memorable signs from what I would have called, at the time, the world of the imagination, as though it was a place I had yet to discover. One of the European names was a certain Swedish name, and that same name took my eye on the day before I began this work of fiction, while I was turning the pages of a weekly newsmagazine from some or another year in the 1980s. One of the pages was headed CINEMA, and I would have turned it without reading it if the Swedish name had not taken my eye. I gathered from the little I read that the Swede, late in his career, had directed, if that is the correct word, a film set in a castle, many a room of which was occupied by one or another chief character from one or another of the many films directed by the Swede in earlier years.

I read once that the writer of fiction Henry James got much enjoyment from hearing from fellow guests at dinner parties anecdotes that he later made use of in his fiction. James, however, as soon as he had decided that something he was hearing would later be of use to him, begged his informant not to go further, not to reveal the outcome of what was being recounted. At a certain point, James had seemingly got all the ingredients he needed for a work of fiction and preferred to devise his own outcome rather than merely report the actual. When I closed the pages of the weekly newsmagazine as soon as I had learned what is reported in the previous paragraph and without having learned who are the occupants of the castle or what takes place when they meet together, assuming that they do so meet, I resembled Henry James in my not wanting to learn more than a few ingredients, so to call them, but unlike James I was not yet aware that I had acquired my ingredients. My only reaction at the time was to admire the Swede for what I took to be a considerable achievement and to read no further about him and his film lest I learn that my admiration was misplaced. His achievement, so I supposed, was his having discovered, late in life, that a true work of art in no way depends for its justification on its seeming connections with the place that many call the real world and that I call the visible world.

I would have watched several of the Swede's films during the 1960s, which was the last decade when I still hoped to learn from films. After I had written the previous sentence, I set about recalling whatever images I could recall from those films. I recalled first an image of a white-haired man looking out over a small lake; behind the man is a house of two or, perhaps, three storys. I then recalled a certain expression on the face of a ragged boy of ten or twelve years. The boy and his two ragged men-companions had completed, moments before, the rape and murder of a young woman, hardly more than a girl, after they had met up with her in a forest. Moments after I had seen the face of the ragged boy, he vomited.

I was about to ask the questions: why am I able to call to mind only those two images from the many thousands of images that would have appeared to me while I watched the Swede's films during the 1960s? do those images have for me any seeming connection with the place that I call the visible world? and, if the images seem to have no such connection, what connection, if any, do they have with the place that I call the invisible world or, sometimes, for convenience, my mind? First, however, I had better reassure the discerning reader that I am well aware of the many false-hoods in the previous paragraph—falsehoods that I allowed into the text for the sake of the undiscerning reader, who might have found tedious a strictly accurate account of what is reported there. I reported, accurately enough, that I had recalled an *image* of a white-haired man but thereafter I fell into everyday language, so to call it, such as probably caused many an undiscerning reader to see in their minds images of an actual-seeming ragged boy and actual-seeming ragged men and to forget that what were, in fact, denoted were mental images, or memories, as some would call them, of images projected through film onto a screen fifty years before their recall. At the risk of trying the patience of the discerning reader, I shall add that much else denoted by my everyday language in the previous para-graph has no existence in the world where I sit writing these words. The image of a man looking out over a lake with a tall house behind him was an image of an image of a man pretending so to look. No young woman, hardly more than a girl, was raped and murdered. No ragged boy actually vomited. Even so, I have kept in mind for fifty years images of these nulli-ties. As for the questions that I was about to ask when I began to write this paragraph, I can best answer them figuratively. If ever I should choose to locate those images and many others of their kind at one particular site, as the Swede, late in life, chose to locate the chief characters of his many films, then the site would be at the center of some or another mental land-scape of mostly level grassy countryside and would comprise a house of two or, perhaps, three stories and who knows how many windows.

I would not brand as undiscerning any reader of the previous para-graph who might look forward to reading in this present paragraph what he or she would probably call a description of the house mentioned above. I would expect, however, that any such reader, after a little reflection, would agree that what he or she wanted from me was that I should report not the appearance of a particular house but the detail that first alerted me to the existence of the house in what I call the invisible world, which detail would surely have seemed likely to fulfill some or another long-held hope or expectation of mine. I would expect also that any such reader, after having read my report, would see in mind just such a house as he or she had long hoped or expected to see while reading some or another passage of fiction.

In the year when I became married, in the mid-1960s, I read the first volume of the autobiography of a male writer who was almost thirty years older than I and who died fifteen years later after having been struck by a car when walking drunkenly across a street in a provincial city of this state. I remember my observing while I read his autobiography that the author used the present tense throughout the book and my deciding soon afterward that I ought myself to use that tense throughout the work of fiction that I had been trying for several years to write. After having begun to write this paragraph, I remembered several details from my experience as a reader, nearly fifty years ago, of the autobiography mentioned, but the only one of those details that I was able to remember *before* I began to write the paragraph was my seeming to see dazzling points of light on a distant hillside during the moments while I read that the author claimed to remember his having seen often as a child, while he watched from a balcony in the late afternoon, and when the light from the declining sun fell at a certain angle, what he called sumless distant windows like spots of golden oil.

Given that the book in my hands was an autobiography, I surely supposed, when I first read the report of the glowing windows, that the author himself had seen several times during his childhood just such windows as he claimed to have seen. Today, having read and written much during nearly fifty years since, I suppose no such thing. Today, I understand that so-called autobiography is only one of the least worthy varieties of fiction extant. Given that what I read was in the present tense, and recalling now how young I was at the time and how little I had read, I can hardly doubt that I supposed also, when I first read the report of the glowing windows, that what I was then experiencing as a reader was the nearest equivalent that I could hope to experience to whatever it was that the author would have experienced, nearly thirty years before my birth, when he sometimes saw from a balcony in the late afternoon reflected sunlight in distant windows. Today, having read and written and supposed much during nearly fifty years since, I suppose no such thing.

While I was reading the report of the richly lit distant windows, I would very probably have counted myself fortunate to know the approximate location, in the world where I then sat reading, of the actual balcony where the author of the autobiography was reported to have watched often as a child and of the distant hillside where the windows were thus lit. Earlier in the text, the author had named the street where he had lived during certain years of his childhood. I happened to know that same street and was even able to visualize, while I read, an approximation of the distant hillside where the windows had sometimes reflected the late sunlight. I suspect that I would have paused soon after I had read the passage in which the windows were compared to drops of golden oil and would have speculated as follows: Given that I know the very street where the autobiographer lived during certain years of his childhood, and given further that I am able to visualize, while I read, an approximation of the actual hillside that he sometimes saw in the distance, I am more fortunate than the many readers who do not know the street and are unable to visualize the hillside. I am more fortunate because I am able, if I choose, to visit nowadays the very street from which the autobiographer looked out sometimes at least twenty years before my birth, to wait in the street until a certain moment on a certain sort of late afternoon, and then to assess the aptness of the autobiographer's comparing a number of distant windows to sumless spots of golden oil. Today, having read and written and speculated much during nearly fifty years since, I could never thus speculate.

Once, or it may have been more than once, during the mid-1940s, I traveled with my parents and my siblings by road from a large provincial city in the north of this state to a smaller city in the southwest. We stopped for our midday meal in a large city in the inner west of the state—the same city, as it happens, where the autobiographer, more than thirty years later, would be struck and killed while drunkenly crossing a street. Travel by road was far slower than now, and we spent most of the afternoon traveling farther toward the smaller city, our destination. When the sun was low in the sky, we were still crossing the extensive plains that occupy much of the southwest of the state. If this paragraph were part of an autobiography or a conventional work of fiction, then I might well report at this point that I saw at least once, and far across the extensive plains mentioned, a sight that I surmised was a reflection of light from the declining sun in one or more upper windows of a house of at least two stories. I might even go on to report that my reading, twenty years later, a certain autobiographical passage in which distant windows are likened to spots of golden oil was in some way connected with my reporting, in the next-to-last paragraph of my first published work of fiction, that the chief character of that work, while travelling with his parents across the extensive plains mentioned, is enabled to see in mind certain details that he has previously been unable to see. This present work being neither autobiography nor fiction of the same order as the work that I began to write, in the present tense, in the mid-1960s, I need report here only the detail first mentioned in the seventh paragraph of this present work. I need report here only that the window first mentioned in the first paragraph of this present work of fiction might have seemed, at the moment when it was first mentioned, as a distant window might have seemed on an extensive plain to a narrator of an autobiography or to a chief character of a work of fiction—might have seemed like a spot of golden oil, even though I myself have never seen any window with such an appearance.

Selected Works of Vladimír Godár

Orchestral

Symphony no. 1 (1980/R 1986)
Partita for 54 strings, harpsichord, kettledrums, and tubular bells (1983)
Meditation for violin, strings, and kettledrums (1984)
Concerto grosso for strings and harpsichord (1985)
Dariachanghi's Orchard, a myth after a novel by Otar Chiladze
for viola, cello, and orchestra (1987)
Symphony no. 2, "Ritual" (1992)
Barcarolle for violin (or cello) solo, harp, strings, and harpsichord (1993)
Via lucis (1993)
Tombeau de Bartók (1995/R 2002)
Little Suite for Little David for electric violin, electric guitar, strings,
and harpsichord (2005)

Chamber Music

Ricercar for four instruments (1977/R 1995)
Violin Duets, 72 pieces (1981)
Grave, passacaglia for piano (1983)
Talisman, nocturne for piano trio (1979–1983)
Sonata in Memory of Viktor Shklovsky for cello and piano (1985)
Sequence for violin and piano (1987)
Tenderness for string quartet (1991)
Déploration sur la mort de Witold Lutosławski for piano quintet (1994)
La Canzona refrigerativa dell arpa di Davide for cello and harp (1999)
O Crux, meditation for cello (1999)
Missa pastoralis for violin quartet (2000)
Leoš Janáček: Moravian Folk Poetry in Songs (arr. Vladimír Godár, 2004)
Sonata for violin (2005)

Vocal

Lyrical Cantata for mezzosoprano and orchestra (1981)
Orbis sensualium pictus, oratorio on lyrics by Johann Amos Comenius for
soprano, bass, mixed choir, and large orchestra (1984)
Four Serious Songs for mezzosoprano, piano, and orchestra (1985)
The Lullabies of Jan Skácel for soprano, flute, cello, and harpsichord (1986)
Ecce puer for soprano and baroque ensemble (1997)

Gilgamesh's Lament for bass and cello (1998)
Stabat Mater for low voice, solo violin, and baroque ensemble (2001)
Lullabies for female voice and string quartet (2002)
Magnificat for female voice, mixed choir, strings, and harp (2003)
Regina coeli for female voice, mixed choir, and baroque orchestra (2003)
Dormi Jesu for soprano, choir, and harp (2008)
Querela pacis, oratorio for soprano, baritone, mixed choir,
and baroque orchestra (2009-2010)

Stage

Under the Cherry Blossoms in Full Bloom, ballet-opera (2008)

Film Scores

Angle of Approach (dir. Vladimír Balco, 1984)
A Peacock's Feather (Petr Weigl, 1987)
Fly of the Asphalt Pigeon (Vladimír Balco, 1990)
Tenderness (Martin Šulík, 1991)
Jurošík the Bandit (Jaroslav Baran, 1991)
Strangers (Jaroslav Rihák, 1992)
Everything I Like (Martin Šulík, 1992)
The Garden (Martin Šulík, 1995)
Orbis pictus (Martin Šulík, 1997)
The Idiot Returns (Saša Gedeon, 2008)
Landscape (Martin Šulík, 2000)
The City of the Sun or Working Class Heroes (Martin Šulík, 2005)
The Country Teacher (Bohdan Sláma, 2008)
Gypsy (Martin Šulík, 2011)

Publications

Kacírske quodlibety (*Heretical Quodlibets*, 1998)
Luk a lýra. Šesť pohľadov na hudobnú poetiku
(*Bow and Lyre: Six Views on Music Aesthetics*, 2001)
Rozhovory a úvahy (*Talks and Reflections*, 2006)
Zrod opery z ducha rétoriky
(*The Birth of Opera from the Spirit of Rhetoric*, 2012)
Alla battaglia – príbeh hudobného druhu
(*Alla Battaglia: The Story of a Musical Type*, 2012)
De Musica I., II. (2013–2014)

An Interview with Vladimír Godár

Taylor Davis-Van Atta

Mr. Godár's responses translated from the Slovak by Clarice Cloutier

You are a composer, musicologist, academic, translator, editor, and aesthetician. For some composers of your caliber, composition is their single occupation, yet I understand that you value your musicological writings at least as much as you value your compositions. What do you find to be the advantages and disadvantages of engaging in such a varied set of pursuits?

Few composers today devote themselves solely to composition. Most dip into writing, usually when they want others to better understand their thoughts, approaches, and artistic goals. However, working in different mediums exercises different portions of the brain and requires different ways of thinking. I try as much as possible to address different subject matter and themes through each activity. Within musicology, for example, I concentrate in particular on historical themes and only rarely tie my own composing in with any sort of written rationalization. By engaging in all of these activities, I hope to achieve a multiplication of viewpoints, a proliferation of contexts, but the disadvantage is potential confusion, such as excessive rationalization of composition.

Your music is often referred to as "polystylistic," but in fact both your musicological writings and your musical compositions address and challenge a broad range of traditions, styles, and historical and cultural thought: you push conventional boundaries in each of your pursuits. To what extent does your musicological writing—and the discoveries you make through writing—influence your compositional thinking, and vice versa?

The avant-garde has dissected artistic works into various elements, thereby destroying in each case some layer of the original, integrated whole. This is what happened with abstraction in fine arts and with Schoenberg's musical combinatorics. I have tried to base my new musical message on existing musical styles, which I have more or less understood within music as being the equivalent of language within the literary arts. Thus, my new expression does not base itself so much on a new language, but flows from the new use of an existing language and vocabulary.

As far as my musicological works, I try to address phenomena that are not immediately inspiring for me as a composer. This is why I primarily concentrate on historical themes. I'm not so interested in rationalizing composers' problems, but would rather see the new relations that arise from the confrontation of current versus historical contexts.

You have described Béla Bartók's music as "a kind of milk" for you. Can you elaborate on how Bartók's catalog has informed your thinking and your evolution as a composer?

As a child, I went to a school where I specialized in mathematics, studied piano, and listened to rock music. The worlds of numbers, words, and sounds interested me. I was twelve when The Prague Spring occurred, and it was then, after the occupation of Czechoslovakia, that I realized that the world of words was the main harbinger of shameless lying, so of the two remaining worlds—of numbers and of sounds—I chose the world of sounds. In fact, it was Bartók's music that was the impulse for this decision. Initially, I admired his music's expression, and later on its ideal balance between rationality and spontaneity, expression and construction, between contemporary and historical models, and between rational composition and oral traditions. The synthetic nature of his personality still fascinates me today. And not just me: we can hear Bartók's influence in the ideals of many other composers whose music I enjoy: Lutosławski, Górecki, Ginastera, Piazzolla, Kancheli, George Crumb, and so on. The universality of Bartók was masked for too long by Adorno's assertion that the polarity of Schoenberg and Stravinsky was the key to contemporary music. To discover Bartók's significance, it is necessary to thoroughly critique Adorno's ideas.

One of the most beautiful movements of *Querela pacis* is entitled "A Sad Pavan for these distracted times." This movement seems to me as much an elegy to a bygone era and culture as it is a lament to what that old way of life has been replaced with: that is, a lament to today's disposable culture. Art is highly marginalized in Western culture—and

increasingly so in world culture. Even though many of the major oppressive political regimes of the past century have fallen, it seems to me that we now engage in a form of self-censorship, wishing to remain distracted rather than engaged. Do you believe it is possible for art to engage with the mass public today?

Thomas Tomkins composed his virginal work "A Sad Pavan for these distracted times" two weeks after the King of England, Charles I, was beheaded on February 14, 1649. Perhaps Tomkins wanted to designate that period in history which was without rules, when violence and terror were everyday occurrences. Today, mass murder, possible because of the latest scientific discoveries, is being legalized by journalists, politicians, administrators of justice, and church leaders. The marginalization of art and its function inevitably accompanies our reality. Artists' belief in a better future—a utopian vision of time on a historical scale—is considered mad, like Hamlet's groans. This belief may be crazy and yet it is completely unavoidable. When the Georgian film director Georgiy Daneliya was asked what is most essential in filmmaking, he answered, "The wistful yearning for good." The composers whom I enjoy are those who attempt to search for this "wistful yearning for good" within their sounds and in their music.

In the *Mater* cantata, you borrow texts from Slovak lullabies, Christian verse, Yiddish folk songs, as well as the poem "Ecce Puer" from James Joyce. *Mater* is a living continuum of both music history and literary history. How long were you working on *Mater* and how did you select these accompanying texts?

Mater developed while working on its various pieces, and I did not know ahead of time what the result of these pieces would be. Some were birthed over a period of a decade, others in a few days, when the deadline for the recording of the piece had already been set. So, sometimes I was dealing with chance, sometimes with a specific goal, and sometimes the connections that arose between its pieces I only recognized much later. Today, I can see that the oratorio *Orbis sensualium pictus* (1984), the *Mater* cantata (2005), and the *Querela pacis* oratorio (2009) form a trilogy. *Mater* represents the female principle, *Querela pacis* focuses on the male principle, and the center of attention of *Orbis sensualium pictus* is the child. Naturally, I

Original manuscript of "Miles," from *Querela pacis*

realized all this *post facto*, so today I need to try to get my *Querela pacis* oratorio on the concert stage and the *Orbis sensualium pictus* on CD. Then all the connections linking the three will be quite clear.

Olivier Messiaen once said in an interview that "the union of mother and child, so discredited in our time, is doubtless the culmination of nobility and beauty on earth." Messiaen was speaking within the context of his devout Catholicism and the symbolic relationship of Jesus and Mary; nonetheless, his thought seems to ring true when thinking about *Mater*... Are you in agreement with Messiaen? Is there a symbolic view of human love you wish to convey through the *Mater* cycle?

When I was working on the concept of *Mater*, I had the fixed notion in my head—without a doubt—that our world should not be run by men alone. Women have a strong desire for our world to always be better as a whole, and for us, as a people, to have some sort of future. Men are much less interested in this, or are not concerned about it at all. I consider the Cult of the Virgin Mary to be the most significant conquest in terms of the development for Catholicism, and the cult of the woman stands at the very beginning of modern Europe, forming the main root of the European Renaissance. I do not mean this only metaphorically, but quite literally.

If I'm not mistaken, your first collaboration with Iva Bittová was in 2000 on the film *Landscape*, which you scored. After this experience with Bittová, were you composing *Mater* with her particular voice in mind? What unique qualities did Bittová bring to the recording of the cantata?

I have been fascinated my whole life by the co-existence of written and unwritten music. Both have their pros and cons; the oral traditions create a kind of naturalness which is unavailable to the written traditions, yet the written traditions make use of a level of rationality and contextuality which is likewise unavailable to the oral traditions. When I wanted Iva to sing *Mater*, it was not because of her voice, but because she, in her own music, had been able to successfully synthesize or span the bridge that both divides and unites these two worlds. Thanks to Iva's voice, I linked together episodes from Šulík's *Landscape*. From there, it was a short step to other projects, such as *Mater* and Janáček's Moravian folklore.

In 2004, you released that collaborative album with Bittová (*Leoš Janáček: Moravian Folk Poetry in Songs*). How do your transcriptions and arrangements of Janáček challenge previous arrangements of this cycle?

Leoš Janáček and Béla Bartók are among the most important ethnomusicologists of the twentieth century. Janáček's cycle, *Moravian Folk Poetry in Songs*, follows the most common way of folklore arrangements, scoring folk songs for voice and piano. I wanted to bring these songs closer to their original form by connecting them with a string ensemble. I could do so because the first violinist from the Škampa Quartet (Pavel Fischer) was an expert in Moravian folk music, which is in turn so germane to Iva Bittová's musicality. So the recorded version unites all these "manuscripts" (folk, Janáček's, Iva's, Fischer's, and my own) into a unified whole.

You have been concerned with reviving the music and reputation of nineteenth-century Slovakian composer Ján Levoslav Bella. Can you please elaborate on your fascination with Bella's music? What has Bella taught you through your efforts to re-establish his work?

The nationalization of Europe that which place throughout the nineteenth century was the main source of each nation's self-recognition and actualization. One of the main reasons for the delay in the Slovaks' social awareness was the fact that our history has almost never been written by Slovaks themselves. Historicism has taught us that each fact has its current, universal, and historical facet. It would be possible to characterize my work as an attempt to give back to the Slovaks their very history. Since I am trying to give back to the Slovaks their history on the basis of my belief in historicism, I have to first absorb these historical values myself. And only then, when the Slovaks have absorbed their own history, can they ask others to take note of their values and add them to the universal whole. This is an extremely interesting road for me, because in reality there are no dead values. The resuscitation of history is always the resuscitation of the present and the formation of new knowledge; in the Talmud, it is written, *He who is wise is he who learns from everyone.*

In all of your music there seems to be a humanistic quality, that is, a plea for global decency, equality, and peace. At the same time, yours

Original manuscript of *Stabat Mater*

is intensely intimate music. Are you concerned with conveying a "message" as you compose your music, or are you only concerned with a composition's aesthetic and technique?

I think that an artistic work becomes great when its creator has been able to incorporate not only his entire personality but also his reality and even his dreams. Great musical works (just as with novels and films) represent utopias for me, helping us—with our limited means—to try to find the road to a better future. This links Tolstoy, Fellini, Chaplin, Shostakovich, Lennon, and Janáček.

I find humor in your music, sometimes because of sudden and unexpected leaps between eras and tropes, at others because you seem to be consciously parodying Renaissance or other overwrought conventions. Do you find humor in your music? Is humor a natural or inevitable result of the music you wish to compose?

I respect humor in music, but I am not sure if I am actually capable of creating it. Caricature and parody are entirely foreign to me, I do not like these words, just as Igor Stravinsky didn't. I am interested in the connections which arise thanks to various codes or various texts (musical styles and languages) confronting each other. Unfortunately, most of the time these connections require a certain amount of explanation and so any humorous effect would only surface for the historically educated listener. This type of humor is rare in written music, but it does exist—several Renaissance masters were capable of creating it; for example, Orlando Gibbons in his *Cries of London* was able to unite within his fantasia both *In nomine*, the highest form of sacred music, and the cries of sellers in the market, into a single, polyphonic whole—and this was three hundred years before Charles Ives and Steve Reich. Georg Phillip Telemann, Heinrich Biber, and Joseph Haydn might be other examples. It is also typical for Igor Stravinsky and Dmitri Shostakovich, the latter of whom—inspired by Gogolian laughter—confronted various types of music in his compositions. His symphonies are polylogues—in the same way Bakhtin characterized Dostoevsky's novel. The novel narration by Milan Kundera is built on a similar basis. (By the way, when Kundera was young, he sought very much to become a composer, and later, after his rebirth as a writer, he began to very seriously study the theoretical writings of the Russian Formalists.)

I often see your name mentioned alongside Tavener, Pärt, and Górecki. Do you feel an affinity with these composers, or with so-called "holy minimalism"? Do you compose, as Pärt does, within a strict, self-imposed methodology and philosophy?

This requires a somewhat more complicated answer. In 1972, the Swedish radio chorus, led by Erik Ericson, came to Bratislava singing Tavener's fascinating work *Coplas*. I became acquainted with Tavener personally in 1996 in London after a concert which featured compositions by Tavener himself (*Tears of Angels*) and Pärt (*Cantus in Memory of Benjamin Britten*), as well as my own (*Barcarolle*). I had known Pärt's music well since the 1960s. Then, in 1978, I was in Warsaw at a concert where his new *Tabula rasa* was performed, and Pärt himself was present. That concert had a significant influence on my life (Schnittke's new *Concerto grosso no. 1* was also performed there). As far as Górecki's work, I knew it well on the whole; we met during his visit to Bratislava for a concert, during which I had played the piano part for his compositions *Muzyczka IV* and *Lerchenmusik*. Thus, I knew these composers' works in terms of their manifold facets and variations, taking into account what they had gained and what had been lost when they had radically transformed the art of their composition.

Perhaps the term "holy minimalism" helps marketers, however it dishonors and trivializes the attempts and results of the creators themselves, so I do not like that term. On the road of this cathartic selection process, Tavener was the first to set out under the influence of Igor Stravinsky's sacred works, yet his own religious rebirth came much later. Likewise, Pärt's reduction consisted, to a great extent, of his own personal catharsis and his political-philosophical conviction, yet the new face of Pärt-the-priest almost completely overshadowed his longtime, childlike playfulness and musical fantasy. Finally, Górecki's reduction happened as a result of the great weight of the Poles' estrangement, against their very essence, during the postwar Russification of Poland. Perhaps these minimalizations are similar to one another, yet they are just as very different in terms of their creative motivations. It is impossible to understand them without knowing the evolution of these significant composers' works.

Various strands link composers. I find an affinity with many composers—some because of their biographies, some because of the decisions they made, which in turn simplified my own search. Our closeness can be seen in our similar selection of timbre or dramaturgy, or in the use of favorite

From *Barcarolle*

intervals. A common element is also negation: what we deny in our musical reality, what we cannot identify with. I wanted to return to music the ancient diatonics, a kind of temporal dramaturgy (in a sense, "music as a story"), as well as the idea that new compositions always have a relationship to existing compositions and the historical forms already present and functioning in music. I feel the greatest connection with the Georgian Giya Kancheli. We share the common, hopeless trauma our little nations experienced and enjoy a nearly thirty-year friendship. We enjoy similar musical timbre, intervals, and a similar understanding of musical time and the mission of art. We laugh over similar situations and jokes. We are not dealing with "minimalism" here, not the "holy" type, and not any other type either.

Giya Kancheli has stated that "music, like life itself, is inconceivable without romanticism. Romanticism is a high dream of the past, present, and future—a force of invincible beauty which towers above, and conquers, the forces of ignorance, bigotry, violence, and evil." What is your view of romanticism in contemporary music? Do you see music as engaging with "life itself" or perhaps music stands alone as an aesthetic statement that does not bear its influence over the rest of the world?

Giya is known in the West as the creator of slow meditations and tragic meditations. Giya comes from a family of physicians and originally began his studies in geology, while his musical dream—thanks to which he finally decided to pursue music—was to found the first Georgian big band. His musical preferences included Shostakovich, Duke Ellington, and Glen Miller. And it wasn't a philharmonic orchestra that recorded his first compositions, but the Moscow big band that was led by a musician with the most miraculous of biographies, Eddie Rosner. Thanks to his musical versatility, Giya became an important figure in Georgian film, a sought-after composer for theater music, and an important contributor to the new wave of Soviet culture which gave voice to this dream of human freedom in all the artistic mediums. Giya was part of that generation and through his music influenced the film, theater, music, and fine arts of his day. I love his music, just as I love Georgiy Daneliya's films or the poetry and novels of Otar Chiladze, and I was so fortunate to have been able to meet these people at the time when I was forming my artistic credo.

What Giya calls "romanticism," I would call "utopia." It is artistic motivation, the dream of freedom which gives our art the reason for its existence, and which motivates our search for artistic beauty and truth. I can identify with this motivation, and that is the main reason that the musical works of Schnittke, Pärt, Silvestrov, Terterian, and Giya Kancheli have played such a significant role in my life.

In 1985, you released *Sonata in Memory of Viktor Shklovsky*. Can you share your thoughts on the importance of Shklovsky's life and work, and how this sonata came into being?

When I was 17, the Slovak translation of Shklovsky's *Bowstring* was published. I was fascinated by his way of viewing artistic problems, his way of thinking, his approaches. I became acquainted with his other books relatively quickly, because the majority of his key literary (*Theory of Prose, Notes on the Prose of Russian Classics, Energy of Delusion, Leo Tolstoy, Eisenstein*) and autobiographical works (*Zoo, or Letters Not about Love, A Sentimental Journey, Third Factory*) had been published in Slovak and Czech. I really wanted music to find *its* Shklovsky, a thinker who knew—via free association—how to convey the most essential items of our craft: the structure of the artistic work and the relationship of the work to actual reality.

When I heard about Shklovsky's death, I spontaneously wrote (in about two weeks) a composition in his memory—"Sonata for cello and piano." Here I tried to apply to my musical discourse the literary approaches he developed from his research of literary plots, which were the key to his lifelong search.

My fascination with Shklovsky was also a way to familiarize myself with the greatest Slavic culture—Russian culture, its obvious and hidden qualities, which were more than once completely taboo (although I had read everything that had come out, I only learned about the execution of his two brothers recently, thanks to the internet).

Perhaps it would be interesting to recall that Shklovsky visited former Czechoslovakia in the 1960s. Our writers wanted to grant him some sort of wish, and Shklovsky asked to go to Brno to the grave of Gregor Mendel and bow to the friar who in the middle of the nineteenth century, in that city's monastery, crossed various varieties of peas and thereby uncovered the laws of genetics, once again newly discovered by modern science at the beginning of the twentieth century. (By the way, Leoš Janáček played the organ at Mendel's funeral ceremony.)

I would also like to add that I am very happy that, thanks to Dalkey Archive Press, readers all over the world can now appreciate Viktor Shklovsky's character. It might interest you to know that in 2014 a collection of my essays will be translated into English and released by Dalkey Archive. I am honored that my work will be published by the same publishing house as Shklovsky's work.

Chin on Palm on Elbow: Listening to Vladimír Godár

Lawrence Sutin

What does Vladimír Godár's music sound like? The candidates for comparison that I've seen mentioned range from Claudio Monteverdi to Arvo Pärt. I could add further names—Igor Stravinsky, Valentin Silvestrov—but the comparisons hardly matter. The music of Godár sounds, to me, like the music of a time in which religious ritual has died and what was prayer is now dramatic exclamation, what was faith is now the enthrallment of beauty. The old ritual forms are often invoked by Godár, for those forms still hold music well, but Godár's music is a renunciation of piety and a restoration, a worship, of the anguish needed to awaken our souls.

So Godár's music sounds to me, at its happiest, even, with hallelujahs faint as angels comforting a child, like anguish. Anguish, like piety, requires form for full expression so as to be released, fulfilled within the ear of the listener, set free to circuit the mind and body, wordlessly to instill the balm of Solomon's magic ring inscribed "This too shall pass," a profound mindfulness, everything passes, but caught within poignant melodies and intense rhythms the anguish passes in its guise of the exquisite beauty of necessity.

That is the theme, I think, of *Gilgamesh's Lament* for bass and cello. In his album liner notes, Godár tells us that he "came to the conviction that it was vital to work with the original text." As that text is in Akkadian, Godár enlisted the aid of a scholar of ancient Semitic languages to create a phonetic version to be sung. Why not instead employ a Slovakian translation? Why deprive his native audience of its native tongue? The answer seems to me to be that Godár hoped for the exact tonalities that Gilgamesh might have let loose over the corpse of his dearest friend Enkidu, a primal man, for the sake of whose companionship Gilgamesh, the warrior-king of Uruk, forsook marriage. To feature these tonalities is to call back to the past as far as one can musically.

Godár observes that he finds what is commonly titled *The Epic of Gilgamesh* "more theatrical than epical," due to the prevalence in it of direct speech. The direct speech of Gilgamesh is directed at a god, is a plea, a loud private prayer. In Godár's setting it becomes a chamber lament played in low darkness with no one to hear but the audience hidden both from the musicians and the god. The solace in the lament is that anguish is ancient and always in essence the same. Gilgamesh must submit to the fact that death awaits not only the friends of great kings but great kings themselves. Yet he did not consent to place Enkidu's body in the grave until, after seven days of grieving, he saw a maggot crawl out of his friend's nostril. And his speech is more tantrum than submission. Godár's music does not seek to convey the tantrum of the text, for that is the business of the text. The music captures the slow cadences of anguish. In this, Godár, who lectures on the history of aesthetics, follows (as I see it) the indications of Gotthold Ephraim Lessing's *Laocoon: An Esssay on the Limits of Painting and Poetry*, in which Lessing argues that the visual arts (and, I would say, music as well) must capture anguish by means of beauty and not by slavish adherence to human reality, which means that, in the famous statue of Laocoon, the seer of Troy, and his two sons wrapped about by thick poisonous serpents sent by Athena to protect the secret of the wooden horse of which Laocoon was warning, all three must possess noble stoic features (even though, as they are naked, the visceral anguish is conveyed by their constricted muscles) rather than contorted howling faces which would have ruined the effect intended— the catharsis of seeing appealing, rather than hideous, persons die. In like manner, Godár did not wish to scream out Akkadian as that would have negated the echo that his call to the past had elicited—Gilgamesh even in anguish would not have shrieked at the god, for the god, Enlil, a god of storm and violence, was already angry at both Gilgamesh and dead Enkidu (it was Enlil who had issued the sentence of death) for their hubris in killing the monster Humbaba who guarded the cedar forest beloved of heaven. Further yelling would have done little good; Enlil had shown his intent and his power. So in Godár's music the vocal tonalities ascend just a bit, enough to be heard on high, then fall to the earth from the weight of their pain and form stones of sound for Enkidu's grave. In terms of the phonological insights of the Prague Structuralists of the 1920s, admired by Godár, the jagged contrasts of the Akkadian phonemes are an onomatopoeia (like the barcarolle form, suggestive of a rocking boat, employed by Godár in a chamber work for violin) as unique as the brickwork of the fortified walls of Uruk, a wonder constructed by Gilgamesh's order, a wonder that, as he says in the epic's conclusion, will survive him.

The Prague Structuralists were influenced by the works of the Russian Formalist (St. Petersburg branch) Viktor Shklovsky. Godár's

Sonata in Memory of Viktor Shklovsky was originally inspired, the composer tells us, by the desire to create "the form of a structured rhetorical composition… This I did not manage to realize, but I think the vestiges of the original conception can still be discerned in the work's final incarnation." What Godár meant by this in terms of this sonata I have no idea, but the topic is a naturally playful one for me. Shklovsky is famous for his insistence that creative writing depends upon the knowing use of devices, skillful techniques, by the artist. To write a good story, one needs to understand how to structure it so that it takes the readers out of their worlds and into the text. That structure has nothing to do with the writer's personal psychology or politics; it belongs to the realm of aesthetics, which Shklovsky aspired to make more empirical, modeled somewhat after scientific research. But the negation of politics as an artistic criterion—and the implicit affirmation of unfettered artistic freedom—had never been a popular view in Russia, not in the days of the Tsar, and not in the days of Stalin.

What I gather Godár means by a structuralist composition shows itself most clearly in a work such as *Mater*. A theme—woman, mother, the eternal feminine—serves to elicit his music. Godár makes his choice of devices—liturgical, literary, folkloric, a Magnificat, a James Joyce poem, Yiddish songs—from throughout time and without regard to their original cultural contexts. (Consider Godár's *Querela pacis* ("The Complaint of Peace"), dedicated to Erasmus, the author of an eponymous 1521 work, with quotations from that work set by Godár to the form of mantras.) The aesthetics of music survive with ease the present shift from the church into theater, the concert hall, films such as those for which Godár writes scores. It is the music, the tones, that are enduring, not the beliefs that they are regarded as serving at a particular place and time. The same will be true two thousand years from now. I look forward as far in time as *The Epic of Gilgamesh* is now distant from us, when samplings from Godár's *Mater* bypass the ear to trigger direct neuronic signals to deep space travelers to enfold themselves with kindness through the long night.

It would be a purist philosophical idealism to conceive for the universe a higher, truer ear beyond our realm. To this ear, music would always be only music. There would be no need for structuralism because the intertwining meanings that inform music as they do all phenomena become irrelevant in the higher truth realm in which the ear abides happily without a head, because all music is interrelated as the medium, sound,

Original manuscript of *Sonata in Memory of Viktor Shklovsky*

is one. No matter what one played for the ear, it would form a kind of infinite occasional oratorio, as best I can conceive it. But here on earth the choices of Godár are vibrant and welcome. But as a grateful, musically untutored listener to his works, I cannot say, though I seem to have written about it, that Shklovsky's devices or anyone's structuralism much matter to me. His music moves slowly, intensely, yearning for the primal ground of Gilgamesh, the tonal grace of the psalmist David. The itinerary is to my liking, the notes take me to places Godár could not have had in mind. Music can be given forms, but listeners can slip free of those and escape with the notes out the window.

Art as Palimpsest: Cultural Exegesis in the Work of Vladimír Godár

Ivan Moody

Dear Vlado,

Thank you very much for "Mater".

When I saw the cover of the CD my first thought was: is the music as good as the design of the CD? And I was so glad to find the music created by an author who had followed the long and difficult way to reach such an outcome. It is the kind of "complicated simplicity" that can be reached only after many years of poignant quest…

—Message from Giya Kancheli to Vladimír Godár[1]

"Complicated simplicity" is an apt phrase to describe Vladimír Godár's recent work. The listener familiar with his *Concerto grosso* or his *Sonata in Memory of Viktor Shklovsky*, both dating from 1985, might be put in mind of the colliding universes of Alfred Schnittke; such simplicity is hard-won indeed, and only won at all by means of dealing with the complex. Though "polystylism"—or, better stated, *thought expressed on several planes simultaneously*—is still characteristic of his work, there is also a new transparency, something easily apprehended but not readily understood in any depth on casual listening. And Kancheli's recognition of the "long and difficult way" that has led to this sort of transparency is quite perceptive.

The sequence of pieces included on *Mater* has finally brought Godár's name to the attention of the West, and critical reaction has frequently been ecstatic. Barry Witherden writes in *BBC Music Magazine* that

> The atmosphere of timeless, serenely enraptured mysticism is maintained beautifully, and is most mesmerising in the "Magnificat" with its gorgeous vocal line hovering over ghostly tolling and a low string drone. Being on ECM, the sound is predictably impeccable, doing full justice to Godár's ravishing scoring and the superb performances: Bittová will break your heart in the "Stabat Mater."

In the *International Record Review*, Peter Quinn observes that

> Entering the world of *Mater*, Godár's hour-long rumination on the subject of motherhood, is rather like stepping into the living continuum of music history. Drawing you into a labyrinth of musical memories, this outstanding overview of the composer's recent work references everything from the ancient intonational patterns of folk music and archetypal Baroque-like textures to the ghostly remembrance of a Monteverdi madrigal and startling dissonances. If this suggests that Mater is no more than an assemblage of cultural bricolage, this certainly isn't the case. There's a powerfully distinctive authorial voice at work here, and a rich arterial force courses its way through the collection... Bittová is a thrilling protagonist. I can think of no other singer whose voice traverses such a vast emotional range, caressing the lyric one moment, raging and wailing the next.

An Italian critic of an authoritative jazz webzine was not only impressed but oddly surprised by the aesthetics of the works recorded:

> Finally, a composer who declares that he does not believe in the avant-garde! It was high time that someone had the courage to admit it! In short, *Mater* is a beautiful work, successful outside conventions but within history, containing music that grasps you by the soul, the entire soul![2]

As the title indicates, *Mater* is a sequence of works linked by the common theme of motherhood, both sacred (the Mother of God, Mary) and secular (in the form of lullabies), as well as encompassing the idea of the past giving birth to the present as part of a cosmic tradition. In his composer's note, Godár states that "under the influence of Thomas Mann, I lost faith in the avant-garde vision of art's progress and instead came up with the idea of a sort of musical archaeology. Art, just like Antaios staying in touch with Mother Earth, builds on existing texts. It is like the exegesis of the text, and a new work of art is its palimpsest."

Godár is far from alone in his disillusionment with the processes of modernity and his interest in rapprochement with traditions of the past— a phenomenon Eduardo de la Fuente has described as "musical reenchantment." Three composers who are frequently linked together—Henryk Mikołaj Górecki, Arvo Pärt, and John Tavener—have each famously experienced similar transformative moments, which have had correspondingly dramatic effects on their creative output. Their work, thereafter, has been routinely and all-too-conveniently considered almost as constituting a single artistic movement.[3] Such a view fails to take into account the substantial stylistic and technical differences between the three composers, and when a considerable number of other composers who have had similar Damascene experiences, or who have even undergone a gradual sea change—one thinks of figures as diverse as Giya Kancheli, the Australian Ross Edwards, and the Latvian Pēteris Vasks—are also taken into consideration, the picture becomes more complicated still.

It would be disingenuous, notwithstanding, to deny that parallels may be found between these composers. If art, as Godár states, "builds on existing texts" and new works are the exegetic "palimpsests" of those texts, then this is inevitable. What differs is not only the way in which that exegesis is carried out, but precisely what its subject is. For Górecki, the "texts" (literally and figuratively) were those of Roman Catholicism and of the rich heritage of Polish culture, while for Tavener they came to be those of the Orthodox Church and, to some extent, Greek and Russian literature (though his recent music has moved in the direction of perennialism). In Godár's case, the texts are those of Roman Catholicism and, more broadly, his national identity as a Slovak.

While the use of Latin liturgical texts is the most obvious means by which the first of these finds expression, Godár's sense of national identity, the "palimpsesting" of Slovak history, is made manifest in various and complementary ways in his work. The use of Slovak as a sung language is the most apparent of these, not only as an emblem of nationality but as a direct connection with the history of the language, as it had been in such earlier works as *Tri piesne na ľudové texty* ("Three Songs on Folk Texts," 1972) or *Žalostné pesničky na slová starej slovenskej poézie zo zbierok 18. a 19. storočia* ("Sorrowful Songs on Old Slovak Poetry from Eighteenth- and Nineteenth-Century Collections," 1979). In *Stabat Mater* (2001), Godár makes use of a medieval Slovak translation of the Latin text, and in *Magnificat*, written two years later, the text comes from the earliest Slovak translation of the Bible (the Camaldul Bible), prepared for press in 1758 by the Camaldolese Benedictine monks at the Červený Kláštor Monastery on the Dunajec river, but forbidden to be published.[4]

At its opening, *Magnificat* employs the Gregorian tone 1 for the "Magnificat," over a low D drone, though the text is in Slovak rather than Latin ("Velebí duša ma Pána") and, as sung by Iva Bittová, acquires as much kinship with folk music as it has with the liturgy.

Magnificat, page 1. © Faber Music.

Latin appears with the entry of the choir (accompanied by strings and harp), which repeatedly intones the word "Magnificat" in a slowed-down, harmonized version of the Gregorian tone. In fact, this is the only word the choir sings (it is repeated sixteen times) until the full phrase, "Magnificat anima mea Dominum," finally appears before the soloist's echo of it (in Slovak) and the instrumental coda.

Magnificat, page 14. © Faber Music.

A comparison might be drawn to some extent with true single-word compositions such as Górecki's *Amen* or Tavener's *Dhoxa*.[5] Even though Godár also frames this central section with the full text at the beginning, and a repetition of the opening phrase at the end, the use of a different, hieratic language and the sheer insistence on the glorification of God by virtue of repetition makes this work indisputably dedicated to the expression of a single theological idea. It is interesting, too, that the work ends purely instrumentally: the final intonation of the soloist gives rise to something that sounds like a sixteenth-century fantasia for viols, though its contrapuntal meanderings remain grounded by the constant low D drone.

Stabat Mater takes liturgy even further into folk tradition. It is a setting of the "Stabat Mater" in Slovak, for alto solo (Bittová), solo violin, and a chamber orchestra comprising strings, harp, chittarone, and harpsichord. Another parallel with Górecki is immediately suggested here, in the use of the "shadowing" of the modal vocal line by chords or clusters in the orchestra.

Stabat Mater page 4. © Faber Music.

The ritualized, cumulative sorrow of the Polish composer's celebrated *Symphony no. 3* is brought particularly strongly to mind, as is a more distant ancestor—Szymanowski's *Stabat Mater*, a work similarly rooted in Christian liturgy and, by means of its modal vocabulary and quotations from Polish hymns, national identity.

The "palimpsesting" of styles is another Godárian technique. In the *Mater* sequence it is particularly evident in the sprightly baroquery of *Regina Caeli*, and it is even more present in the recent *Querela pacis*, an oratorio written in homage to Erasmus of Rotterdam. Movements such as "Miles" and "A Gran Battaglia" evoke Monteverdi and Vivaldi, but while making the transition from the repetitive figuration of such writing to both folk-infused writing (as occurs in the latter) or to the suggestions of minimalism found, for example, in "The Lament," seems entirely natural, moments such as the emotionally weighted and lush coda of "Obsidium Urbis" are entirely unexpected. It is as though the palimpsest is unintentionally revealing part of another layer—a palimpsest of a palimpsest.

The risk in this kind of undertaking is obvious: it would be easy for the music to be no more than an assemblage of stylistic clichés or reminiscences, a feeble attempt at a postmodern rejection of "progress." To mold them into a coherent identity expressive of a particular cultural stance, as Godár attempts to do, requires a singular musicality and consistency of vision. The composer thus avoids both the alienating effect of his earlier polystylism, and that of Schnittke (as also the postludial world of Silvestrov), just as he avoids the total but temporary absorption of a particular style— the stylization of a style—that one finds in the recent work of Vladimír Martynov. With Godár, the style stands not for itself, whether as an ironic commentary or a painful nostalgia, but is rather an eminently positive symbol upon which he may build. A palimpsest cannot be a palimpsest if it is written upon a clean sheet. Godár's "palimpsesting" makes deliberate use of the symbols inscribed previously on the sheet, but for those symbols to be exegetically explored, they must be invested with strength. Contrary to any view of postmodernism as the end of "metanarratives," any recycling of earlier styles that wishes to do more than merely ironize must either seek, like Schnittke, to work through the moribund metanarrative(s) or to accept those styles as part of a huge quarry of available constructional possibilities to be called upon when needed, so that fragments of past metanarratives are built into a new one. The strength or fragility of that new metanarrative is resolved in each case by the quality of the composer's exegesis.

"Obsidium Orbis," page 6. © Faber Music.

A further level of exegesis in Godár's catalog is attained through his collaboration with the singer, violinist, and composer Iva Bittová. While Bittová has participated in crossover projects that have brought her to international attention (most notably her work with the Nederlands Blazers Ensemble and Bang on a Can), and while her collaboration with Godár led to the release of her solo recording for ECM, her origins as one of the three daughters of a hugely talented musical family in Czech Silesia are what define her musical activities. She has said that "it has always been everyday life that inspired my music and interpretations…

Its inspiration has been total silence and an absolutely positive atmosphere."[6] Her studies in Brno and subsequent success have merely made her sources more important to her.

Though Bittová's "palimpsesting" of her native culture is perhaps more radical, in that her stylistic non-conformism makes full use of a wide range of avant-garde techniques, including a combination of extended vocal techniques and humor that suggests the late Cathy Berberian, the correspondence with Godár's work is obvious. Indeed, the composer mentions in his notes for the *Mater* sequence that

> the compositions for female voice and period instrument ensemble were in many ways inspired by Iva Bittová, her art, personality and perhaps even her life. A 'depth of time' is very much present in her art, going back to the very beginnings of music and reaching all the way to our problematic present.

This "depth of time," it seems, is the starting point for cultural and, consequently, spiritual exegesis.

If, as Phillip Blond has claimed, "art should be an account of, and a meditation upon, our relationship to what we are given," then Godár's work fulfills this condition completely, in a way that is postmodern and positive.[7] Blond notes further that "apparently, for us moderns, it is entirely appropriate to separate ideality from reality, as reality has nothing of the ideal in it."[8] Godár's reality, on the other hand, is entirely constructed from the exegesis of the ideal, found in the "depth of time." In the *Mater* sequence, as in much of Godár's recent work, glimpses of the vanished past become an almost-stable present and thereby show us a possible future.

A Personal Tribute to Vlado

Peter Breiner

In 1974, amid the worst of the post-1968 "normalization" in Czechoslovakia, Vladimír Godár and I, then eighteen-year-old music students, met at the admission test for the Academy of Performing Arts in Bratislava, both hoping to study composition. We were admitted, and a lifelong friendship between Vlado Godár and myself began.

We entered the school together, graduated together, and we both married our wives on the same day. Our understanding of one another borders on the uncanny: only Vlado could know what was going on when, many years ago, a telegram was received by his flabbergasted father, who could not understand why the Karamazov brothers would ask him to pickle the oranges in casks. Indeed I, quoting from Ilf and Petrov's *The Golden Calf*, had sent the telegram, and Vlado got the joke immediately. As Montaigne once wrote, we are friends because he is he, and I am I.

To this day we are able to communicate in our own shorthand language. Despite the fact that we've been living on different continents for over twenty years now, our connection is as strong as ever, and whenever we meet, even after many months, we continue our conversation as if we had met just the previous day.

Vlado's depth of knowledge and understanding of such a diverse set of subjects is extraordinary. Between all his work, teaching and raising his children, and taking care of a household, he still manages to remain up to date with the world of classical, world, and pop music, literatures from around the world, movies, politics, historical research... The stream of recommendations I receive from Vlado is vast and virtually endless. I am unable to follow even a fraction of that which comes my way from him, even as he has already incorporated it all—and all the resulting ramifications—into his latest writing. His mind's capacity to find the most unbelievable and yet strongly logical connections and associations is a continuing source of wonder; if there ever was a polymath, a Renaissance man, it must be Vladimír Godár.

I often imagine the pleasure of being Vlado's student. He doesn't merely teach a subject; his discourses come complete with multiple contexts, unexpected yet crucially important connections and associations, and, on top of it all, a spirited and humorous delivery.

I know his musical output intimately, having performed many of his pieces. It is always a creative adventure to pick up one of his scores and, moreover, a pure *physical* pleasure, since his music is both incredibly beautiful and beautifully crafted.

Far from what you might call a "practical" man (Vlado does not drive, and I don't think he would be capable of any manual labor; in fact, there is an infamous story about a clerk at a hardware store who refused to sell Vlado a chainsaw just from looking at him...), he is an incredible organizer and an inspiring force to anybody who has had the luck of collaborating with him.

Countless times Vlado has inspired me and given me new ideas for my own work. It was during our university days that he started suggesting, and later insisting, that I should be playing jazz piano more seriously. Luckily enough, I listened to his advice, and continue to do so, whether it is a suggestion of a possible musical partner or an opportunity to present a piece I've written. But I'm far from the only one who has benefitted from his generosity. Vlado has a keen eye and ear for discovering extremely talented musicians. Besides discovering them, he takes on the responsibility of helping them kick-start their careers, often organizing concerts to feature their skill and compositions. In the same way, he's made a veritable trade of discovering forgotten or neglected composers and helping to revive their reputations and compositions, and presenting them anew to the public. The service he has provided in preserving important composers of Slovak and European music history and their output would be difficult to overstate, even if, so far, it has gone underappreciated.

As a conductor with an extensive record of performing contemporary music, I cherish Vlado as a composer, because he strives to make his music accessible and, before all else, beautiful. No matter the subject, whether a composition is a very serious one that focuses on themes of history and societal change, or is just a short musical joke, the music always maintains that most important attribute: Beauty. His compositional craft remains at the highest level possible, regardless; I must stress this most perfect union of qualities, because they are so seldom found in contemporary music.

Since the beginning, I believe, we have shared the same opinion about what music should offer its public. Within the ivory confines of today's academia, despite the proven fact that audiences are quite uninterested in it, our colleagues, firmly rooted in outmoded theories of Adorno and those that emerged from Darmstadt, have tried to ignore, ostracize, boy-cott, and harm Vlado. Instead of appreciating his merits, our colleagues—whether composers, writers, or teachers—have tried to exclude him from their institutions; however, Vlado's work and music eventually, it seems, maneuver clear of these petty squabbles, the intriguing nature of his work always finding the light. His audiences are now beginning to recognize the value and deep humanity of Vlado's music and its message. His music stands firmly on the shoulders of history, yet it is nonetheless innovative and original, often taking as its starting point the best works of world literature throughout history, from folk poetry (whether Slovak or African) to the works of great Slovak, Chinese, and other poets, such as Jan Amos Komensky, Erasmus of Rotterdam, James Joyce, Viktor Shklovsky, or Chiladze, through to the most important texts, such as *The Epic of Gilgamesh*, among so many others.

Vlado refuses to create music aimed at the pseudo-intellectual crowd, those who pretend to fall into a trance over three minutes of silence or those who are excited by three hours of the same five notes on repeat, even when such music is put on a pedestal by tasteless media outlets and critics who live in fear of being exposed as promoters of the emperor's new clothes. He has long understood that it is of utmost necessity and a matter of the artist's responsibility to carry the torch of tradition, to stress and highlight the focal points in human history, and to strive for peace, beauty, and compassion.

All of the above can be as justly said for his writing as a scientist and historian, as well. His ability to isolate and then uncover links between various points in history that are not only invisible but often completely unknown to most of us, is almost eerie. In doing so, Vlado is able to arrive at new strands of logic and theories which are often quite surprising, and always relevant. They help the rest of us to understand, at least partially, the message that the quest for discovering meaning in human existence remains important, even if we will never arrive at a lucid answer. And his music somehow lets us feel that, all of a sudden, everything, at least for a fleeting moment, makes complete sense indeed.

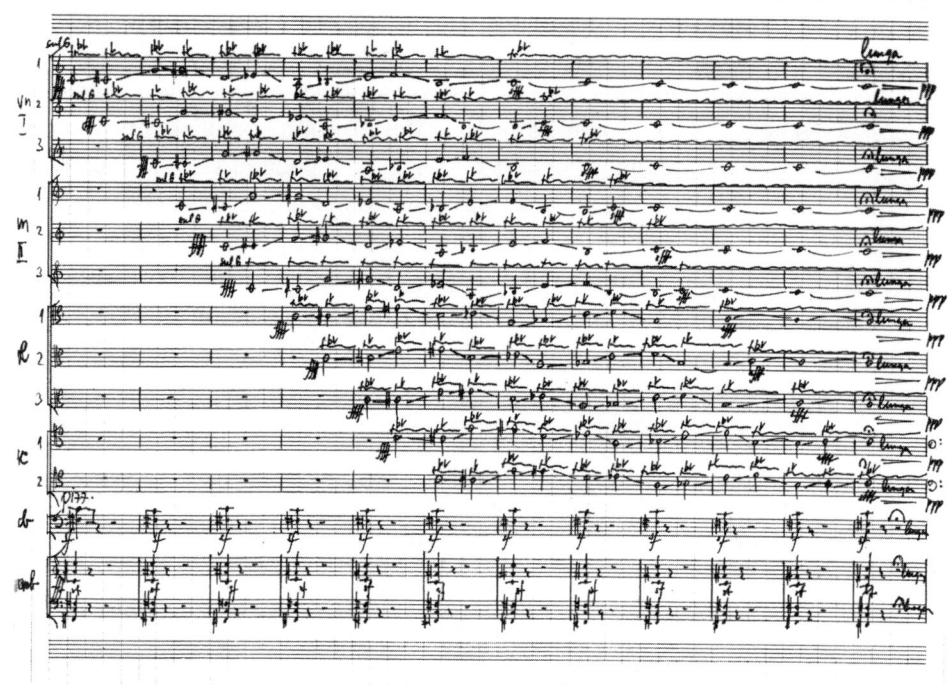

Original manuscript of *Concerto grosso*

Recording *Mater*

Tomáš Šelc

I came across the name Vladimír Godár in music reviews in magazines before I began hearing his recordings on the radio and discussing his work with my mother, who is a musicologist herself and a colleague of Godár's. When Dušan Bill, the conductor of the Bratislava Conservatory Chamber Choir, brought new scores to rehearsal and one day announced that we were to record a piece composed by Vladimír Godár, I was very pleased, and it wasn't long before we realized that *Mater*, as a whole, is a masterpiece, and that it would be a true success. I immediately thought it could be a perfect match not only for classical music admirers but also for those who prefer more mainstream contemporary music. We were looking forward to having our first rehearsal with the chamber orchestra (Solamente Naturali, led by Miloš Valent) and were especially excited to work with the lead soloist, Iva Bittová. It seemed impossible to me at first to successfully combine a classical score with a singer whose domain was predominantly contemporary interpretation; nevertheless, Iva immediately removed all doubt. Over the last few years, I have come to the conclusion that even a masterpiece can fail if it lacks either musical innovation or a solid promotional strategy. Both are needed to attract listeners who typically stick to music styles outside that of a given recording.

Vladimír Godár composes wonderful music, seamlessly overlaying Renaissance with contemporary features, with oriental ornaments included throughout. What makes *Mater* special to me are the references to traditional Slovak music, especially those fragments written and sung in the language originally used in now-Slovakia hundreds of years ago. The orchestral instrumentation is very simple but appealing, and therefore fully in line with Godár's characteristic mode of composition. Here Godár fully employs his enormous musical knowledge, keeping the style crystal clear and avoiding any disruptive experiments. The score bears his exceptional and distinctive seal.

The performance of Solamente Naturali during the recording sessions is to be admired as well. The orchestra members have shown their flexibility and professionalism, especially Miloš Valent, who insisted on the absolute purity of sound and just interpretation. The ensemble dedicated no fewer than ten minutes to flawless tuning before each recording session.

Similarily, Iva Bittová arrived superbly prepared. She brought to the recording a fresh and, I believe, unintended dimension. Her interpretation lent Godár's score a strange, unusual, yet very appealing character. Iva Bittová devotes herself completely to her musical interpretations, which helps her captivate and involve her audience and thereby all at once achieve absolute involvement of all elements. I think that this unconditional devotion to just interpretation, in combination with Godár's terrific scoring, makes *Mater* exceptional.

At present, I am very happy to enjoy Vlado's close friendship. Moreover, in cooperation with Andrew Parrott and Solamente Naturali, we worked together on *Querela pacis*. I was even given the honor of singing the solo part.

Every time I visit Vlado in his flat, which is dominated by a piano and a large bookcase packed with unfinished, forgotten, or recently discovered scores and hundreds of scientific books, I feel deeply honored to know the man personally. I admire his unprecedented wisdom, which he generously shares with anybody he talks to. Vlado Godár, on top of his superb qualities as a university professor and as a composer, overshadows his contemporaries with his inexhaustible knowledge as a musicologist, not only in terms of Slovak but also global music. I dare to say that, without Vlado, many scores would have been irrevocably lost or would never have been discovered at all. Vlado's work is especially meaningful for Slovak culture and music since he is one of the few who realizes that without knowing one nation's music history and legacy there can be no cultural emancipation.

On the Work of Giya Kancheli

Vladimír Godár

Translated from the Slovak by Clarice Cloutier

The roots of Georgian culture date back to the ancient past. Three millennia of cultural advancement on native soil have made the Georgian nation one of the most significant bearers of human memory. Historians have documented direct ties between ancient Georgia and Mesopotamia, the Hittites, and ancient Greece, while general mythology recalls the Colchian King Aeëtes with his relatives Mino and Circe, and his daughter Medea, striking fear into the hearts of the ancient Greeks. Likewise, the character of Prometheus appears in Georgian mythology as Amirani. The first mentions of Georgian music are also ancient, written by Xenophon in fourth century B.C.

The development of civilization has continued through to the modern era. In 355, Georgian was Christianized with its own Catholicos, a script drawn from the Biblical Aramaic, and with its own literary tradition. The dynasty of the Bagrationi (dating from the ninth through the thirteenth centuries) represented the Georgian's greatest period of prosperity. During the reign of King David the Builder and his queen Tamar, Georgia had a population of ten million, and its national income was multiple times those of England and France over that period. Lectures on Christian theology were held at academies in Ikalto and Gelati, accompanied by lectures on Greek philosophy, Arabic mathematics, astronomy, and Buddhism. Its religious and literary traditions culminated with the epos of Shota Rustaveli, "The Knight in the Panther's Skin," toward the end of the twelfth century, before the time of either Dante or Thomas Aquinas. Thus it was not by chance that when Cyril enumerates the nations with their own written cultural traditions he mentions not only Armenians, Persians, and Abkhazians, but also Iberians, i.e. Georgians, as examples in his defense of the implementation of writing for the Slavonic nations.

Yet this prosperity ended during one of the crusades when, in a battle with the Arabs, Georgia was befallen from the north by Batu Khan's horde, which went on to annex the whole of Georgia between 1230 and 1240. The following centuries were plagued by battles for power, raids, and uprisings that ushered forth the various stages of continued genocide against the Georgian nation, its economy and culture, first by the Mongols, then the Turks and Persians, ending with the annexation of Georgia to Tsarist Russia in 1802. During this historical peripeteia, Georgia's population had been diminished to one million. The eventual annexation to Russia secured relative stability but marked the end of the royal dynasty, the fall of the nobles and armies, as well as the loss of church autonomy. The genocide continued into the twentieth century. During the fatal years of the Second World War, Stalin took a particularly suspicious stance toward his own native people. The Georgian population at the time was 2.4 million, and from them six hundred thousand young Georgians were sent to war.

Consequently, antiquity and tragedy are main attributes of Georgian history. This historical introduction is imperative, because when trying to understand any phenomenon it is impossible to appreciate its function without first knowing its history. And the essential within the subject is found in its function. The characteristics of a cultural phenomenon or artistic work of a certain society are determined by the function which it fulfills within the given society. And this function is set forth by history.

Today, remnants of the cultural upspring begun in the Ancient Kingdom of Egypt do not exist; all that remains of the Hittite Empire are fragments pieced together by historians, while the culture of Ancient Greece is likewise non-existent. Cultures which do not pass the baton, so to speak, eventually disappear from the face of the earth, their remains to be discovered by archeologists. That we can be thankful to the Phoenicians for the concept of money we know from archeologists, not from the Phoenicians themselves. Thus, the chief question to be posed in an essay on Georgian history is the following: How is it possible that the Georgian nation still exists? To this there is only one answer: despite the centuries-long genocide, they were able to foster integrated factors and institutions, which in turn enabled them to survive the imperialistic zest of all those in power, and thanks to this, even in the most unfavorable conditions, to strengthen their national sovereignty and distinctiveness. Their high esteem for the past and for human greatness, their high esteem for saints and significant ancestors, their high esteem for Rustaveli—all of these are active factors that inform the idea of Georgia's national sovereignty. Respect for manual work, respect for children, and a continuing moral credo became the backbone of an unparalleled tradition. Indeed, over the centuries of genocide, epics, poetry, music, social rituals, religious life, art, and myths have all established a framework for enduring demonstrations of national sovereignty. Earlier, I recalled Rustaveli's "The Knight in the Panther's Skin." While the poem's European counterparts, such as "La Chanson de Roland" or the lyrics of the troubadours, are merely titles from the history of literature for most Europeans, and apart from a few experts hardly anybody can recall the name of even one of the numerous Provençal lyrics, Georgians hold an annual competition for the recitation of Rustaveli's 6,348 line epic from memory, while a troubadour-like gentility has become an enduring norm for how a man behaves toward a woman.

Thus, although a nation may lose its army (its physical means of defending its national sovereignty), other societal means of integration may yet endure—art among them. During the period of its vassal relationship with Tsarist Russia (in the nineteenth century), Georgia founded its national culture on an ever-growing contextual basis, eventually giving rise to its modern, universal manifestation, which in turn is based on world and national cultures at large. The nineteenth and twentieth centuries saw the integration of European culture into Georgia with amazing results. In fact, the Georgian film school had achieved a global reputation by the 1960s with top Georgian actors and directors, including Georgiy Daneliya, Tengiz Abuladze, Otar Iosseliani, and Robert Sturua. Significant prose writers likewise emerged: Otar Chiladze, Tamaz Chiladze, Chabua Amirejibi, Nodar Dumbadze, as well as the composer Giya Kancheli—all of whom have helped bring Georgian culture to the world stage.

The main question, then, is not: What is national culture? Likewise, the corresponding answer is not: Like nation, like culture. The main question is different: What function does culture have within a nation, and how do the representatives of a national culture understand this function? For the representatives of national values, culture may be a lifelong trough, of sorts, or, conversely, it may be the object of the highest national consciousness, conscience, and honor, since we know that true culture may also serve as the safeguard of a nation, ensuring that it does not go extinct. For the artist, this question is twofold: What art does a nation's government need? and What art does the nation need? Perhaps the artist would appreciate if the answer to both of these questions were the same. However, such an instance in history has not yet taken place.

Governments tend to view art as decoration, pretending that art has no other function. If the artist agrees with this, he will become the keeper of the trough assigned to him, but for the nation he becomes useless and contributes only to the degeneration of art. Oskar Kokoschka once stated, "All official art is kitsch." Likewise, the Arabic historian Ibn Khaldun wrote in the *Muqaddimah*, some 600 years earlier, in 1377, concerning the function of poetry:

> Poetry was the archive of the Arabs, containing their sciences, their history, and their wisdom. Leading Arabs competed in it. They used to stop at the fair of 'Ukaz to recite poetry. Each would submit his product for criticism to outstanding and intelligent personalities... Then there came great royal authority and a mighty dynasty. The Arabs approached the Caliphs with their laudatory poems, and the Caliphs rewarded them most generously according to the quality of the poems and their position among their people... Thus, the predominant purpose of producing poetry came to be mere begging and asking of favors, because the particular use, that, as we have mentioned, the early Arabs had made for the poetry, no longer existed. This is why people of ambition and rank among later Muslims disdained poetry.[1]

Thus, nations never needed panegyrics, and it seems they have no use for them now. A nation needs an art that will be able to overcome the limiting restrictions of a given period and pose essential questions while also holding its place vis-à-vis the art of other nations. Paradoxically, national art is indeed the art which every other nation takes as its own. And to this day, a nation has always been ready to easily distinguish between artists who respond to the essential questions and those who bow to their providers.

This was the artistic goal for the generation of which Giya Kancheli found himself a part in 1960s USSR. Again, antiquity and tragedy are two of the main characteristics we observe when first coming into contact with Kancheli's art. The mission of Georgian artists at large has become to bring Georgian culture up against global culture. Just as Georgian film directors base their poetics, craft, and credo on the masterworks of world film traditions, and Georgian prose writers put their efforts into engaging with the biggest literary phenomena, so it is with the music of Giya Kancheli, who has drawn on the most important European musical traditions and composers, such as Beethoven and Stravinsky. His catalog does not contain "recreational" compositions, but is instead completely focused on the axial European musical forms of symphony and opera. Kancheli has composed nine orchestral works (seven of which are symphonies), one cantata-oratorio, and one opera. This is all.[2] An orientation around the essential, the human elements, so to say, is also evident in the very structure of Kancheli's compositions. There is almost no reason to discuss how his symphonies are put together, because we will only discover that he is not concerned with the problems of double counterpoint, the use of national folklore, or the dramaturgy of sonata form. He is interested in the final outcome alone to which the orchestral medium is subordinated with his infallible sense. His artistic direction, as well as his style, bear the mark of decades of work, labor, and thought, and yet the composer has never offered any written explanations.[3] Kancheli is not interested in readymade recipes, and we will not find in his scores analogies to the work of other composers. The essential suggestiveness of his compositions results from his dramaturgic infallibility, the key to which will likely forever remain his secret.

We might think of Kancheli's compositions as being constructed through the use of "musical montage," based on film theory, not realizing that this device is typical not only for cinematography but for all process arts. Elsewhere I have written about Kancheli's music in connection with the so-called Kuleshov effect, a film editing technique in which the director precedes a still shot of a laughing child with several different shots—a running creek, a man serving ice cream, etc.—resulting in a different meaning being associated with the child's face after each. The effect proves that man associates or projects his/her own emotional world onto the actor's face. Kancheli may well have successfully applied the Kuleshov effect to music. Particular fragments of his compositions have their own qualities that are transfigured by a higher context to which they pertain. The effect is a multi-layering and multiplication of contextual sounds, and this forms the basis for the unusual richness and human quality of Kancheli's credo. It is only the seeming "simplicity" of the base elements that disguise the pharmacist's balancing scales, which weigh all the composition's elements and create the semblance of some kind of primary simplicity. However, simplicity is merely the starting point, not the end goal. When speaking about a simple starting point, we must also take into account that composers, graphic artists, and poets are all fighting their greatest battle in determining the direction their reduction should take such that a work might achieve a desired form, and not the form that the material dictates through technological convention; I speak of the well-earned simplicity of Beethoven's Fifth Symphony, for instance, a simplicity that serves the intended integration.

Another quality often associated with Kancheli's work is its seeming archetypal nature. Thanks to his understanding of musical time and his mastering of dramatization, Kancheli creates—despite his rich multi-layering and the multiple meanings coming from his various material confrontations—musical events that seem equally as likely to take place today as yesterday or ages ago. His expressions of aggression, tenderness, and sadness are like pure water—a sure and constant accompaniment to a person on his journey through time. The stoppage (or delaying) of time in music can be understood as a typical compositional device, intended only for the captivation of the listener's perception, or as a symbol of an "eternal stage" where various human conflicts play out in all their yearnings and trials, with lightness and darkness, and thus as a specific cosmological archetype.

I am not acquainted with a composer whose music fuses so many contrasting elements. In Kancheli's music, sets of extreme opposites exist side by side: expressive opposites (forte, piano), structural opposites (diatonic melos, clustering), and temporal opposites (unlimited time and the ever-vivid present). We could also add to this list historical time: the confrontation of the oldest and newest musical structures. All of these help us to see the determinants of Kancheli's musical world. We cannot understand how it is possible that the artistic whole created by these elements does not fall to pieces, that the aforementioned contradictions mutually strengthen rather than diminish one another. Each of Kancheli's symphonies is a kind of one-act drama that takes place on the stage of eternity. Each solves elemental conflicts, those of being itself, which the composer encounters differently every time according to the new scenario at hand and with the undying strength of his masterful statement.

My initial engagement with Kancheli's music produced in me an incredible desire to write about it, to verbalize my experience. Yet I feel a great awkwardness when writing about it today. This description of his material, devices, and situations does not draw us any closer to his compositions (or to my own experience of them), but only pushes us further away. By uttering my associations I deprive myself as well as others of their (perhaps even more adequate) reinterpretations of Kancheli's world. The deeper I come to know Kancheli's music, the greater aversion I feel to describe it with words. I am left with the impression of having created some sort of futile verbal improvisation that, even at best, will only insult the legacy of Kancheli's music.

A similar sense of futility arises when I consider other aspects of Kancheli's musical legacy. For example, although his work began in those legendary years of the 1960s, I am not able to specify its relation to the musical explosion that took place during that decade. It is possible to speak of him as the only composer who emerged from that time who did not have to carry the millstone of an artistic change of direction, which has indeed been a major burden for so many of his contemporaries. He did not have to undergo the complications arising from a change of artistic direction, a new definition of self. Perhaps it was also because he (much earlier and at a younger age than his other composer colleagues) knew how to substantiate himself, even if in a tortuous way and against the much larger opposition of contemporary tendencies. Once a misunderstood figure, if not a laughing stock, at avant-garde festivals, Kancheli and his music, former outsiders, have, without any change of orientation, *become* today's avant-garde, influencing changes of artistic direction in various other important contemporary composers.

I am not interested in confronting Kancheli's work with the opinions of those who formed the stalwarts of the so-called avant-garde and so-called communicative music. Likewise, I am not interested in commenting on the labels of "hedonism" and "populism" with which his work has been designated, but which stem more from deafness than from opinionated positions. In the face of his work, the dichotomy of avant-garde vs. communicative music is clearly exposed as incompetent.

That is why I am able to concentrate only on the composer's attitude. Kancheli's solutions and responses to the questions of his day result from the function of art in Georgian culture (even if he was blamed for denationalization) and from the function which he himself assigns artistic work. His responses stem from the traditions of the Georgian artist's moral stance and also from attempts at a personal statement, both of which began developing at the start of the 1960s in the USSR, when a general humanization with regard to how art was interpreted began taking place, including its goals and the means of creative artistic work. In fact, it was this humanistic orientation, avoidance of marginality and conformity, and imperatives of the times, including the attempt to search for answers to the existential problems of man—these aspects represent the most significant achievements of Georgian art and the greatest contributions Georgia has made to the treasure chest of human culture.

Contemporary aesthetics suggests that art serves multiple functions in a society, from a recreational function to aesthetic and cognitive functions. Yet, largely due to the arrogance of contemporary aesthetics, the very function that art had—whether recreational, ritualistic, or mythical—in its beginning, has been all but forgotten. And this is the function of integration. Even in the earliest times, myth, ritual, and riddles were integrative in their function and so, despite the long period in which they developed differently, the original integrative function of art itself did not disappear. And even if it remains hidden, it does not cease from being a central argument for the very existence of art. Perhaps it was because of Georgia's historical tragedies that it remains as a permanently present ideal in Kancheli's music and in Georgian art as a whole. And it serves as the greatest gift for us—we chaotic inhabitants of the twentieth century—as well as a most important lesson that we as creators can have. We do not need to learn from Kancheli how to write two-voice counterpoint or how to score compositions, but thanks to him we can reflect on what we are actually writing and what it serves. "Music is what unifies."[4] It is with these words of the Chinese sage Seu-Ma Tsen that Stravinsky closes his *Poetics of Music*.

This unification is also the very source of the pure water which Georgian art offers all of us, whether in the films of Tengiz Abuladze or Eldar Shengelaia, the novels of Otar Chiladze, or Kancheli's music. I am very thankful for the lesson on the greatness of the human soul which infuses Georgian art. Even the lesson itself is transferable: Georgian art offers us a cure for the disease of our time, that is, the disease of disintegration, and that cure is *integration*, which stems from the approach taken by Georgian artists toward art, the world, being, and toward themselves.

In *Convivio*, Dante writes:

> It is necessary to know that writings can be understood and ought to be expounded principally in four senses. The first is called the literal, and this is the sense that does not go beyond the surface of the letter, as in the fables of the poets. The next is called the allegorical, and this is the one that is hidden beneath the cloak of

these fables, and is the truth hidden beneath a beautiful fiction…
The third sense is called moral, and this is the sense that teachers
should intently seek to discover throughout the scriptures, for
their own profit and that of their pupils… The fourth sense is ana-
gogical, that is to say, beyond the senses; and this occurs when
a scripture is expounded in a spiritual sense which, although it
is true also in the literal sense, signifies by means of the things
signified a part of the supernal things of eternal glory…[5]

If we attempt to interpret Kancheli's music, we cannot forget to incorporate Dante's interpretation and to take into account all aspects. In
Kancheli's own words, music itself is supposed to be a composer's
"conversation with God and not with himself."

Encountering the Poet

Vladimír Godár

Translated from the Slovak by Clarice Cloutier

In memory of Jan Skácel (1922-1989)

On Christmas day in 1985, I wrote a cycle of three songs for female voice, flute, cello, and harpsichord, which I named *The Lullabies of Jan Skácel*. I did not ask for approval from the poet or from any qualified institution. The following year, our musicians introduced the composition in concert in Brno, yet I was afraid to meet the poet in person, so I did not personally attend the concert. Indeed, Mr. Skácel did come to the concert and afterwards went up to talk to the musicians, who later passed along to me word that he enjoyed it. This was my encounter with the poet Jan Skácel...

My first contact with the creative work of Jan Skácel came much earlier in life, through the writings of Milan Hamada. My father worked as a warehouseman for Pravda, the publisher of state newspapers and books, and he brought home all of their publications. When I was thirteen, he brought home a recently published collection of Hamada's literary essays entitled *A Poet's Transcendence*, which contained a study called "Concerning Truth, Beauty, and Jan Skácel." This essay in fact further developed a previous study ("Dispute with the Poet"—the poet being Miroslav Válek) that documented the possibilities for a socially in-tegrative mission for art based on the work of Jan Skácel.[1] Hamada argues that art's capacity for integration is central to its mission: art connects people. Válek, however, had established himself, according to Hamada, as a poet who did not believe in this mission and whose art had lost its humanistic character. Hamada's "Dispute with the Poet" had serious consequences; after reading it, I was able to borrow a single collection of Skácel's poetry, *Grief Song (Smuténka)*, but beyond this it was impossible to find Skácel's other books in libraries and bookstores. Soon my father was no longer a warehouseman, Hamada was no longer a literary scholar and critic, and Skácel was no longer an editor and poet: throughout the country, almost one million people had been forced to leave their jobs. Válek had been made Minister of Culture. The era of Husák's consolidation had begun.

Later, as a high school student, I understood this as the Era of Great Misunderstanding, and ever since, misunderstandings that augment chaos have become synonymous for me with sin. The rapid consolidation of power in our region inevitably fostered a certain pathology among the people, and the phenomenon of so-called "social autism" was born. Those who had something to say remained silent, while those who had never had anything to say were screaming. Even Skácel was among those who went silent...

"One can't believe impossible things," Lewis Caroll's Alice said to the Queen. "I daresay you haven't had much practice," replied the Queen. "Why, sometimes I've believed as many as six impossible things before breakfast." Bruno Bettelheim, a psychoanalyst who was among the first to specialize in the treatment of autism in children, took into account his own experiences in Dachau and Buchenwald when developing his therapeutic methods of treatment. He felt a deep affiliation between the prisoner who is completely subjugated to the will of an outsider and an autistic child. For Bettelheim, both represented utterly lost hope in terms of their submission to an exterior power which limits their own personal activity—and thus compulsory agreement with the replacement of their own subjectiveness. When you exist as an object to the world around you, rather than as a subject, the world becomes a kind of hell. A person thus starts believing not only in impossible things, but also starts living them out. In 1976, the poet-minister published his manifesto on "state autism," which he entitled *The Word*. At that time, I did not read *The Word*, since I was busy reading the silence, and that is when I got to know Skácel...

While deliberate misunderstanding is indeed a sin, we may say that understanding is not pieced together by simply adding up various meanings but also needs to be affirmed by reality. Saint-John Perse expressed a similar sentiment in a letter to Archibald MacLeish:

> At the entrance of a Mongol yurt in the middle of the Gobi Desert, I asked for the translation of a wonderfully guttural sentence pronounced by a migrant high lama of the Red Sect: "Man is born in a house, but dies in the desert..." For days and days, during the long, silent hours on horseback, I kept ruminating this sentence, so delectable to the palate of an Occidental who can never be sure of having his mouth sufficiently rinsed of all romantic aftertaste. Until the day, in a lamasery, on the edge of the desert, I was given this trivial explanation: "A dying man must be

Original manuscript of *The Lullabies of Jan Skácel*

exposed outside the tent so as not to infect the dwelling-place of the living."[2]

It is impossible to understand the word of the poet condemned to death, nor the word of the poet-minister, nor even the silence of a poet without that projection of the reality onto singular elements of the text, which may even be silent...

The disease accompanying our post-communist society still lives on today in the fact that while we encounter almost every day the alibi-like justification of the actions of Válek and other executors of the will of the established party, it is still impossible to seek out Skácel's collected works.[3] Jan Skácel was Czechoslovakia's only poet who remained immune from the pervasive idea that poetry was to be used as a tool for snitching. This corrupt use of poetry stems from Mayakovsky's form of Futurism, and in his poetry it reached a climax. Termed "critical or socialistic realism," and later on, "engaged" art, Mayakovsky's idea of art was consecrated by Stalin himself. And the authority Stalin commanded allowed our domestic leaders to successfully introduce it to our soil as well. Propogandists for the new reality—with their seemingly noble vision of amending the wrongs in society—did not discern their own transfigura-tion from snitching in the creation to the snitching in life itself. Even today, this identification with positive criticism still blocks them from seeing that true poetry is something completely different. If you do not agree, ask yourself: What does Homer have to do with critical or engaged art? And, more specifically, who was Homer ratting out, and to whom and for what? Skácel did not mix politics and poetry, and that is why he does not fit within any political sphere or philosophy, nor can the influence of politics be found in his poetry...

My friend, the Georgian composer Giya Kancheli, was once asked a question concerning the presuppositions of creativity, and to this he gave an entirely unexpected answer: "If you want to write music, you have to love something immensely, incredibly, but just as strongly, just as incredibly, you must hate something." Is it possible to generalize Kancheli's oxymoron according to which any artistic work is motivated and defined at once by extreme love and extreme hate? Are we dealing with a modern formulation of mythology after which Harmony was the out-of-wedlock daughter of Aphrodite and Ares? Are these the contrasting characteristics at work in Sophocles' tragedies, Michelangelo's frescoes, Shakespeare's dramas, Bach's passions, and Beethoven's symphonies? Is the secret to creation found in an ability to carry both of these burdens while not succumbing to either? This oxymoron, which might help connect the searches of Pythagoras and Buddha, church fathers and atomic physicists, was the same oxymoron that Skácel found in a wheat field:

> Once, a long time ago, the painter Bohdan Lacina asked me if I knew what the words *mitmem* and *mítmavo* meant. During his childhood in the village, he had heard these words spoken from the lips of old people. For a long time, I pored over dictionaries until I finally found that, in certain dialects, *mitvy* means *to put something one way, then to put it the opposite way the next time*. For example, the way in which ears of grain lie in the field. The roots of these words are old and mysterious, and in them I hear much quietness, and sense the need for poetry: "'Neath quietness alone / there is some other sound / and 'neath that other sound / some other kind of quiet / Mítmavo / Words clutch together / one tight against all others / shifting them this way, now that way."[4]

According to communist propaganda, *the new man of the future* will be raised with the help of the cultivation of class hatred. While Communist propaganda resorted to rhetorical claims of Heraclitus' eternal fire, the flame of class hatred fueled most of its actual activities. Bruno Bettelheim defined the basis of autism as the inability to love, which was, to him, the equivalent of hatred. According to Lewis Caroll, meanwhile, a fairy tale is "a gift of love," and this creates a dilemma for Bettelheim: Is the story of Oedipus a gift of love? Is the story of Goldilocks a gift of love? A positive response would classify the story as a fairy tale, while a negative one would place it alongside the myths. If autism is an expression of lost hope, then the fairy tale represents a medicine that must be given, a symbol of care shown by an older person for the sake of the child's soul. This is what Jan Patočka has cited as the accomplishment of ancient Greek philosophy (a means of "caring for the soul"). Narrating fairy tales helps develop a sense of self-worth in children and creates models that encompass hope, laying the foundation for the maturation of the soul. The cultivation of fairy tales is the cultivation of hope, serving as a path toward personal integrity—not just some discovery of modern psychoanalysis. The great poets already understand this. As Pushkin writes,

"Independence and self-respect alone can lift us above the trifles of life and the storms of fate."[5] Likewise, modern biologists recognize this axiom. François Jacob writes,

> Hope and possibility give us the strength needed to develop our own rationality; hope for the future is our only guard against inevitable fate. The scientific attitude has a well-defined role in the dialogue between the possible and the real, and we must not forget that man has equal need for both. It is hope that gives meaning to our lives. And hope is based on the prospect of being able one day to turn the actual world into a possible one that looks better.[6]

The scientists and artists of the twentieth century have already summoned the courage to acknowledge and integrate their newly acquired knowledge with the knowledge preserved in myths. The Moravian Jan Skácel went even further. In the era of state autism and stoking the fires of hatred, he listened to a voice within and began creating fairy tales...

During the years under the communist regime (1971-1989), Bohemian and Moravian literature experienced a sharp divide between permissible and forbidden or dissident literature. Skácel's fairy tales undoubtedly represented an escape, a breakaway, or desertion. Such statements often accompany not only his work, but also Hrabal's, yet these assertions are as absurd as a law forbidding the creation of poetry. Is it possible to consider the cultivation of faith, hope, and love as an *escape*? How can we understand the strengthening of human positivism as *desertion*? Can we possibly call the fostering of the capacity to distinguish good from evil a *breakaway*? Despite it all, the situation did in fact concern escape— an escape to truth, goodness, and the future, the realization of which the great poet did not live to see...

The journey of every artist is set forth according its own set of laws. Yet Beethoven's path from his first piano sonatas to his last, Bach's journey from his youthful organ toccatas to *The Art of the Fugue*, the difference between the adagios in Bartók's *Piano Concerto no. 2* and *no. 3*—all of these share a common denominator. Young artists tend to use every artistic and creative means at their disposal, but as they grow older each finds a road that leads from this youthful richness to the selectivity of older age, when they tend to use only a section of that rich palette of their youth. Yuri

Mikhailovich Lotman describes this course in his study *On Rhetoric* as one from rhetorical expression to style. Skácel's creative path enables us to realize yet another aspect of this metamorphosis. Perhaps the reverence for silence, from Skácel's very beginnings, is the most characteristic aspect of his poetry, and while reading his first collections it would be impossible to speculate as to how the selective reductionism of his mature work would eventually appear. The cycles entitled "The Flaw of the Peaches" and "Nuts for the Black Parrot" from the small book *Hope with the Wings of the Beech Tree* demonstrate that Skácel's maturity took the form of a specific type of miniature: quatrains, which sought to concentrate an entire universe of meaning, expressed through a most rigorous set of laws. These are Skácel's haikus, his realization of the well-worn aphorism: to see the world in a grain of sand. Here we find both the first prattling of childhood as well as the gallows that symbolize violent death at the hands of another. The artifact of the poem may be small, however it possesses in itself an entire *universum* of meanings, as does a grain of sand. Its reading may last only several seconds, but it forces us to think quietly for a much longer time. A similar condensation occurs in Webern's mature work, as well as in Stravinsky's wise *Requiem canticles*, which the 85-year-old composer wrote for himself...

I simply love Skácel's poetry and that is probably the reason why I cannot write about it. I love Skácel's Man—at once hunter and prey, farmer and harvest, a creator of words and the creator of quietness. His Oedipus is older and more experienced than Jesus Christ, he understands that it is not only God who must forgive man, but man has reason to forgive God as well. Skácel knows that even though Rocinante will end up in a slaughterhouse, Jesus Christ himself will accept Don Quixote into Heaven, and that Horatio must finish the drama even after Hamlet has died...

After I finished my *Symphony No. 2*, I added to it the motto, "I love the drum and hate the drum sticks," a line borrowed from Jan Skácel's poem "Voice." This was thus my last encounter with the Brno poet, at least for the time being.

Vladimír Godár (left) with the Georgian writer Otar Chiladze in Bratislava
on the occasion of the premiere of *Dariachanghi's Orchard* (1988)

Vladimír Godár (right) with Giya Kancheli in Dolná Krupá, Slovakia,
where "On the Work of Giya Kancheli" was read (1988)

Vladimír Godár (left) with Julian Lloyd Webber in Kensington Gardens
before the premiere of *Barcarolle* for cello and orchestra (1996)

Vladimír Godár (center) with Andrew Parrott (left) and Vladimir Mendelssohn
preparing for the performance of *Dariachanghi's Orchard* (2000)

Vladimír Godár (left) with film director Martin Šulík (2002)

(From left to right) Peter Breiner, Vladimír Godár, Andrej Šeban, and Stanislav Palúch after the premiere of the *Little Suite for Little David* (2005)

Peter Breiner (left) with Vladimír Godár rehearsing
the *Concerto grosso* in Bratislava (2011)

(From left to right) Pavol Maruščák (producer), Juraj Kováč (cello),
Miloš Valent (violin and leader of the Solamente naturali ensemble),
Peter Spišský (violin), Iva Bittová, and Vladimír Godár, after finishing
the recording of *Mater* (2005)

Selected Recordings of Iva Bittová

Solo

Iva Bittová (1986)
River of Milk (1991)
Ne, nehledej (1994)
Kolednice (1995)
Iva Bittová (1996)
Divná slečinka (1996)
Solo (1997)
Iva Bittová (2013)

Collaborations

Bittová & Fajt (with Pavel Fajt, 1987)
Svatba (with Pavel Fajt, 1987)
The Danube (with Dunaj, 1989)
Pustit musíš (with Dunaj, 1996)
Béla Bartók: 44 Duets for Two Violins (with Dorothea Kellerová, 1997)
Bílé inferno (with Vladimir Václavek, 1997)
Classic (with Škampa Quartet, 1998)
Dance of the Vampires (with the Netherlands Wind Ensemble, 2000)
Echoes (with Andreas Kröper, 2001)
Čikori (with Čikori, 2001)
Leoš Janáček: Moravian Folk Poetry in Songs (with Miloš Valent,
arr. Vladimír Godár, 2004)
Mater (with Vladimír Godár, Miloš Valent, Marek Štryncl, Solamente
Naturali, Bratislava Conservatory Choir, 2006)
Elida (with Bang on a Can All Stars, 2006)
Moravian Gems (with George Mraz, Emil Viklický,
Vladimir Václavek, and Laco Tropp, 2007)
Zvon (with Prague Philharmonia, 2012)

A Conversation with Iva Bittová

Mark Molnar

This conversation took place on 17 July 2013.

The first release of your music was a 7-inch record in 1986, and it has three very different pieces: *Ukolébavka* for violin and voice; *Plavil Janko Koně* for guitar, violin, and voice; and *Boží Dárek* [*Gift of God*] for drums, violin, and voice. Was this the first recorded document of your work, outside of your performances?

These are the first pieces that I wrote myself for voice and violin. Then we added percussion with Pavel Fajt, and *Plavil Janko Koně* was done in cooperation with my dear friend Karel David, who has written lyrics for me through all of my work, and continues to do so today. He is playing guitar, and I am singing with him. There are connections between all three pieces. I took traditional lyrics from old Czech folk songs and adapted these for myself. I don't think that *Plavil Janko Koně* has a melody associated with it. A melody for this was written for this adaption. This was the first release, yes.

What kind of work were you doing musically leading up to this?

Before this, I had an idea to work with violin and voice, and this was the beginning. I was already twenty or twenty-one years old, and I was practicing violin about nine hours a day. I tried to sing with my violin playing. I was practicing classical music, but I took those lyrics and composed those songs. I tried to work with my voice. I was inspired by these lyrics, these folk songs, and I decided to work with folk poetry. This was the beginning of using both violin and voice.

The music you were practicing, was this classical music learned through private teachers or through a conservatory system for performance?

It was classical music. All of my life I worked with my teacher Rudolf Šťastný, who just died last year. He was taking care of my technique. He was a teacher in Brno with the Academy of Music and Performing Arts, and he gave me private lessons for thirty years.

Was he supportive of your move away from that foundation in classical music and in the direction of using your violin and voice?

I practiced scales, etudes, and concertos. When I was a bit more comfortable and ready to bring out my new compositions, he was the first to listen and to say critical things. He was very helpful. From the beginning, he was quite surprised with the sounds that were appearing with voice and violin both, but he slowly developed a huge respect for what I was doing. From there, he was more precise to help me as a violinist, and at the same time, he was sure to help out with what I was doing with singing. But he did not take care of the voice of the compositions. He was always taking care of my technique on the violin.

What was your experience of playing these pieces in public at the time? Was there a community of people working with sound in similar ways at the time, or were you doing this alone and trying to find your way?

I was doing most of these things on my own.

What was the public reception like when you started performing?

It was very strange, very difficult. That is why I have always said that at the beginning of one's work and process, [wide exposure] is always more difficult. If you achieve huge success immediately, then all of those things could die very soon. But, that is just my thinking. It was strange because my first productions and presentations were usually in Folk Festivals in the Czech Republic. I was acting at that time with *Divadlo Husa na provázku* [Goose on a String Theater], an important avant-garde theater. The director and the people in the theater group knew what I was trying to do, and I was given the chance to play some characters on stage, where I could include my violin and different sounds with my voice. It was fantastic. When I started my career as a musician, I only acted for a few more years and then I completely stopped because I was not happy. I was really hoping that music was the right thing for me to do. I was not meek on stage as a musician, but the audience, especially young girls, sometimes they would be smiling and saying, "What is she doing? She is completely crazy! What are these sounds? What does this mean?" But they were smiling, and I was trying to keep going and to play the whole piece. It was not like fighting, but your self-confidence leaves suddenly because you do not get a reaction that you want to accept. But I was not waiting for praise. I was thinking too much about what I was doing. And I was practicing more and more. I did not want to give up the idea. I was trying to be stronger and stronger. After about two years of performing, I started to get more respect from the audience. But that was my process.

When people would hear you play your songs, would the audience recognize the lyrics as poems or common folk songs that offered them a way into what you were doing?

In Czech Republic, yes, but the style of it was a huge shock.

Was there anyone else doing what you were doing at the time? Did you feel like you were coming out of a tradition or a community of this work that the wider public was not aware of, or did you feel that you were on your own starting out with this?

It is bad to say, but it felt like I was on my own, and it still is today. I don't like to talk much about it with other people because after thirty years I know what I am doing, but sometimes they ask, "Is this Czech traditional music?" I have to say, "No, it is very different."

When did you start working with others and adding percussion? There are two records done shortly after this, one that appears in the Czech Republic as *Bittova & Fajt*, and then another duo record that appears as *Svatba* (*The Wedding*). Were these done at the same time?

No. The problem with the appearance of these is that they were done at a time of deep Communism in the Czech Republic. When I started, I was completely solo, and then I met Pavel about a year later, and we started to enjoy working together. The agreement was that he would work with my music if I would work with his rock band Dunaj. When we started to play live as a duo, it was a huge step to be able to tour across Europe at festivals. The opportunities and contacts came very fast. We came into contact with Fred Frith, Tom Cora, and Chris Cutler, and all of those musicians. We were very lucky at the time. It was received very well all over. We met Hubel Greiner in Germany, and he asked us to record in his studio for a release in Germany. At that time, it was complicated to bring recordings from out of the Czech Republic to other places in Europe. We did the first record, and about a year later, we did another similar record that was recorded live in the studio in Germany, and it had some of the same songs on it.

What kind of venues did you work in during this time?

We performed in all kinds of places. I like both large and small places, but I prefer intimate spaces. The sound in open air spaces was very hard. It was difficult because I used to only use the acoustic sound of my violin. I don't like even the smallest changes that happen with a pickup. It was quite difficult to get a really good sound, and we were always fighting to have a good sound. Pavel was not able to hear me at high volumes, but if our performances were inside small venues we were able to control the sound more and hear each other.

You moved away from strict duo work in your recordings shortly after, with the release of _River of Milk_.

This was my next solo recording. Pavel was helping me to work on the sound at the time. We went to several churches to get these sounds and to build the pieces up through those spaces. The solo _Iva Bittová_ record on Nonesuch was recorded at that time too, and then a Japanese label EVA released it there. That label no longer exists. Then we released it again in the Czech Republic. Finally, Nonesuch put the solo album out by choosing a series of pieces that I had recorded.

The sound—and your approach to your voice and violin—changes dramatically in your work at that time. The first _Iva Bittová_ record, which was re-released as _River of Milk_, appeared in 1987 and is a powerful leap forward from the first collaborations. Your use of voice is specific to each piece, wrapped up in the songs and melodies. The earlier works seem to be performing to an audience, and the recordings capture that spirit and energy, but these pieces are complexly orchestrated with

different sounds and refined details. And you seem to use your voice as an instrument unto itself. There are elements of that in the earlier recordings, but there is an intimacy with these pieces that has turned away from the self-conscious presentation of recording and is now focused on the nature of the pieces in those spaces, the reverb, the response to the way your violin and voice interact with the cavity of the spaces you are working in. What changed in your approach with these pieces, and your artistic process in writing them?

For me, it is a simple explanation. I had gone deeper, in my way, into what I was doing with violin and voice, and I had many different experiences as a soloist on tour. I was trying to draw on those things, and I was more free to not have to think about the violin and the playing. I think you can hear the difference in the experiences that I was drawing on.

The newest ECM record, as well as the Nonesuch release in 1996, are similar in that the pieces on each are all related, and they do not deviate too far from one another. The music on those records is beautiful, but in the context of your other work, they sound like one of several collections of pieces that have come out over the years. They are great documents, but they do not have the arc or the impact like the original sequencing of *Iva Bittová/River of Milk* or *Bílé inferno*.

The pieces for each of those records were compiled by the label from longer sessions. The pieces that are not on the newest ECM record will come out later this year on the Pavian label. I am curious how you would compare my last solo work to that time, and whether there are any differences?

The change that took place and that is on display on *River of Milk* has not left your artistic expression: each of the records after still maintains that intimacy and a respect for the pieces, with the audience as witnesses to the work; whereas on the first two records with Pavel Fajt, the audience, as witnesses, seems to be the primary concern, and the songs are projected and captured as performances. This is something that I find to be the hallmark of a more refined and genuine artistic expression, which is that someone is working from an artistic voice that is governed by their inspiration and their creative integrity, and that the abstract considerations of who the audience may be, or where the work will be listened to, or how listeners will use it as a tool in their own development, is secondary. This intimacy and integrity, even in the most left-field work, is something that I feel your work shares with some of the musicians you have mentioned. How did you come to experience their work living in the Czech Republic under Communist rule, where the State had a strong interest in controlling the work that was presented?

[Unsanctioned artistic expression] was a secret underground experience during Communism because it was not officially sanctioned. You would wait for a phone call and then get on a waiting bus. It would bring you to a restaurant to see a private concert. The first time I saw Fred Frith and Tom Cora as Skeleton Crew was at a restaurant in Brno.[1] I was completely amazed and so happy to hear that music. When I met them at festivals years later, we were able to perform together, and now we know each other and are like one family, which is beautiful.

It makes sense to consider your work in that context. The work that you were doing, and the folk melodies that are at the root of what you had done, seem to have a kinship with some of the more historically rooted elements at the heart of Skeleton Crew. You seem to be drawing from the same types of melodies and phrasing that Tom Cora was trying to weave into the music that he was making with Fred Frith. The touchstones of his sensibilities sound so similar to your approach.

We understood each other, and I think that we were inspiring to each other. Fred Frith was one of the first who helped me to be more free on stage, to improvise, to keep going, and to play something that was not composing. This was a big help. In the beginning, it came from listening to him and what they do in performance. Then we had a chance to play on stage, and they invited me to play something together. Those were the first steps. In 1989, they invited me to the Knitting Factory in New York City to play with them.

Are you still working with traditional works as the basis of your recordings, or are you trying to write things for yourself?

These days, I have a huge collection of different kinds of lyrics. Some come from my friends, and some just appear to me. I have my favorite Czech writers. Sometimes my shyness disappears and I write a few little lyrics for myself, but if I am ready to write songs, I go through my binders and pages to find lyrics that I can use with the melodies I am working on.

Who are the Czech writers that you continually go back to?

They are all different. It is hard to say. I know it is hard to understand when I am singing in English because I put in so much emotional content, but I am working to be more precise with my pronunciation. I want to use different languages because I can feel different intonations and little details. Every language has a different core. For my process, I will spend some time studying and going deep into an idea and books. Then I come to a time when I need to make more music and it comes to me as feedback from what I was reading before. It shifts me and brings me somewhere. I do those things by instinct. I realize there is always one period where I cannot play and practice so much, when I am touring and listening, which is when I am reading more. Then there is a period where I start to vibrate, to bring to life the vibrations of the violin and voice, and to create something new.

Jordi Savall has said, "It is no longer possible to work completely divorced from all early music, from all of history... It has always been quite natural to imagine that the great works of art from the Middle Ages or the Baroque period could provide fresh sources of inspiration for modern composers, allow them to give their work new dimensions."[2] I would go a step further and say that we have an obligation to the continuity of our history and to shaping that continuity in a respectful and generous manner. In the work that you have done in the last twenty years, this has been a reoccurring theme, and now with your present schooling toward a degree in Music History with a focus on Early Music, it is taking on a new presence. What has been your relationship with this tradition?

I just finished my first year in school. It is completely different, and it shows me new things. There are some things that I already know to be true, but at the same time it brings new dimensions and new spaces for me. There is a lot of inspiration because I am trying to read old notation from original manuscripts, and I am going to hear the old songs. I always try to transform it, absorb it, and adapt it to my way.

Are you finding a kinship with that work? Are you finding that you recognize it as part of the way that you naturally hear music?

Yes, for sure. But the problem for me comes when I hear the recordings. I am more excited to read the notation because I don't agree with a lot of the interpretations, and what amazes me is that there is so much freedom in how you read the notation. You can see how simply it was written, and you can see how much space, huge space, there was for all musicians on the page. This is what brings me new inspiration that I can play with, and I can change it, and hopefully no one will say, "That's not how Janáček or Bartók wrote this!" I hope that this experience allows me to change a bit. I try to go deeper into the theory to try to find my understanding and communication, to take this material and translate it through my creativity. Maybe I am stealing a bit.

Well, with the case of what is referred to as Early Music, the notation was often there to provide a structure or a core to work from, but not to limit them. People were expected to improvise around it based on their time, their expression, and their voice. When you hear this music performed now by orchestras, it does not sound the way it would have then. I have some recordings of Mozart pieces that are performed on the instruments as they would have been at the time, and they sound strikingly modern and ferocious in their expression compared to how they sound now, if you go to hear a typical orchestra perform it for a contemporary audience on a program that is contributing to reifying the canon. We have lost some of that freedom and the sense of these pieces as modern, not just in their time but in the nature of their expression.

I think so, and I hope this study will open me up to some ideas for how to work. I think that what was important at that time was that many students and young children knew this music, and how to play in these ways, but this is something we miss now. I think the knowledge and how we teach is different now, and I am not sure if it is right. This kind of original presentation and space for improvising is missing, and I think it would be nice to find specific ways to teach differently from what we have now in schools. It may only be that we need tiny things that could be different.

You have mentioned before that you played a great deal of music with your mother and father and sister growing up. Was there a space for improvisation when you played together?

If I remember the picture of the atmosphere of playing together at home, I can say that what was most important was that we played the music and the songs as they were written, but what is connected to me today is that we were very happy, and there was a lot of joy to play music together. I think that this was the most important thing. I don't remember how much we improvised at the time, but we were very free to play all different kinds of genres. It was very open. The joyful feeling to just play and be together and to communicate with music was the most important thing. I know that everyone has individual problems and that we all have to fight with too many things. The music helps me to stay in a good mood, and I want to share those things with the audience. It always depends on each of us as artists. For me, it is the most important thing to bring part of my joy and positive energy when I start to play, and they immediately get it. People then try to be happy with me, and we can find a positive communication. I never brought any difficulties to the band. Evan Ziporyn always says that I am easy going, but it helps me not to be stressful. I know people are always in some stress, and music is one of the things that can help people to forget and just enjoy it. You can present this to the audience, and they can absorb it and forget their problems. I am so happy to see the audience. I always ask for more light in the audience so that I can see their faces, and I can see that their eyes are smiling. It happened on my last tour that the audience started singing with me. They feel so much freedom to show themselves, and for me at this moment, with this kind of communication, this is more important than showing how good my technique is as a musician or how good I am as a singer or anything else… It is more important to me to see this part of our life, and how we can be free to bring out positive emotions.

Has this always been your experience as a musician?

I don't think so. I just realize it more and more as I see the reaction of people and as I get older. It is not easy, but it still works.

Knowing, Feeling… : An Oral History of Iva Bittová

Ian Patterson

Iva Bittová is a rare talent. She has developed a personal idiom and vocabulary that is almost entirely her own. Her sound, her very personal language, forged from the union of violin and voice, cannot be categorized, yet is immediately recognizable. Bittová is, quite simply, inimitable.

Though she is not the first artist to create a hybrid language that draws from different roots, nobody has forged quite the same path as Bittová. Her artistic idiosyncrasies and virtuosity as a singer often draw comparison to Icelandic singer-songwriter Björk, though Norwegian Sami singer Mari Boine and Portuguese singer Maria João may also serve as references to some degree. Bittová's innovative techniques with both voice and violin, her attraction to minimalism, and her multi-disciplinary career perhaps draw closest comparison to another allrounder, Meredith Monk. However, it is unknown whether Monk has ever used a ping-pong ball as an *objet trouvé* to alter her voice, as Bittová has done on occasion. In the end, these comparisons hardly matter. Bittová's performances, whether solo or accompanied, contain a dramaturgy that is every bit as natural as her improvisations. It is impossible to separate the actor from the musician, the entertainer from the artist.

"In the language of an actor, to know is synonymous with to feel," notes Russian actor and theater director Constantin Stanislavski, and *feeling* is at the core of Bittová's expression, whatever setting she may find herself in. Clarinetist Evan Ziporyn, who first played with Bittová when she collaborated with the celebrated New York ensemble Bang on a Can in 2000, observes:

> When Iva first appeared in the U.S., I think there was some sense that here was this deeply Eastern European music, but I don't think it's that; she's a cosmopolitan person. She was very much at the center of Czech urban culture. She was a film star and kind of a pop star. She knows jazz, she knows rock 'n' roll, she knows classical music—she knows Janáček and she knows Mozart… Hers is an honest hybrid music that just reflects all of her musical experiences. She's not putting up any boundaries. She just responds to the whole sonic fabric of the moment.

Responding to the sonic fabric of the moment comes close to capturing Bittová's unique gift. One need only watch Bittová's unique interpretation of the jazz standard "My Funny Valentine" at the Isole Che Parlano festival in Sardinia, 2011 (available on YouTube), to gain a sense of the in-the-moment essence of Bittová's art. The megalithic, Bronze-Age Tomba dei Giganti provides the ideal setting for the singer's performance. Bittová seems to draw energy and inspiration from the silence that enfolds her and that frames her almost Shakespearean drama.

Bittová conveys her feeling for Richard Rogers' tune and Lorenzo Hart's lyrics in gesticulations and body language that exude balletic grace and theatrical magnetism. Her voice runs a gamut of emotions, from susurrus, lullaby-delivery to the ululations and cries of a tortured soul. It's a performance that transcends genre. The small crowd, mere feet away, is spellbound by the singer's seductive and sometimes startling idiom.

Bittová's improvisations would no doubt have been a bit too avant-garde for the crowds who flocked to see the 1937 musical *Babes in Arms*, which introduced "My Funny Valentine" to the world. In Europe, in another century, her performance might have brought forward accusations of demonic possession. But at the Tomba dei Giganti, her performance inspires wonder. To borrow from Meredith Monk, Bittová's voice dances and her body sings.

Even in the early twenty-first century, however, Bittová's more outré music may initially dissuade people more used to mainstream music, but Ziporyn, who also currently plays with Bittová and guitarist Giyan Riley in the trio Eviyan, has seen Bittová's powers of musical persuasion first-hand:

> The thing about Iva is that what she's doing is so transparent and so real that everybody gets it. I've performed with her in front of classical audiences, avant-garde audiences, and indie rock audiences. Everybody understands what she's doing because it's deeply personal; it's connected to the core values of music. Everybody understands, and it's true folk music in that sense.
>
> As a result, she can take people to places that normally they don't believe they are willing to go. Because Iva's music is rooted in this simple, earthy style, she can suddenly do things that are completely avant-garde and experimental, and people will go with her, and vice versa. You can get a very hardcore audience that

wants to be wowed, and because there is that side of her that's so intense, once she gets very simple and personal, that audience will also go there with her.

Both of Bittová's parents were musicians. Her father, Koloman Bitto, was a well-known bassist and multi-instrumentalist versed in classical and Slovakian folk music. Bittová took violin and ballet lessons as a child, but dropped the violin when her family moved to Brno in 1971. She later graduated from Brno's Conservatory in drama and music, and throughout the 1970s, she acted in films and television. Much of her future inspiration was gained from formative music and acting experiences in Brno's experimental Goose on a String Theater.

Bittová returned to music in 1981, quickly developing a very personal style, with the violin serving as an extension of her voice. She soon came to the attention of percussionist Pavel Fajt, who invited her to join the rock band Kolektiv (later Dunaj). Bittová also collaborated with Fajt to record two albums in 1987, *Bittová & Fajt* and *Svatba*.

The intimacy captured in these musical vignettes reflects the deep connection between Bittová and Fajt, and the spare arrangements serve to accentuate their songwriting craft. Bittová's panoramic vocal articulations and her emotive violin voiced a new age soundtrack to a timeless Moravian fable. Fajt's percussive accents accentuate the drama. This is progressive folk music, sometimes tremendously lyrical (as in the beautiful "Morning Song"), at other times veering toward post-punk dissonance ("Trifonov").

Their second album found the ears of former Henry Cow percussionist Chris Cutler, who re-released *Bittová & Fajt* on his label Recommended Records. Cutler's former Henry Cow colleague and improvising partner, the guitarist Fred Frith, filmed Bittová and Fajt performing as part of his documentary film *Step Across the Border* (1990). The two releases were key in introducing Bittová and Fajt to an international audience.

That Bittová and Fajt's unconventional yet arresting idiom should appeal to Cutler and Frith is unsurprising; the music's eclectic roots and contrasting textures, the spontaneity that is a Bittová trademark, were all elements to be found in the progressive Henry Cow. Bittová and Fajt's duo recordings came out a year before the debut Dunaj release, but in the meantime, the six-piece band continued to carve a fearlessly personal musical path. At the distance of over a quarter of a century, it can be difficult to fully appreciate the originality of Dunaj and the impact it had on the Czechoslovakian music scene during the dark years of Communist oppression.

Dunaj's bassist Vladimír Václavek recalls those times:

> When we started, it was our intention not to copy any style of music. We were uncompromising. We really wanted to make our music something new. We went our way as far as was possible at that time. Our music never touched politics, but it was not easy during Communism because there was no freedom.

Fajt concurs that Dunaj had no overt political agenda:

> Dunaj was never about making political statements. We had no obviously political lyrics. But everybody who listened to Dunaj and heard the expression we put in to this music and those abstract lyrics was sure how much we hated the political situation in our country.

The censorship and travel restrictions of those times meant that it was impossible for Dunaj to tour abroad. Fajt and Bittová, however, did manage it as a duo. In fact, the duo's second album, *Svetba*, was recorded in Konstanz, Germany, in Hubl Greiner's studio. Their proposed tour to Germany didn't go without a hitch. Fajt explains:

> You have to imagine the preparation before that first tour. We had to play before the commission from Pragokoncert, the state artistic agency, and the only one that could provide visas and police papers for us to cross the border. I think we succeeded because we pretended to be a strange folkloric duo. Also, maybe because they took half our fee!

The papers, however, did not come in time and the German organizers had to cancel the tour. A rescheduled tour went ahead, initiated by Herbert Jugel of the Exquisite Music Agency and managed by Greiner. Fajt is quick to acknowledge Greiner's role in making the tour happen:

> The tour was a great success, largely thanks to Hubl Greiner's

extraordinary help. Probably nobody expected such avant-garde music—and such *warm* music—from behind the Iron Curtain. It was a rare privilege to cross the border two years before it crashed.

Feeling, warmth, and freedom are themes that recur frequently when Bittová's musical collaborators talk about her. "The freedom in her music has always touched me," says Václavek.

> She was a very important part of Dunaj. She would never do a song the same way twice. She always transmitted a very special kind of feeling. I would say this feeling is connected with the heart—it's something very alive. It was always fascinating to see, and it was something that I was learning myself.
>
> I love the first Dunaj album. The music we made with Pavel and Iva was superb. There were several bands that were part of a special scene, but somehow Dunaj became legendary in the Czech Republic and beyond. With Dunaj, we started a new style, a new musical language for the Czech Republic. From these roots, there is now some kind of scene, an alternative scene.

Fajt also points to Bittová's part in the band's success:

> Iva was unique. There were other woman singers at this time, like Dáša Andrtová-Voňková, maybe some others, but they were more like folk singers than performers. Iva's own musical language was already very developed. She had this huge artistic background from avant-garde theater and films. All the time she mixed together her acting and playing music. I think that this was the strongest part of her.

As for Bittová's significance on the Czech music scene, Fajt states: "I think that for a certain artistic movement, her influence has been pretty fundamental."

Bittová left Dunaj in 1990, returning briefly in 1995/6 to record on the album *Pustit Musíš,* and reuniting once more in 2002 for a series of concerts in tribute to vocalist Jiří Kolšovský, who died in 1998. Bittová's post-Dunaj career falls broadly into two categories: her solo career, which yielded six albums between 1991 and 1997, and her collaborative projects, dating roughly from 1997, when Bittová began to consciously expand her talents musically.

Her eponymous debut *Iva Bittová* already carried many of the hallmarks of her later solo work: music whose rootsy minimalism defies conventional contours, with her voice and violin now inseparable. It was an impressive debut, plaintive and lulling, in turn urgent and soaring. Bittová's Romani-tinged songs dance in the shadows between folk and modern classical music. Blessed with an arresting voice of great purity, Bittová's vocal improvisations swing between visceral and comic. Her violin playing—a mixture of lyricism and rhythmic pulse—is soft as spring rain one moment, and rages like a storm the next.

Some of Bittová's most outstanding work pitches these elements in collaborative settings, beginning with the striking duo recordings with Fajt. In 1997, Bittová once again aligned with former Dunaj co-member Vladimír Václavek to produce what many consider to be the real gem in her discography, *Bílé inferno*. For Václavek, the record holds a special place: "For me, it's one of the best, if not *the* best record I made in my life. In music, you can never plan that something will turn out so good. The spirits helped us with this."

As Václavek recalls, the double album took about ten days to record: "It was very fluent and easy. I had some guitar motifs and some ideas. Iva worked on her parts, and we built something very nice together." Guest musicians, such as cellist Tom Cora, trumpeter František Kučera, double bassist Jaromír Honzák, and pianist Ida Kelarová, add subtle textures. A children's choir works a little magic into the seams, particularly on the epic "Uspávanka." An inspired Bittová, who has rarely sounded so relaxed—though there are flashes of her fire—plays kalimba, viola, African lyre, and that most ethereal-sounding of instruments, the waterphone.

Surprisngly, Bittová's violin is only heard on a few tracks, throwing the spotlight more on her voice. "I think Iva felt freer as a singer on this record," says Václavek. "She didn't need to use violin so much because my guitar brought a harmonic environment to the music. She could feel free to use only her voice... There was more space. It was not so full like our earlier music." Certainly, the unforgettable melodic motifs are framed by beautifully spare arrangements.

The magic of this album lies in the chemistry between Bittová and Václavek. It is no surprise that it sold well in the Czech Republic, gaining gold status. "Yes, it was very successful," says Václavek. "Whenever I play concerts, people come up to me and tell me how *Bílé inferno* touched them in some period of their lives."

The success of *Bílé inferno* led Bittová and Václavek to form the band Čikori with Kučera, Honzák, and drummer Miloš Dvořáček. An album, simply titled *Čikori*, followed. Though the record can be seen in some ways as a natural extension of *Bílé inferno*, the music is quite distinct. "The spirit and feeling were already different, because we tried to build a band," says Václavek. "But, yes, it was like a follow up to *Bílé inferno*."

The music on *Čikori* is more urgent and has a darker soul than *Bílé inferno*, and ranks as one of Bittová's most striking works. For non-Czech speakers, Bittová's music can be frustratingly inaccessible, since the meaning of her lyrics is lost. "The lyrics are very important in our music," says Václavek. "They're not just to fill out the music. But if you are sensitive to music then somehow it's complete even if you do not understand the words."

After *Čikori*, some years passed without any further collaboration between Bittová and Václavek, as the singer embraced new musical challenges. Václavek has watched Bittová's progress with interest and is no way surprised by her versatility and success:

> Iva Bittová is one of the most important figures in the history of Czech music. I can't think of anybody on her level, with her power. In Czech today, people follow styles; they play *like* somebody. Iva's way is really original and she follows her way with complete conviction.

Three decades after first playing together in Dunaj, Bittová and Václavek continue to play duo concerts and have recently reactivated Čikori, with a new album planned for late 2013 or early 2014.

The range and diversity of music that Bittová has turned to over the years is remarkable. Her chameleon-like musical persona increasingly defines Bittová as an artist. She has recorded an enchanting collection of children's songs with child musicians, *Kolednice*, which includes a delightful re-interpretation of "Ave Maria." With Dorothea Kellerová, she gave a stunning performance of Béla Bartók's *44 Duets for Two Violins*, leading to international tours. Bittová's album *Classic* saw her interpret the music of Czech composer Leoš Janáček alongside the internationally renowned

Škampa Quartet, with whom Bittová would further explore Janáček's catalog, six years later, with *Moravian Folk Poetry in Songs*.

The distinguished Slovak composer Vladimír Godár contributed special string arrangements for the Škampa Quartet on *Moravian Folk Poetry in Songs*. It was a reunion of sorts, since Godár had composed the music for the film *Tenderness*, which featured Bittová as its lead actress. Bittová and Godár solidified their working partnership in another stand-out performance of Bittová's career, on Godár's modern classical masterpiece, *Mater*.

The sixty-minute suite, based on religious and secular texts, was almost stillborn before it began. Godár explains: "For a long time, I had been dreaming of setting the text of 'Stabat Mater' to music. However, when I heard Arvo Pärt's *Stabat Mater*, I gave up the idea, as this piece appeared to me so impeccable—there was nothing more to say."

The inspiration finally arrived while Godár was working with Bittová on the music for the film *Landscape*.

> I started once again to occupy myself with *Stabat Mater*, as the juncture of the voice and violin embodied in one person inspired me. I chose the old, Slavonic church translation for my *Stabat Mater*, and I wrote it for Iva... At the premiere, Iva was singing and simultaneously playing the solo violin, but for the recording I divided these two tasks between two performers. Thus, my *Stabat Mater* was inspired by her musicality joining string and vocal renditions, her intonation and the emotion with which she performed the music. The whole of *Mater* was later based on the knowledge of her extraordinary musical skills.

The *Mater* project assembled the talents of violinist Miloš Valent's baroque chamber ensemble Solamente Naturali, conducted by Marek Štryncl, and the Bratislava Conservatory Choir, led by choirmaster Dušan Bill. The live premiere took place at the Bratislava Music Festival in 2003. To see Bittová bring life to his compositions was clearly an edifying experience for Godár: "This concert was an immensely moving event for me. It fulfilled many of my long-held contemplations as well as actual expectations."

Three years later, the recording of *Mater* was released on Manfred Eicher's legendary ECM label to widespread critical acclaim, bringing global attention to Godár and Bittová. For Godár, this release held special significance:

> I have to admit that this was one of my age-long dreams. ECM has released music of many composers who were always very close to me and who were very important for my own development. I was very happy to find myself among the people who I have related to for a long time already.

In a nice piece of symmetry, Bittová also joined the prestigious label when her solo ECM debut, simply titled *Iva Bittová*, was released in 2013.

For many years, Bittová has enjoyed a degree of fame throughout much of Europe, but it wasn't until her first American release on Nonesuch Records in 1997 that she began to make major inroads into the country that would later become her home. The record was a combination of songs from Bittová's first solo recording and *Ne, nehledej*. The CD came to the attention of Evan Ziporyn, the innovative American clarinetist who has collaborated with the likes of Ornette Coleman, Phillip Glass, Brian Eno, Terry Riley, Meredith Monk, Nik Bärtsch, and Don Byron. Of Bittová's early music, Ziporyn recalls:

> I connected with it immediately. I felt I understood what she was doing on a very intuitive level. There was something very natural about the way she approached her music—the combination of how simple it was and how avant-garde at the same time. It didn't seem to be forced or artificial in any way. I immediately felt like I knew her, or understood her.

Ziporyn had been closely involved with Bang on a Can since 1987, and the group asked Bittová if she would be interested in a collaborative project. The music she subsequently wrote, inspired by a poem by Czech poet Vera Chase, debuted on the recording *Elida*, a beguiling work which marks a high point in Bittová and Bang on a Can's respective discographies.

Live dates followed the recording. Recalls Ziporyn:

> The music morphed, at least for some of us, in a more improvisational direction. We were all just getting to know each other, and with Iva, it's all about personal connection and intimacy. To me, that's the essence of her music and playing with her. That's how

she connects to the audience and that's how she connects to the other players. That, frankly, is what draws me to working with her, because it's very important to me also. When you feel that way of making music, it's very hard to not want to do more of it. I find working with her incredibly pleasurable and stimulating, and part of that is always being challenged. She just makes you want to play better.

Ziporyn began doing side projects with Bittová (as did Bang on a Can's pianist Lisa Moore) and arranged some of her pieces for the group. Around this time, Zipory had met guitarist Giyan Riley (son of minimalist composer Terry Riley), and an idea began to ferment in his mind:

> I felt a similar connection to Giyan that I felt to Iva, so I just asked the two of them to meet with me. I just felt this was going to be a really nice combination, or at least a combination that I would want to be in. So, we all went to Iva's house in upstate New York and spent a day together, but really within about an hour we knew we had a band.

The three began writing, rehearsing, and gigging. The trio's name, Eviyan, is an amalgam of their names, a simple but effective metaphor for the close symmetry at play within their music as well as the confluence of influences that makes the music impossible to hang a name on. "What draws us together is that all three of us are somewhere between genres," says Ziporyn. "You can't really call it jazz, you can't really call it New Music, you can't really call it World Music... It's somewhere in between all those things."

Eviyan is quietly making waves. The band has played at the Lincoln Center and the Festival of Experimental Music in Quebec. Summer festivals and European tours are lined up, and public and critical acclaim has been glowing. "Our live sets are a combination of composed and improvised music," Ziporyn explains, "but there's fluidity between those things, and sometimes I think it's hard for a listener to tell which is which, and that's the way I think we all like it. It's all about the spontaneity."

Bittová is the perfect fit for Eviyan's fluid idiom, one that embraces discipline and freedom, but for Ziporyn she is much more than just an intuitive playing partner:

What I like about playing with Iva is that she reminds me to be absolutely present and absolutely honest. When I'm playing with her, I never think about anything other than wanting to make the sounds we make together really amazing. I don't think, "This is how the tune will go," or "What will the audience think of this?" The strength of her musical persona reminds me what music is all about.

Given Bittová's virtuosity, her improvisational flair, and her openness to all music, it's somewhat surprising that she hasn't often ventured into—or been more courted by—the world of jazz. It was perhaps inevitable, then, that Czech jazz pianist Emil Viklický recruited Bittová to record a program of jazz arrangements of Moravian folk tunes with bassist George Mraz and drummer Laco Tropp.

Viklický, dubbed in some quarters as the "Janáček of Jazz" for his adaption of folk melodies, had previously given the jazz treatment to *Morava* with Mraz, drummer Billy Hart, and vocalist Zuzana Lapčíková. The success of that album led to a proposal for a follow-up several years later. Viklický wrote new arrangements, but unfortunately Lapčíková was unavailable to record. Viklický then was asked if he could find a suitable replacement.

Viklický knew Bittová from a recording session over fifteen years previously:

I recorded two CDs from one session in 1986 with [bassist] František Uhlíř and [drummer] Cyril Zeleňák. One was called *Homage to Juan Miró*, and the other, which came out in 1990, was called *Beyond the Mountains, Beyond the Woods*. A year before, in 1989, I added one song with Iva. It was a version of "Beyond the Mountains, Beyond the Woods." I asked Iva to do the folkish melody with me in a different style. She did it fantastically, her emotions were so strong. She did all that experimental stuff with Pavel Fajt and rarely did any traditional folk, but it's inherent in her.

Bittová provided a new challenge for Viklický:

It wasn't all that easy for me because all the material I had already prepared for Zuzana. I had to change to different keys because

Iva has a different voice. Iva is more emotional and has a greater range. Zuzana is fantastic, very soft, very mellow, but it's missing that emotional *outburst* which Iva exemplifies.

Bittová's lack of hands-on familiarity with the jazz idiom was no obstacle during the session, and Viklický now laughs at the memory of how she sailed through the material that became *Moravian Gems* in her inimitable style.

> She comes from folk, not jazz, so she doesn't improvise on changes. But that doesn't really matter because she's a natural improviser. The classic example is on "A Little Bird Flew By..." She doesn't know the changes. She improvised and it *sounds* like she knows the changes. Her level of musicality is so high that we didn't even talk about the changes or how the harmony goes. We didn't even talk about the *forms* and yet she fulfilled all the forms. She would look at me and I would signal with an expression, with my eyes, and that was enough. That's what she has inside. It's natural, you know.

The quartet played a handful of concerts in America and some festivals in Europe to widespread acclaim. One particularly memorable performance took place at a giant rock festival in Slovakia. "We came on stage at midnight," recalls Viklický. "There were thousands of people there. It was Iva's fiftieth birthday. Václav Havel, our former President, came on stage to greet Iva on her birthday."

Viklický remembers too Bittová's penchant for theater wedded to her music:

> We played a church in Ostrava at the Colors of Ostrava festival in 2008. Some people collapsed because it was totally packed. The concert started with me, George, and Laco playing jazz, a fast song called "Austerlitz," about Napoleon. We played for four or five minutes before, all of a sudden, from the back, Iva came into the church and started walking between the people and singing, crying, without a mic. She used the natural acoustics of the church. She walked slowly through the crowd and got on stage. The people were absolutely flabbergasted. They were open-mouthed. It was fascinating to watch.

Bittová has been grabbing audiences and collaborators alike for thirty years. The twelve pieces on *Iva Bittová* (2013) are titled "Fragments" I-XII, reflecting somehow the deceptive simplicity and the mystery that their music contains. This is arguably Bittová's finest solo recording to date, for while all her signature sounds are present, there's a depth in her voice that comes from all these years of *knowing*, all these years of *feeling*.

What is this primal music that soothes one moment and makes the hair stand on end the next? What name to attribute to Bittová, this guardian of Janáček's spirit and a thousand years of Romani folklore, this classical Siren? Somehow the term "avant-garde" seems inadequate to describe a musician whom composer Vladimír Godár deems "totally unparalleled." Perhaps Gertrude Stein's poetry, which Bittová incorporated into song with "Fragment III," provides as good a description as any of a musician who recognizes no boundaries other than the limits of nature: "Listen to me, I am I."

Mesmerizing Bittová

Béla Jávorszky

Translated from the Hungarian by Sue Foy

Whatever Iva Bittová picks up turns instantly to music. Her most irresistible and overpowering quality is, of course, that thousand-faceted voice, which she handles as creatively, freely, and convincingly as any other—Björk, Laurie Anderson, Diamanda Galás, Meredith Monk… Her music is self-determining and self-identifying, difficult to measure in terms of anyone else's, difficult to draw comparisons to. She plays almost exclusively her own compositions, which are integral to her, which pour out of her, in such a way that others don't even attempt to perform them. She boldly roams the extremes: at once raw and refined, full-blooded and intellectual, passionate and modest. We know, of course, that the theater is definitely in Iva Bittová's past and in her blood, yet when she performs she does not put on foreign guises, she presents herself in full, displaying all the while glimpses of her many different sides.

The last time we met, in May 2013 at the Mediawave Festival, Iva became a floating diva, swathed in a red veil, mesmerizing in a mysterious atmosphere of theatrical fog. It took a few minutes for those in the furthest reaches of the packed room to realize that if they wanted to enjoy the infinitely intimate music Bittová was illustrating with delicate movements, they'd be best off keeping silent. From then on, the spell was in full effect, the soaring sonic flight took off, and the anticipated state of clemency arrived.

Iva has a bewitching command of space, of the distances between her voice, her instrument, and the microphones, and of the changes in the very air that accompany her shifts in volume. She played, whispered, shouted, chirped, or snapped according to her mood, at times with her back to the lights, other times leaving the stage to walk freely among the audience. Now over fifty, she sometimes needs her glasses, but she performs with precisely the same fire, humor, and sensitivity as any time in the past thirty years. She is a performer whose weaker productions still have the power of revelation.

In addition to a proper command of her instruments, she has an innate feeling for theater and dramaturgy, a childlike playfulness and healthy sense of humor. She is often like a child making up stories with two characters: her violin and her voice.

Bittová's music is feminine through and through: it is graceful, delicate, velvety soft to the touch. She inhabits a supreme sound universe that is comparable to nothing else, of which she herself is both alpha and omega. The ease, fluency, and naturalness with which she handles her voice and instrument is difficult to put into words. She is playfully serious and seriously playful, a ham with an innate sense of self-irony. Her playing nonetheless springs from a spirit deep within, so much so that tears run down her face in more spiritually charged sections.

One of Central Europe's most important international film and arts festivals, the Mediawave Festival, is special terrain, a venue that offers Bittová a great deal of exposure. It is held in a superb location on the Hungarian-Slovak border, one that is befitting of the eclectic mix of traditional and avant-garde acts on display. The audience, composed mainly of residents from Budapest who attend the festival for days on end, basks in a sense of timelessness brought on by the deep history inherent in the performances.

Over the past twenty-three years, Iva Bittová has appeared at Mediawave at least a dozen times. And knowing her, it was not just out of politeness, that three years ago when she accepted the festival's Parallel Culture award, overwhelmed by emotion, she said:

> No matter how many times I come to play at Mediawave I feel like I have come home. Of course in the Czech Republic the people recognize and respect my art, but perhaps because of Béla Bartók's music, or because of my father's blood, the audience here perfectly understands what I play. I have gotten several awards from the Czech Academy of Music, but have never gone to the award ceremonies. But now I am quite proud of that. And I am proud to be here now.

In Iva Bittová's case, it can be said that music runs in the blood. Many of her ancestors were musicians. Her father, Koloman Bitto, who spoke both Slovak and Hungarian, was from the town of Galanta, Slovakia. He was a renowned Roma double bass player who was just as comfortable playing at village weddings as he was playing classical music in big city concert halls. He surrounded his daughters with music from birth, while they also inherited their mother's all-pervasive love of the theater. The family lived in Bruntál in northern Moravia, and chamber music was a daily event in their household, sometimes playing jazz or folk music instead of classical. So it is understandable that all three sisters ended up staying close to music. The eldest, Ida, is a successful singer who teaches singing workshops all over Europe. The youngest, Regina, directs children's musical theater. While the middle child, Iva, is a composer-performer with one of the most original sounds of her generation.

Of course, Iva's path has been of varied intensity and by no means linear. In fact, as a teenager, it seemed she would give up music. Her father wanted to make her into a violinist that could even "play as well as a man." At fourteen, she grew terribly frustrated, hung her violin on the wall, went to Brno, and concentrated solely on theater for the next ten years. She graduated from the Academy of Drama, acted in a dozen films, and won numerous national and international awards. She didn't, however, feel like she'd found her calling, and couldn't really identify with the roles she was getting. She realized that music—once, not so long ago, such a burden—was, after all, her ideal artistic medium. At twenty-two, she came full circle and returned to her violin, which she now supported with her singing voice. And because she hadn't been trained in singing, she was able to soar above convention, in complete freedom.

Ever since, she has acknowledged that decision as the most important of her life. But it took another ten years to develop her unique musical language from the myriad of traditions, experiences, and influences whirling inside and around her. And from the beginning of the 1990s, her musical language became irresistible. Her own personal world of music has fed mainly off of contemporary and classical music, as well as Roma folk and to a lesser extent experimental jazz. Some feel that Iva Bittová should officially be declared part of world heritage.

She declared some time ago, as her *ars poetica*:

> My violin and I sing together, and I compose my music. I perform at home and all over the world. This is my calling. The violin is one of the most beautiful instruments—it forms my reality, awakens my emotions, my feelings, aesthetically it fulfills a mission, it is capable of producing the highest values, speaking between me and the rest of humanity. That's why I love the violin. And to love is to live.

Bittová plays not only with her voice and her instrument, but with her whole body. Sometimes it's synchronized; sometimes it's asynchronous. Her self-expression has never been restricted by the instruments: any object she picks up becomes a musical instrument, whether a rattle, comb, beer can, or blow-out noisemakers. Once she received a kalimba as a gift from a friend, and though she had no idea how to play it she plucked it as she saw fit and immediately composed a tune on it.

Iva Bittová's career has had its own sonic phases and characteristic periods. She spent the early years when she was still finding her way, playing in her ex-partner Pavel Fajt's rock band Dunaj, which, for lack of a better term, could be categorized as *alternative*. During this time, Iva came in contact with the Anglo-Saxon experimental avant-garde of the period, playing with Fred Frith, Chris Cutler, Tom Cora, and John Zorn, and appeared in the documentary cult film *Step Across the Border* and on the accompanying double album. On both fronts she was memorable, but still did not feel she had come into her own.

After her younger son was born, she disappeared from the spotlight for a while, reappearing in the mid-90s, now clearly a soloist, with a matured and characteristically unique voice. Since then, she has been polishing and enriching her style with new tones and timbres. Yet, it cannot be said that she has gotten stuck in her own style. In fact, from concert to concert, record to record, she always comes up with something new, and more surprises.

One can never be sure what her concerts will bring. In 1998, the Mediawave Festival rediscovered her for itself and for us Hungarians. She brought two different shows: in one, she performed her own pieces with guitarist Vladimír Václavek; in the other, she reinterpreted Bartók's violin duets with Dorothea Kellerová. In the following decade, she performed at least a dozen times in Hungary. She has arrived at each concert with a different collaborative project: with a village girls' chorus (Lelky); a German pianist, Barbara Maria Willi; British contemporary band Bang on a Can; Czech DJ Javas; or with the experimental Netherlands Blazers Ensemble, which whom she performed both Leoš Janáček's and her own compositions.

Why the frequent changes of music partners, and how consciously were her musical impulses changing? "Too many opportunities arise to play with superb musicians and bands, and I simply don't want to miss out on any of them," Iva told me years ago. "Anyway, I work relatively quickly." Later on, she added:

> For many years, I have worked in a range of musical genres, including jazz, rock, classical and opera. Deciding on a name for my style of music is far from over yet. Whatever it is, many of my listeners have long considered it highly original. It has always been everyday life that inspired my music and interpretations. Its inspiration has been total silence and an absolutely positive atmosphere. Those are the most important conditions and surroundings in which my ideas spring into life. I believe they have a significant impact on my music.

But Iva Bittová has not worked only in collaboration. Many times her strongest performances, at least of those I've seen in Hungary over the past few years, have been her solo acts—supported only by her own voice and violin.

On her most recent record, *Iva Bittová*, again she plays by herself. Appearing on the heels of *Mater*, it is her second recording under the aegis of the legendary ECM label. Most of the pieces on her new album have been played in concert (at Mediawave, amongst others), but the twelve "fragments" are so nicely linked here that they bring surprises even to those well acquainted with her artistry. And yet again, more powerful and original colors successfully intensify her extraordinarily rich and varied sonic oeuvre.

According to custom, her voice dominates on this album. Mainly she accompanies herself on violin—drawing, pulling, plucking, and at times gently hitting the strings. The forty-two minutes of material also include the earlier-mentioned kalimba: its ethereal sound sets off "Fragment I," gradually developing from silence into a lullaby-like though dramatic performance. The kalimba's dreamlike tinkling also accompanies her voice on the way out, on the concluding "Fragment XII." In the improvisation-like compositions, which can only loosely be referred to as songs, Bittová, as usual, happily and freely uses Roma folk, Byzantine choral works, or Moravian folk music. But, in "Fragment VI," she sings, stringing texts by Gertrude Stein and Chris Cutler together to melodies by Joaquin Rodrigo. These sources, however, function only as inspiration or impulse; in her performance, they become completely personal, flowing organically into an autonomous whole.

Over the last twenty-five years, at least twenty-five records have been released that include her name, the most recent one being her ninth solo album. And though all of them are collections of beautiful, artistic, original material, with regards to her full artistic power, *Bílé inferno* from 1998 with guitarist Vladimír Václavek, rises far above the rest.

Many guests appear on the seventy-seven-minute double album (spread out on black and white disks)—amongst them, the American avant-garde cellist Tom Cora, who often played with John Zorn; one of the best Czech wind instrument players František Kučera; and Iva's older sister, pianist Ida Bittová. The record is listed together with Vladimír Václavek's name and the folk roots are clearly audible. Nevertheless, *Bílé inferno* is one of Iva Bittová's most personal and original sounding albums. The repetitive and percussive accompanying instruments, strongly picked guitar, briskly plucked violin, smoothly and sculpturally bowed cello, firmly played piano—are all there to support Bittová's irresistible, thousand-faceted voice. Naturally, she takes full advantage of the opportunity—whispering and yelling, chirping and cracking, cajoling and shocking. Endlessly creative, she freely, frankly, unreservedly, and convincingly uses her voice, but is never self-centered. One thing is certain: her rich and colorful formal solutions never turn into filler music. The childlike playfulness of "Sirka v louži" or "Moucha"; the longing of "Uspávanka"; the polyphonic, superb counterpoint vocal of "Zvon"; the dark tones and tormented and noisy world of "Moře"—all remain magnificent and fascinating, even after fifteen years.

Bittová, to this day, continuously seeks out new challenges and inspiration. This is one of the reasons she left Brno after living there for decades, moving to the United States in 2007. Now she lives in upstate New York with her youngest son—of whom she is extremely proud, and who in the meantime has been accepted to Bard College, so adding another musician to the family tableau.

Iva Bittová lives and works next to the Hudson River in a house surrounded by forest, only a couple hours from one of the world's most important music centers, where, as she has emphasized to me on many occasions, the musicians are different, the listeners are different, the expectations are different, the experiences are different. Not to mention the fact that such significant changes in and of themselves, generate huge amounts of stimulus and energy. This is what keeps her open, fresh, and young, and this is why she today still plays with the same fire, humor, and sensitivity as she did in the mid-90s.

I have been lucky to hear Iva Bittová in many different kinds of formations and venues over the past twenty years. But still, I can never get enough of her. She pulls me along time and time again. With a touch of euphemism, I would nevertheless put it this way: for me, Iva Bittová has been a part of world heritage for a long time.

Iva Bittová and the Question of Eclecticism

David Auerbach

Musical conventions themselves depend on the development of shared feeling.

—Naomi Cumming[1]

Iva Bittová's long career of eclecticism—encompassing rock, jazz, folk, improvisation, classical, and the avant-garde—does not make it easy to classify her. Bittová's accomplishment is by no means a trivial or common one, even though her cross-cultural proficiency appears effortless. The challenge of eclectic music is to integrate the vital characteristics of folk forms without becoming either a purist or a dilettante.

Bittová made a DVD entitled *Superchameleon*. I take the title to be half-ironic, because Bittová's voice is always immediately recognizable and her violin only a little less so, yet her flexibility represents a model for embracing eclecticism without sacrificing a singular identity. As to why this cosmopolitan eclecticism is a *good* thing, I'd like to explore her relation to classical music and the folk tradition, as well as the historical interaction between them.

I. Eclecticism as Resistance

The eastern half of Central Europe contains a huge mix of cultural influences: the West and South Slavic, Magyar, Vlach, Romani, and, until World War II, Jewish. This cultural interchange gave rise to many overlapping cultural forms, and perhaps also to the grim worldview reflected in folk lyrics such as these:

> *My mother put a curse on me,*
> *When she gave birth to me,*
> *In her birth pangs she cried out,*
> *That I should never be happy.*[2]

Consequently, Bittová has stood with feet in multiple musical idioms since childhood. She grew up in Moravia and Brno, but her influences are not at all confined to the current geography of the Czech Republic. Moravia exists right on the border between Eastern and Central Europe, absorbing influences from both, and Bittová's musician father Koloman Bitto was originally from Southern Slovakia, with roots in Magyar and Romany culture. Bittová's sources come from all across a region best described (by Paul Magocsi) as "East-Central Europe's Alpine-Carpathian zone," geographically comprising much of the Danubian Basin and encompassing parts of countries from the Czech Republic to historical Transylvania in Romania.

Looking for a dominant folk tradition in Bittová's music beyond a general Alpine-Carpathian ethic is counterproductive. She calls her music "my own personal folk music." Another term might be *cosmopolitan folk music*, one based not in a particular culture but in the spaces between them. Bittová transforms her material so as to be quite far from its varied roots.

I discovered Bittová via the key figure of guitarist-composer Fred Frith, who shares with Bittová a tireless eclecticism and fluency in both popular and classical forms. When Frith began to play with the Swedish band Samla Mammas Manna, and particularly its co-leader Lars Hollmer, he said, "I re-learned not to be afraid to be simple, not to be afraid to be passionate, and not to be afraid to have fun—things that I didn't need to think about when I first started playing in rock 'n' roll bands."

Most members of Samla did not read music, yet were capable of playing fluidly in eccentric time signatures and of focused collective improvisation: their 1977 LP *För äldre nybegynnare* consists entirely of live improvisations. Technical skill does not dominate their playing, nor do the folk influences stand out from the musical gestalt. Rather than grafting Scandanavian folk music on top of rock, at their best they achieve an integration that makes use of melodic and rhythmic aspects of folk while intrinsically transforming them into a hybrid possessing its own structural integrity.

Similarly, eclectic groups sprung up in the 1970s and 80s under Communism. Some of the better-known include Hungary's Kampec Dolores and its progenitor Kontroll Csoport, the Czech Republic's Uz Jsme Doma, Slovenia's Begnagrad, and Estonia's Ne Zhdali. Many of these bands were promoted in the West by Chris Cutler, who had played with Frith in the Henry Cow and the Art Bears, but who was also the head of Recommended Records and a tireless promoter of experimental rock in his own right. All made use of East-Central European folk forms while playing electric rock music, also borrowing bits and pieces from everything from bossanova to Afrobeat.

Bittová, who sang in the Czech band Kollectiv in the mid-80s, likewise has found success in adapting to wildly different playing contexts without confining herself within them. Comparing the two versions of the album she recorded with Dunaj (a renamed Kollectiv) is instructive. Bittová plays the part, more or less, of a rock singer on the first recording, *Dunaj a Bittová*. Her trills and register shifts are there, but she generally adopts a less inflected style and sometimes sings lower than she ever has subsequently. Her contemporaneous duet albums with Dunja's Pavel Fajt are far more unhinged, so Bittová is consciously modulating herself on the Dunaj recording. Bittová's control over the degree to which she assimilates classical and rock styles into her vocals prevents any homogenization of her voice.

Bittová dominates the 1996 recording with Dunaj, entitled *Pustit musíš*, bringing in a wider vocal range and more acrobatics, not far from her performances on the album I still consider to be her masterpiece, *Bílé inferno*. (Her performance the following year on Pavel Fajt & Pluto's "Pro Johanku," on the other hand, is far more subdued.) Yet Bittová's two different negotiations of the same material reveals the degree to which she has taken care *not* to conform to a chosen idiom, except on her own terms. This applies to rock as well as it does to classical.

Her eclecticism poses a challenge to her collaborators. Someone like Frith or Vladimír Václavek (her collaborator on *Bílé inferno*), who share her eclecticism, can successfully negotiate the uncertain spaces between musical idioms. But habituation can make subtle conventions difficult to shake, even with the best intentions. I suspect this is the reason why I find *Elida* to be one of Bittová's less successful albums. Despite their best efforts, the talented and virtuosic Bang on a Can All Stars do not mesh with her idiosyncratic playing—the rhythms are a bit too stiff, the textures too lush. Surprisingly, a later orchestral performance of the title track (on *Zvon*) fares better. Despite the instrumentation being far grander, the musicians on *Zvon* complement Bittová's timbre far better, they swing with her and the performance gels while the earlier does not. So the problem is not the recontextualization, *per se*, but simply a problem in stylistic negotiation between the players. As further evidence, the jazz performers on *Čikori* adapt quite comfortably to Bittová's esoteric sensibility, even as she takes a few steps toward them.

Today's fetishization of "authentic" performers encourages such artists to resist experimentation rather than engage in it, lest they "water down" their "native" voice. But Bittová's example shows that it is not any particular cultural background or training that permits or limits musical fluency in a particular idiom, but eclecticism and a willingness to engage music in different contexts with wildly different musical values. Yet specialization is the norm today, running the risk of the sort of acculturation Naomi Cumming discusses in *The Sonic Self*:

> If the Romantic violin is the instrument in which a sounding identity has been formed, the value attached to its sound is inevitable, reflecting the work that has been invested in attaining it. It can, nevertheless, be a source of freedom to discover that identity is not singular, but multiple. An addiction to one kind of sound may actually lead to a cloying of sensitivity to other sounds.

Yet by examining two of Bittová's classical inspirations, Janáček and Bartók, it becomes clear that the embrace of pluralistic eclecticism has been a positive musical force for quite a long time.

II. Folk Inside and Outside the Classical Idiom

> The situation of folk music in Eastern Europe may be summed up thus: as a result of uninterrupted reciprocal influence upon the folk music of these peoples there are an immense variety and wealth of melodies and melodic types. The "racial impurity" finally attained is definitely beneficial.

> —Béla Bartók, "Race Purity in Music"

Folk music originates within a specific, local cultural context, serving certain types of social functions. Whether at clubs, weddings, funerals, or churches, folk music does not survive removal from its context without a loss of meaning and character. That isn't to say that it becomes "inauthentic," as authenticity is a bugbear usually invoked by those who fear they lack it themselves. Classical music, too, has its own cultural context. But appropriation of folk music into novel contexts must be done carefully. A player simultaneously trying to mimic the music of a foreign culture while coming to it from his or her own training and background runs the great risk of making a mess of things, unable to integrate diverse traditions with any sort of coherence.

Béla Bartók wrote:

> This influence can make itself felt most efficiently if the musician encounters folk music not from printed collections, but as it lives untrammelled among the people themselves. If he allows himself to surrender to the impressions of living folk music, and if he can mirror the effect of these impressions in his works, then he has recorded a piece of life.

It's a tall order. Yet what Bartók speaks of may simply amount to living enough with the music to absorb more than its notes and approximate durations, but the intimate relations of all its characteristics, which defy easy notation or hearing and which must be assimilated subconsciously and instinctually.

The absorption of "popular" folk material into the high classical tradition is a longstanding practice, but the folk material has always been disguised or drastically transformed. The mazurkas of Chopin, for example, are far removed from the original idea of a mazurka, borrowing the rhythm and certain scales but overlaying such compositional complexity as to be quite far from the mazurka as folk dance music. Scriabin's mazurkas are even further removed from their formal inspiration. Yet the idiomatic characteristics of the mazurka have vexed many pianists; even superb Chopin players like Arthur Rubinstein, Martha Argerich, and Arturo Benedetti Michelangeli feel less certain in the mazurkas, while others simply play them as lurching waltzes, conflating one dance form with a drastically different one. The unmatched mazurka performances of Maryla Jonas are quite different from most others in their rhythms, tempi, and rubato. (Jan Ekier's excellent renditions are similarly distinctive.)

Folk song and exoticism became a marker of the Romantic idea of "authenticity" in the nineteenth century, but this rarely amounted to a genuine investigation of folk tradition. So-called "nationalistic" musics, like the Spanish school of Albéniz and Granados, made use of local influences as well, to say nothing of the mercurial borrowings of Liszt. But the notion of folk music remained ill-formed. Noting similarities between Grieg's *Nordic Dances* and Bizet's "oriental" *Djamileh*, Carl Dahlhaus drolly remarks in *Nineteenth-Century Music*:

> Regardless of the milieu being depicted, exoticism and folklorism almost invariably make do with the same technical devices: pentatonicism, the Dorian sixth and Mixolydian seventh, the raised second and augmented fourth, nonfunctional chromatic coloration, and finally bass drones, ostinatos, and pedal points as central axes.

In other words, there was often little difference between folklorism and exoticism in high classical music.

Nonetheless, *some* local influence does make itself felt in the classical players of a given culture. The timbral particularities of East-Central European folk music can be noted in their classical string players. I hear something in common between this music and the thinner tone of the Vegh Quartet, the roughness of Szigeti, and the lightness of George Enescu. All are far from the rounded romantic sound of Fritz Kreisler, even if they are still stylistically closer to Kreisler than to Bittová.

For our purposes, though, the significant change occurred in the Fin-de-Siecle, when the phonograph and ease of transport allowed for a boom of research and documentation. In Central and Eastern Europe, composers began to intensely study folk music of their own nations and sometimes others: Kodály, Janáček, Szymanowski, and above all the towering figure of Bartók.

The Czech Janáček and the Hungarian Bartók are crucial figures for Bittová. She has played the music of both, adapting them to her own idiom, using their own folk borrowings as a common language with which to negotiate a new style. The cover of her album *Classic* shows her putting on the mask of a refined woman with a bow on her head, her face peeking out underneath, and it is not a bad analogy for its contents. Bittová brings out the innately non-classical character of the source material to a greater degree, but while she resists assimilation to the classical idiom, neither is she returning the material to its origins.

Consider the interpretations of Janáček's *Moravian Folk Poetry in Song*, recorded by Bittová and the Skampa Quartet. Arranged by Vladimír

Godár for voice and string quartet instead of voice and piano, the treatments are so different as to be nearly unrecognizable. In Magdalena Kozena's 2000 renditions, they sound like representative post-Romantic classical lieder with some touches of folk melodies. Kozena's full-throated operatic voice sounds stately in the slower pieces but somewhat ridiculous in jaunty pieces like "Stálost." (Indeed, she takes some of them more slowly than Bittová to mitigate this problem.) Bittová's piercing tone is far more agile and matches the sharp attack of the strings, drawing out the fundamental role of *dance* in the source material. For comparison, Dagmar Pecková's performances take a middle path, preserving the original arrangements but uses far sharper phrasing rather than smearing the words together, as Kozena does. Yet Bittová's voice is utterly foreign to classical norms, drastically shifting registers in "Stesk" from a bird cry to a wolfish howl, that she breaks down far more fundamental sonic barriers than Pecková. The strings, while possessing more of a fiddle-like quality than most classical performances, remain more genteel than the sawing drones of dedicated folk groups like Muzsikas or the Okros Ensemble.

Similarly, on her performances of Bartók's 44 *Duets for Twin Violins* with Dorothea Kellerova, the violin tone is thinner and far less vibrato-laden than any other version I've heard, and more strikingly, Bittová sings some of the violin lines. Yet one other performance goes further from the classical idiom: the Hungarian group Muzsikas played a few of the duos on *The Bartók Album*, which mixed in Bartók pieces with some of the original folk source material. The performance of #44, "Transylvanian Dance," played by Mihály Sipos with guest violinist Alexander Balanescu, is more rhythmically irregular and texturally raw than Bittová and Kellerova's, though there is no singing.[3] The point, again, is not to get into a contest of authenticity. Indeed, comparing Bartók's pieces with the source material and field recordings on *The Bartók Album* shows that Bartók's material doesn't *permit* such a return to "authenticity." In *Bartók, Hungary, and the Renewal of Tradition*, David Schneider writes:

> Just as Bartók makes peasant music suitable for the stage in the Rhapsodies by distancing the melodies from their folk models, animating these tunes in performance requires the ability to conjure an imaginary peasant performance through the contortions of virtuoso artifice. For Bartók, then, successful concert arrangement was far more than a transcription. A series of

peasant dances for violin and piano or orchestra had to be transported far enough from their roots so as to create an illusion of a peasant ritual brilliant enough not to fade under the spotlight of the modern concert stage… Bartók's music stands apart from that of his Hungarian predecessors less because of its greater fidelity to authentic folklore than because it asserts more elite standards of craftsmanship, originality, and modernity.

And thus I conclude that it has never been Bittová's aim to bring Bartók and Janáček back to their supposed roots, but to interpret them eclectically and uniquely. She does not translate their sources back into their original idiom, but into her own idiom.

In their time, Bartók and Janáček were doing exactly that as well, bringing in diverse material not to subject to an existing classical style, but to forge a new synthesis. Their respective folk elements had not penetrated into classical composition, and so there was a fundamental eclecticism to their efforts that is more difficult to hear today, now that their influence has been integrated into a classical mainstream. As with the best and most adventurous contemporary composers and performers, Bittová's single-minded pursuit of a personal and unique synthesis follows more truly in the vision Bartók and Janáček pursued.

Notes

THE THREE ARCHIVES OF GERALD MURNANE

[1] These notes are provided by Gerald Murnane. They have been rather heavily condensed by the editor due to space constraints. Mr Murnane's complete detailed listing of the contents of his Chronological Archive, in particular, runs many pages in length.

ART AS PALIMPSEST: CULTURAL EXEGESIS IN THE WORK OF VLADIMÍR GODÁR

[1] Via an e-mail dated 22 June 2006, as quoted on Godár's website.
[2] Translation by the author. Quoted from the *All About Jazz* webzine.
[3] Josiah Fisk's damning assessment of the "new simplicity" has proved a particular beacon for those uncomprehending of such aesthetic shifts. See Josiah Fisk, "The New Simplicity: The Music of Górecki, Tavener and Pärt" in *The Hudson Review* vol. 47, no. 3 (Autumn, 1994), 394-412.
[4] See Eva Kowalská, "Language as a means of transfer of cultural values," in Peter Burke and R. Po-chia Hsia, eds., *Cultural Translation in Early Modern Europe*, Cambridge: CUP 2007, 61-62.
[5] *Dhoxa* was subsequently incorporated as the first movement of the longer work *Ikon of Light*.
[6] Quoted from Bittová's website, www.bittova.com/biografie.php
[7] Phillip Blond, "From modern painting to the vision in Christ," in John Milbank, Catherine Pickstock and Graham Ward, eds., *Radical Orthodoxy: A New Theology*, Abingdon: Routledge 1999, 200.
[8] Ibid.

ON THE WORK OF GIYA KANCHELI

[1] The *Muqaddimah*, translated by Franz Rosenthal; chapter VI, 58, p. 792-793.
[2] Since 1988, when this lecture was originally delivered, Kancheli has written tens of other compositions.
[3] Since 1988, a book has been released entitled *Giya Kancheli v Dialoghach s Natalej Zeifas* (*Giya Kancheli Conversing with Natalia Zeifas*), in which Kancheli addresses some of these issues. The book is published in Russian by Muzyka in Moscow, 2005.
[4] *Poetics of Music*. Harvard University Press, Cambridge 1947, p. 147.
[5] Book II, chap. 1

ENCOUNTERING THE POET

[1] "Concerning Truth, Beauty, and Jan Skácel" was originally published in *Slovenské pohľady* no. 5, 1967.
[2] Perse, Saint-John. *Letters*. Trans. Knodel, Arthur. Princeton: Princeton University Press. 1979. 449-450.
[3] The complete works of poetry by Jan Skácel was finally published in 1996, three years after

this essay was written, by the Brno publishing house Blok. Its publication was made possible by a gift from Milan Kundera.

[4] Excerpted from Jan Skácel's poem "Mitmem" from the collection *Millet*, 1981.

[5] *PSS*, vol. VIII, p 81.

[6] From *The Possible and the Actual*.

A CONVERSATION WITH IVA BITTOVÁ

[1] Skeleton Crew was a duo between Fred Frith and Tom Cora that was active between 1982-1984, and then as a trio with Zeena Parkins from 1984-1986. They released two studio albums (*Learn to Talk,* in 1984, and *The Country of Blinds,* in 1986) along with several cassettes on tour, and a bank of source sounds (*Etymology* in 1995).

[2] "A Conversation with Arvo Pärt." *Music & Literature* no. 1, August 2012.

IVA BITTOVÁ AND THE QUESTION OF ECLECTICISM

[1] From Naomi Cumming's *The Sonic Self: Musical Subjectivity and Signification*. Indiana University Press, 2001.

[2] A lament from the Kalotaszeg Region.

[3] Itzhak Perlman and Pinchas Zukerman's fine performance makes a sprightly compromise between folk and classical technique, while Sandor Vegh and Alberto Lysy take a more rough-hewn approach. Both performances have strong rhythmic inflection while remaining within the classical idiom. The recent, dour recording by Andras Keller and Janos Pilz, drowned in reverb, slurs the rhythm so much as to be unidentifiable as dance music.

Notes on Contributors

David Auerbach is a writer and software engineer. He is the author of www.waggish.org and has written for *The Times Literary Supplement*, *n+1*, *The Nation*, and elsewhere. He lives in New York.

Iva Bittová was born in Bruntál, Moravia, in the former Czechoslovakia. As a violinist, singer, and composer, she has recorded many solo albums and collaborated with major international talents, including Pavel Fajt, Vladimír Václavek, Škampa Quartet, Miloš Valent, and Vladimír Godár.

Peter Breiner is a composer, conductor, pianist, arranger, and journalist. One of the most recorded musicians in the world (over 200 CDs), he studied composition with Alexander Moyzes, a founding figure of the modern Slovak music. Since 2007, he has been living and working in New York.

Clarice Cloutier is a translator from Czech, Slovak, Russian, and French. Having taught at Charles University (Ph.D., 2005), and New York University in Prague, she is currently on sabbatical and has recently guest taught courses at AGH University in Krakow, Poland.

Teju Cole is a writer, art historian, photographer, and Distinguished Writer in Residence at Bard College. Born in the U.S. to Nigerian parents, he was raised in Nigeria and now lives in Brooklyn. He is the author of a novella, *Every Day is for the Thief*, and a novel, *Open City*.

Scott Esposito is the co-author of *The End of Oulipo?* (Zero Books, 2013). His writing has appeared widely, including in *The White Review*, *Tin House*, *Bookforum*, the *Washington Post*, and the *Los Angeles Times*. He also edits *The Quarterly Conversation*, an online journal of essays and literary criticism.

Tristan Foster is a writer from Sydney, Australia.

Sue Foy has been living in Hungary for the last twenty-four years, where she does translation in the film industry and in the areas of traditional music and dance, culture, and tourism.

Vladimír Godár is known as a composer of symphonic, chamber, vocal, and film music, and as a writer of a huge number of texts on music and art.

Will Heyward is a writer and editor from Melbourne, Australia. His reviews and interviews have been published by *The Australian*, the *Australian Book Review*, *BOMB Magazine*, *Arena Magazine*, and others. He is an editor of *Higher Arc Magazine*.

Ivor Indyk is Whitlam Professor in the Writing and Society Research Centre at the University of Western Sydney, and founding editor and publisher of *HEAT* magazine and the award-winning Giramondo book imprint, which includes Gerald Murnane among its distinguished authors. A critic, essayist, and reviewer, he has written on many aspects of Australian literature, art, architecture, and literary publishing.

Matthew Jakubowski is a short story writer, essayist, and literary critic based in Philadelphia. He is a member of the National Book Critics Circle and has written extensively about translated fiction for various publications worldwide.

Béla Jávorszky is a writer, journalist, music critic, and editor specializing in jazz, folk, rock, and contemporary music. Between 1996 and 2005 he worked for the leading Hungarian daily newspaper, *Népszabadság*. His books include *The History Of Rock* vol. I-II, *The History of Hungarian Rock* vol. I-II, *The Sziget Story*, and *The History Of Hungarian Folk*.

K. Thomas Kahn is a writer based in New York City whose criticism has appeared in the *Los Angeles Review of Books*, *The Quarterly Conversation*, *Book Slut*, *3:AM Magazine*, *The Millions*, and other venues.

Hari Kunzru is a novelist based in New York. His latest publication is the novella *Memory Palace*, which is the basis of an exhibition at the Victoria & Albert Museum, London.

Wayne Macauley is a Melbourne writer. He is the author of three highly acclaimed novels, *Blueprints for a Barbed-Wire Canoe*, *Caravan Story*, and *The Cook*.

Mark Molnar is a composer, musician, and a teacher of literature and history. He is the founder of Black Bough Records, and a member of Kingdom Shore.

Ivan Moody is a composer, musicologist, and Orthodox priest, and is Professor of Orthodox Church Music at the University of Eastern Finland.

Gerald Murnane was born in Melbourne, Australia in 1939. He is the author of eleven works of fiction, including *Barley Patch, Inland, The Plains,* and *Tamarisk Row,* as well as a collection of essays, *Invisible Yet Enduring Lilacs.* Murnane has been a recipient of the Patrick White Award and the Melbourne Prize.

Ian Patterson is a freelance writer based in Ireland. He writes for the webzine *All About Jazz* and goes to far too many concerts.

Tomáš Šelc is a young baritone from Slovakia. Winner of eight international singing contests, he has participated in several festivals in Europe, Asia, and Africa. With a focus on concert repertoire, he performs operas and has recorded several albums.

Emmett Stinson is writer and literary critic. His collection of stories, *Known Unknowns* (2010), was shortlisted for the Steele Rudd Award, Australia's only prize for books of short fiction. He is a Lecturer in Publishing at the University of Melbourne.

Lawrence Sutin is the author of two memoirs, two biographies, one historical work, and one novel. He teaches at Hamline University and Vermont College of Fine Arts.